The Politics of Lying

The Politics of Lying

Implications for Democracy

Lionel Cliffe
Professor of Politics
Department of Politics
University of Leeds

Maureen Ramsay
Senior Lecturer in Political Theory
Department of Politics
University of Leeds

and

Dave Bartlett
Department of Politics
University of Leeds

First published in Great Britain 2000 by
MACMILLAN PRESS LTD
Houndmills, Basingstoke, Hampshire RG21 6XS and London
Companies and representatives throughout the world

A catalogue record for this book is available from the British Library.

ISBN 0–333–71738–4

First published in the United States of America 2000 by
ST. MARTIN'S PRESS, INC.,
Scholarly and Reference Division,
175 Fifth Avenue, New York, N.Y. 10010

ISBN 0–312–23139–3

Library of Congress Cataloging-in-Publication Data
Cliffe, Lionel
The politics of lying : implications for democracy / Lionel Cliffe and Maureen
Ramsay; with case studies by Dave Bartlett
    p.   cm.
Includes bibliographical references and index.
ISBN 0–312–23139–3 (cloth)
1. Official secrets—United States.   2. Official secrets—Great Britain.
3. Official secrets—United States—Case studies.   4. Official Secrets—Great
Britain—Case studies.   5. Deception—Political aspects—United States.
6. Deception—Political aspects—Great Britain.   I. Ramsay, Maureen, 1948–
II. Bartlett, Dave, 1947–   III. Title
JK468.S4 C58   2000
320.1'01—dc21
                                                        99–053561

This book is printed on paper suitable for recycling and made from fully managed and sustained
forest sources.

10   9   8   7   6   5   4   3   2   1
09   08   07   06   05   04   03   02   01   00

Printed and bound in Great Britain by
Antony Rowe Ltd, Chippenham, Wiltshire

For Maxine, who always faced the truth

Contents

vii

Preface and an Introduction

This book had its genesis in a course with a similar title taught by Lionel Cliffe at the Department of Politics, University of Leeds. Its original aim was to follow a workshop approach which would encourage students to do their own investigations into a few of the more notorious cases of government dissembling or deception in recent years. But its popularity forced a widening of the net to excavate more cases for students to work on. That exploration in turn gave rise to a research project which involved a deepening as well as a widening of the investigations, as a whole hidden side of political life in English-speaking countries was increasingly laid bare. Growing awareness of the submarine parts of this iceberg prompted analytical questions of how such incidents were to be explained. Much of this volume is given over to an analysis of some of these notorious cases on both sides of the Atlantic. Each case-study covers familiar ground in the course of attempting to 'nail' the lie by comparing initial official announcements with what is later revealed. But the significance of each case for our understanding of politics and the kinds of calculations that are made by governmental actors that might 'explain' the deception are also probed.

The more cases that are brought out, the more one realises that what also has to be explained is the seeming pervasiveness of the phenomena. If they were merely occasional if spectacular exceptions to normal democratic and open practices, then the 'exceptional' circumstances surrounding a particular case would be central to any explanation – although, even in that light, comparative analysis might allow isolation of the types of circumstances which are likely to give rise to government lying. However, as more cases come to light, the possibility that they are the common stuff of 'democratic' politics, at least in some countries, in turn poses the need for a different level of explanation. Are such practices of deception systemic? And to the extent they are, is that to be understood in terms of the character of certain political leaders that give a regime its character or of politicians and power-holders generally, or of more structural characteristics or contexts of particular political systems? Or is the phenomenon to be explained as a more fundamental element in the conduct of politics in contemporary democratic polities?

The original scope of the course and the book has in fact been limited to *democratic* political systems. Principally this is because there is little intellectual challenge in accounting for the extent of lying in dictatorial or repressive systems. Regimes that are not elected, that do not depend on popular support for policies, and that are in no sense accountable, do not have to worry overmuch about public reaction to what they do. In so far as they do seek popular acclaim, much as a football team prefers applause from its fans but in no way seeks a mandate from them, they usually have the means – monopoly of radio and television, controls on the press – to indulge in straightforward propaganda, without fear of public exposure of their deceptions. Conversely, in authoritarian states citizens often react with a cynical disbelief of every pronouncement of government. In a state that claims to be democratic, governments want people to believe they are acting in the best interests of their people, so the explanation of why there should be lying is less obvious. Keeping people in the dark or giving out deliberately false or misleading information flies in the teeth of various tenets of liberal democracy: accountability, the right to know. Moreover, it seems to cut across the rationale of electoral and especially 'opinion-poll' politics: if government is there to serve the interests of the people, or at least a majority, and if governments that want to be re-elected have a self-interest in doing so, why are they engaged so often in activities that have to be kept from the public? It is that disjuncture that has to be explained in democracies, and posing the question in that way underscores the need to explain both the lying and the actions or policies that are lied about. As we shall see, those questions can be analytically distinguished but are often related. Indeed, the short answer to our problem is that deception is most often about actions that are indefensible – but that is only the beginning of a full explanation. A related puzzle about this aspect of democratic politics also has to enter the analysis: the *how* as well as the why of deception. How is it possible, where there is freedom of the media and apparent openness of government, that governments can still limit their citizens access to information? If that possibility were excluded by some combination of effective rights to information and media and public vigilance, then there would be no need for elaborate explanations of motives or imperatives for lying: it would seldom happen.

These issues about deception in democratic politics in turn raise questions not only of political analysis but of political theory. First are those to do with *justification*: how do those who deceive justify their actions? Are their reasons in any way valid? And how far does the 'justification' relate to or depend on whether the actions that are covered up are justifiable? A second dimension concerns *democratic theory*: what are the arguments about full and accurate information as a requirement for democracy? How great an impediment is lying and secrecy to the proper working of democracy? These basic matters of principle became part of our agenda when Maureen Ramsay joined the Leeds research programme, bringing her insights from political philosophy to the subject. These themes are dealt with in general and theoretical terms in the opening chapters, but the insights derived from that discussion are used to develop criteria for assessing justifiability in individual cases in the second part of the book.

The case studies that are afforded full treatment are selected from those which have attracted major attention in recent years in Britain and the USA. The Iran–Contra affair of 1985–86 (or affairs, according to Draper, 1991) involved a grand-scale cover-up of a set of actions which had been explicitly prohibited or at least inhibited by Congress, and were kept secret from the State Department and even the CIA as well as the legislature, and, of course, the American public. Two major pieces of deception in the area of foreign policy by the British Government are also scrutinised: first, the executive sanctioning of the supply of arms to Iraq, and second the coupling of an aid-package to build a dam in Malaysia to a deal for that country to buy arms, both of them actions in apparent contravention of the Government's own stated rules and guidelines, as reported to Parliament. The British cases also include two that relate more to domestic policy. The internal security problem posed by Northern Ireland is explored to see to what extent there was a practice if not a policy of pre-emptive shooting of the country's own citizens in a manner that was unlawful in terms of any policing role, and even by the special rules of engagement employed in Northern Ireland under the state of emergency laws.

That latter case inevitably prompts questions about what the generalisation of such 'emergency' practices and the role of the security services in them have done to shape the overall character of British government and politics. Issues about the consequences for the working of the polity as a whole of what might seem abhorrent practices are also raised by any exploration of the recent revelations of the growth in the buying of political favours through Parliament. Very different implications are raised by government's handling of information about and responses to the crisis of 'mad cow disease', or BSE, and its possible transference to humans. Dramatic in its own right and in its wider repercussions, on British relations with the European Community for instance, the case poses broader issues of how open governments are or should be about threats to environmental health and how they handle risk. Unpalatable facts and even policy errors were covered up, but it offers an example of a much broader process whereby government seeks to manage the flow of information, including scientific facts and evaluations, about a topic. In this respect the second of the major US cases, the 'war on drugs', invites comparison. There, too, our analysis illustrates not just a particular set of denials but a whole policy area and the considerable propaganda surrounding it that arguably has elements of a 'charade' – a major campaign premised upon a debatable diagnosis of the problem, and one wherein the actual activities do not fully square with the image presented.

The cases presented here are thus exploring a wide range of different contexts and policy contents – domestic as well as foreign, to do with issues of power, economic and environmental issues, and concerned with 'national interest' and security, with vested interests and personal corruption. They also offer examples of differing kinds and degrees of deception: denial of some facts or of some action or policy – or of responsibility for them – *denials;* suppression of covert activities or politically embarrassing actions or of disturbing information about the economy or the environment – *cover-ups;* routine massaging of information to hoodwink or lull public perceptions – *manufacturing consent;* and even the undertaking of action for nothing more than those purposes – *charades.*

This volume is therefore more than a study of 'lying' as a neglected dimension of politics. It also offers a different 'take' on the nature of political institutions and the way they work, and especially on relations between governments and publics, that pinpoints a crucial deficiency in the operational character of democratic politics. The significance of studying instances like those documented here, where the hidden workings stand revealed by some opening, is stressed by Draper's (1991) comment on the plethora of evidence brought into the public domain by the volumes of reports and documentation about Iran–Contra: 'seldom has such a window been opened on to the actual inner workings of government'. A similar comment could be made about what the mass of evidence unearthed by the Scott Inquiry into arms to Iraq revealed about the workings of the corridors of power in the UK.

The tortuous revelations about one scandal has dominated media coverage and commentary on US public affairs in the last months of finalising this volume: President Clinton's affair with Monica Lewinsky and the Report of Independent Counsel Kenneth Starr into it and other presidential indiscretions. However, we should make it clear that it is not the proximity of a publication deadline that leads us to give this incident scant attention in this book. Even though it has been clearly established that Bill Clinton repeatedly lied, even apparently to a grand jury and under oath, the events lied about are not intrinsically *political*. The 'impeachable' offences outlined in the Report (Starr, 1998) do not include any that involve policy matters or the misuse of power, for anything other than avoiding personal embarrassment – or even concern actions that could be seen as those of the officeholder rather than the man. Thus our judgement is that the case falls outside our remit. Its inclusion would not be consistent with our emphasis on the *politics* of lying, on what is being lied about and justifications and explanations of it, and on how such actions shape political life, rather than the mere act of falsehood. The volume is concerned in particular with the implications in undermining democratic accountability by lying. From that perspective, Clinton's denials, although clearly self-serving, were of a different order from some of those actions of US presidents given detailed consideration here (although the context set out in Chapter 4 is relevant to an understanding of the post of Independent Counsel). Clinton was not covering up an act in the arena of policy debate, nor his responsibility for covert operations. His lies were not taking decision-making out of the public realm. One could argue that he ought to be made to account for his peccadilloes to his family, and to his god, but not necessarily to the American public.

Covering as it does theoretical issues, both normative and analytical, and empirical case studies, the book is organised into two Parts which correspond to this basic divide. Part I contains two chapters dealing with the normative evaluation of justifications for lying in politics and three chapters which are concerned with different levels of explanation of the phenomenon. Chapter 1 explores the basic issues of morality raised by political deception and critically examines the arguments used to justify it. Chapter 2 enlarges on the problem of ends and means raised by the use of 'consequentialism' as justification, particularly when used in a democratic political order, and concludes that the deepest questions are posed not by efforts to justify, or the deception itself, but by the actions or policies which are the subject of dissembling and by the political context in which it arises. Chapter 3 then focuses on those contexts, seeking to offer explanations as to how and why the practices occur in democracies, and apparently so commonly, at the most general level of the nature of power and interests in democratic systems. Chapters 4 and 5 supplement that account by considering possible explanations by documenting the patterns of political deception that characterise the two particular political orders with which the book is mainly concerned, the USA and the UK.

The detailed case-studies which make up Part II include two major episodes in US foreign policy – Iran–Contra and the 'war on drugs' – and then two chapters to do with British foreign affairs – arms to Iraq, and the aid-for-arms issue at the heart of the Pergau dam affair in Malaysia. Chapter 8 is a study of security practices in Northern Ireland. The last chapter deals with the BSE issue.

In a brief conclusion there is a reflection on some of the broader political justifications and explanations of these cases and their political implications and how far they shed light on the moral issues and types of analytical explanations considered in Part I. It also discusses what can be learned from the revelations of these cases about how people and popular bodies can engage in 'intellectual self-defence', as Chomsky calls the ferreting-out of the truth. These suggestions are offered following a discussion of what can be done to promote political reforms so as to promote less official lying and secrecy, and greater openness and more accountability in government.

Successive cohorts of students taking Cliffe's course in 'The Politics of Lying' have provided great stimulation to the conception of this volume and their investigations and classroom discussions have provided valuable material and insights which need to be acknowledged. So does the contribution of Dave Bartlett to the teaching of that course, to the development of the general ideas of the book, as well as his authored case-studies. The broader intellectual debt in charting the field and indicating the crucial importance of this obscured dimension of politics is owed not so much to academic predecessors, except the classical writers on political theory, but to that vital, but diminishing tradition of investigative journalism, embodied in the work of I. F. Stone and David Wise (whose own work of a generation ago gave us the title), and the 'crossover' academic and investigator, Noam Chomsky, in the USA, and Richard Norton-Taylor, Paul Foot and others in the UK.

Leeds

LIONEL CLIFFE
MAUREEN RAMSAY

Part I

Justifying and Explaining Political Deception in a Democracy

1
Justifications for Lying in Politics

Maureen Ramsay

Definitions – lies and deception

A lie is defined here as a statement intended to deceive others. Telling a lie is not simply the opposite of telling the truth because telling the truth and being truthful are not the same thing. Nor is saying what is false necessarily to deceive. To see this, we need to distinguish between truth and falsity, truthfulness and deception (Bok, 1978, 6–13). Questions about truth and falsity belong to the ontological and epistemological domain and involve questions about what is the case and how or if it can be known to us. A statement is true or false if what is said to be corresponds to what actually exists or is. Questions about truthfulness and deception belong to the moral domain of intention. Someone is being truthful when what they say, they believe to be true. If they intend to deceive, they are not being truthful – they are lying. They say something they believe to be false (or not true) with the intention that someone else should believe it to be true. The liar pretends that circumstances are other than they are.

Following from this definition, someone can tell a lie that contains true statements. This is either because the statements are in fact true and the liar intending to mislead, inadvertently tells the truth, or because the deceiver selectively uses true statements to intentionally mislead. Conversely, someone can think they are telling the truth, but be mistaken. Here they are being truthful, they are not lying but what they have said is false. The essence of lying then is not the truth or falsity of the statement, but the conscious intention to mislead. Whether or not someone is lying depends on their intentions and beliefs, what they believe to be true or untrue.

This definition of lying follows a long philosophical and theological tradition. St. Augustine wrote 'for a person is to be judged as lying or not lying according to the intention in his own mind, not according to the truth or falsity of the statement' (St Augustine 1952:55). St Thomas Aquinas elaborates:

> If we say what is false thinking it to be true, it is false materially, but not formally, because the falseness is beside the intention of the speaker; so that it is not a perfect lie – If … one utters a falsehood formally, though having the will to enunciate what is false, even if what one says be true, yet in as much as this is a voluntary and moral act, it contains falseness essentially and truth accidentally, and attains the specific nature of a lie. (Aquinas, 1922: 11–111 Q110, Article 1)

Bok sums this up: 'The moral question of whether you are lying or not is not *settled* by establishing the truth or falsity of what you say. In order to settle this question, we must know whether you intend your statement to mislead (Bok,1978: 6)'. Theologians, moral philosophers and political theorists have wanted to distinguish between those lies which are justified and those which are not. This has led some to attempt to define lying in a different way, so that some intentional falsehoods do not count as lies. This arises from the recognition that not all lies are equally bad or wrong and the desire to avoid blanket condemnation of all and every lie on the grounds of the intention to deceive alone. For example, Grotius argued that speaking falsely to enemies, that is to those to whom truthfulness is not owed is not lying (Grotius, 1925, Bk.3, Ch.1).

These approaches, though, confuse reasons to defend some lies with lying itself. They conflate justifications for lying with definitions of lying. Lies may be justified with reference to the type of intention that motivates them, the purpose for which they are told and the ends they are designed to achieve. Well-meant lies where the intention is to protect, avoid harm or bring about some other good are often defended, sometimes even applauded. But excusing some lies and making a moral distinction between benevolent and malicious lies is separate from defining what counts as lying. Morally evaluating an intentionally misleading statement is different from whether or not a statement is intentionally misleading.

If a lie is an intentionally misleading statement then it is clear that lies can be both written and spoken. But making others believe what you do not believe to be true can also be communicated by gesture, disguise, action and, more insidiously, by inaction. Omission, evasion and silence can be ways of misleading people. People can be deceived by conscious deliberate lies which are directly communicated to them by word or deed. Typically in politics this takes the form of denial, an explicit lie which claims 'this did not happen', 'the policy has not been changed'. They can be systematically manipulated by propaganda designed to spread particular ideas which influence the attitudes of large numbers of people. The public can be the subject of governments 'manufacturing consent', a process of managing and orchestrating information received by the public so as to set and limit agendas and colour opinions. They can be deceived by other forms of institutionalised lying, by misinformation, the distribution of official lies to give a misleading account of the truth; or by disinformation, the spreading of false information to conceal the truth. Rather than an explicit lie being told, the truth can be evaded by manipulating information and presenting it in such a way so as to disguise a problem from public view. The truth can be hidden. Official secrecy can be used to control and suppress information to prevent democratic debate about matters of substantive significance. Government cover-ups to ensure that a covert action or policy remains secret can be used to create an atmosphere of apparent normality in order to avert suspicion of the truth. All the above can be classed as lies since they are actions or inactions which express deceptive intention. Whether of not any of these forms of lying can be justified is a problem to which we now turn.

Justifications

Machiavelli

There is a long tradition of justifying lying and deceit in politics. In various ways, past and present writers justify lies and deception in the political domain with reference to the good consequences they can bring about. In the history of political thought though, the case for lying in politics and for immoral behaviour of all kinds is nowhere more forcefully stated than by Machiavelli in *The Prince*. Here Machiavelli is associated with advocating the doctrine of moral expediency and deviousness in political action; the divorce of politics from private morality; the justification of all political means, even the most unscrupulous on grounds of reasons of state and the use of fraud, force, coercion and deceit in order to achieve political ends.

Although the words Machiavellian and Machiavellianism have entered the language as terms of reproach and dishonour, Machiavelli's arguments in *The Prince* have been echoed and endorsed by writers and statesmen from his own time to the present day. All subsequent justifications for lying and deceit in politics are in one way or another elaborations, defences or reinterpretations of Machiavelli's ideas.

Machiavelli wrote *The Prince* as a practical advice document in the genre of treatises dealing with the problems of princely rule. In princely literature from the Middle Ages to the Renaissance, theologians and political theorists had compiled a list of the cardinal and princely virtues a good ruler ought to have. The prince, like his subjects, was advised to be liberal, generous, merciful, truthful, kind, chaste, religious, tolerant and devout. Public and private virtue were identical, ethics and politics interrelated and inseparable.

Machiavelli radically broke from this tradition, arguing that such advice could only apply to perfect princes living in ideal and therefore unreal situations. He aimed to analyse actual political events in order to reach the truth about practical politics and to provide useful advice to those who govern. His new approach was based on a realistic assessment of human nature and the political situation and was to apply directly to the problems of the real world. Machiavelli saw himself as an innovator and claimed that his novelty lay in talking about 'man' and the state as they are, not as they should be. He therefore aimed to examine human nature and political events to bring out what was typical and general and from this to establish rules and maxims for political behaviour and successful political action.

Machiavelli rejected the metaphysical and theological underpinnings of his predecessors' arguments and claimed that his conclusions were based on facts drawn from history, his own observations and practical experience. In doing so he undermined the links they had made between Christian morality, moral virtues and healthy political life and statesmanship.

Machiavelli assumed that the goals of politics are the acquiring and holding down of power, the stability and longevity of the state, the preservation of order and general prosperity. Therefore he was concerned to show how these ends had been, and could be, achieved in the real world where political leaders could not afford the luxury of acting according to the dictates of private morality. He was not concerned to define moral rules or to explain why they should be obeyed, nor was he concerned with the rights or duties of princes and citizens. Rather, he was concerned with the kinds of qualities rulers must have and the actions they must take to achieve the ends of political life. These qualities were psychological and social, rather than moral. Actions were to be governed by prudential technical rules about means to ends, rather than by moral rules. Consequently, Machiavelli overturned the idealised conceptions of the virtues found in humanist catalogues.

Machiavelli admits that it would be praiseworthy for a prince to display those qualities which are usually considered good. He does not deny that liberality, mercy, honesty, truth, chastity and religion are virtues. He does, though, draw attention to the fact that no ruler can practise them, because the realities of the human condition and the political situation dictate behaviour which by conventional standards would be considered immoral. The irony of the political situation is such that practice of virtue can be destructive, whereas actions that are usually considered to be vicious can bring security and well-being (Chapter 15: 101).

Machiavelli draws on historical examples to illustrate the point that supposedly morally good actions can lead to evil results, and that so-called immoral actions can have beneficial consequences. The classical virtue of liberality is considered to be a good, yet its consistent practice can be damaging. A liberal prince may use up all his resources and be forced in the end to tax people excessively, making him hateful to his subjects. His liberality injures the many and rewards the few as well as bringing ruin to himself. Whereas if a prince is mean initially he will have enough income to carry out his plans without harming people. Similarly, with cruelty and mercy. Cesare Borgia's cruelty united the Romagna and brought it peace and prosperity. The misplaced loyalty of the Florentine people led to the ruin of Pistoia. Well-intentioned moral actions or refusals to act immorally may have far worse consequences than timely, selective, resolute immoral actions. Machiavelli is not merely arguing that good ends outweigh immoral means or that the prince cannot conform to moral standards if the interests of the state or the common good are to prevail. Implicit in his argument is the suggestion that failure to commit a wrong through 'too much' virtue involves moral responsibility for the bad consequences that result.

Machiavelli does not disregard conventional morality or advocate evil when unnecessary. He urges the prince to live according to the virtues when he can, when the political situation is stable and secure. In these circumstances public and private morality are identical. But the prince must be adaptable 'and have a mind ready to turn in any direction as Fortune's winds and the variety of affairs require, yet ... he holds to what is right when he can and knows how to do wrong when he must' (Chapter 18: 108). The prince must cultivate not conventional virtue, but Machiavellian virtù. He must display those qualities, capacities and dispositions necessary to restore and maintain the stability of the state, win honour and glory for himself, and overcome the blows of Fortune. He must be bold, resolute, flexible, prepared to break promises and act against charity, truth, religion and humanity. The prince must combine the cunning of the fox with the strength of the lion, and be devious, ruthless, violent or cruel as the situation demands.

This is because politics poses questions for which conventional morality is inappropriate. In times of necessity the prince must be unconstrained by normal ethical ideals, and adopt methods which though they are contrary to those ideals lead to beneficial consequences. Political morality frequently demands that the prince must act immorally – he must learn how not to be good. It is not just because of the special nature of the political situation that there is a rift between moral and political behaviour. Machiavelli's scepticism about human nature led him to suggest that there is also a rift between moral behaviour and what people actually do. It is partly because people do not act morally in either their public or their private life that the prince must do the same.

In Chapter 18 Machiavelli argues for the breaking of promises and telling lies to enemies on two grounds. The first is straightforwardly consequentialist and a classic endorsement of deception for reasons of state. Experience shows that princes who break their promises and use trickery have done great things. A prudent ruler should not keep his word when it works against him. The second justification is with reference to the corrupt nature of human beings in general. 'If all men were good, this maxim would not be good, but because they are bad and do not keep their promises to you, you likewise do not have to keep yours to them' (Chapter 18: 107). Similarly, since others are deceptive, this justifies retaliatory lies. Here, it is because of human nature that the prince is not to act as he ought, according to moral values but as other people act.

According to Machiavelli, people do not act morally, nor do they ultimately judge the actions of others by their moral worthiness. The prince need only appear to be virtuous. He must imitate the cunning of the fox to disguise his faithlessness, lies and deceit. In practice he can resort to immoral means because 'as to the actions of all men, and especially those of princes, everyone looks to the result'. If princes succeed in conquest and in preserving stability, they are honoured and praised regardless of the means used. Machiavelli's ideas on the relationship between means and ends, morality and politics must be seen in the context of his pessimistic assumptions about human motives and aspirations. Machiavelli's supposedly realistic view of human beings as natural egoists with a lust for domination and glory led him to see history as an arena of conflict, treachery and violence and to see politics as the struggle for power. The result was inter-state aggression and domestic turmoil. The roots of this conflict were psychological located in the nature of human beings. The solution was social and political. In order to acquire and hold on to power, ensure self-preservation, create order and stability an ethic of consequences must be the statesman's ethic. Conventional morality is inappropriate to the political domain when its practice defeats political goals. Given the state of the world and the nature of human beings, immoral actions are necessary and what is politically valuable depends on prudential calculation. An effective political morality must be one designed for human beings as they are, in the circumstances they find themselves in.

For Machiavelli expediency was not just a feature of certain political conjunctures or abnormal situations, but was the norm of political activity. Fraud, force, lies and violence were normal aspects of political life. Moreover, since Machiavelli thought that human beings in general were fickle, ungrateful, untrustworthy, eager for gain, domination and power, the need for immoral action was for him part of the human condition as well as a feature of the political situation.

Machiavelli stresses more forcefully than any other writer before or since the incompatibility of the demands of traditional morality and the requirements of power politics. And it is this crucial and perennial problem of the relationship between means and ends, ethics and politics that have inspired all subsequent justifications and condemnations of unscrupulous, scheming, duplicitous and cunning political practice.

An amoral defence of lying and deception

Given Machiavelli's recognition of the element of expediency in successful political action it is not surprising that Machiavellianism has been understood as an immoral doctrine that licences the abandoning of any and all moral scruples in the quest for political power. However, if desirable political ends cannot be achieved by moral means, then neither is it surprising that other writers and politicians have tried to legitimate the use of means that normally would be classed as immoral. One way of doing this is to argue that the Machiavellian idea that the 'end justifies the means' is not an immoral but an amoral doctrine when applied to politics.

Some writers interpreted Machiavelli in this way and following Croce (1925) they argue that it was Machiavelli who first recognised the 'autonomy of politics'. According to this view the realm of politics has its own logic and laws, it is a separate sphere 'beyond good and evil'. In politics, actions are evaluated without reference to extra-political or moral factors. Ends–means calculations are relevant and appropriate in politics because politics is rightly concerned with preserving and furthering the interests of the state. Chabod (1958) argued that Machiavelli 'swept aside every criteria of action not suggested by the concept of *raison d'état*'.

The concept of *raison d'état* was familiar in the late Middle Ages and inherent in the practice of fifteenth century politics, though Meinecke (1957) claims that Machiavelli was the first person to fully recognise the element of necessity in political conduct. Arguments for *raison d'état* are premised on the idea that the striving for security and self-preservation at any price is behind all state action, it is its 'fist law of motion'. The state is impelled by egoism for its own survival and advantage. It follows that *raison d'état* refers to what a statesman must do, what it is logical and rational to do in order to preserve the health and strength of the state. Reasons of state then legitimate action that would otherwise be classed as immoral. The necessity of furthering the interests of the state justifies fraud, force, lies and violence. The ends of politics dictate not the morality, but the rationality of the means.

The doctrine of political necessity and the justification of all political means on grounds of reasons of state so lucidly and dynamically expressed by Machiavelli, played a major role in intellectual and religious debates as well as in the political behaviour of statesmen over the next three centuries. This is seen in seventeenth- and eighteenth-century doctrines of the best interests of states, theories of state sovereignty and *raison d'état* which reached their supreme climax in Hobbes' *Leviathan*. It is explicit in the behaviour of ministers and statesmen from Richelieu to the monarchs of the eighteenth century and to both Napoleon and Bismarck who acted alike in ruthlessly pursuing state interests and national objectives without regard to any moral law in foreign policy. There were attempts, during this time to assert the rule of law based on Christian morality in international relations, but it is not evident that *raison d'état* was ever abandoned in practice or that moral principles actually conditioned relationships between states.

Though the term *raison d'état* is now seldom used and the doctrine rarely defended in its original form, its spirit continues to the present day in the terminology of the problem of power, power politics and the power state. It is seen in utilitarian calculations regarding the best interests of states, in the idea of the rationality of the politics of interests and in the political realism or *realpolitik* that dominates international relations theory.

Political realists, like apologists for *raison d'état* assume that the struggle for survival and security, power and dominance by sovereign and self-seeking states characterises and propels international politics. The very structure of international society creates situations of irreducible conflict. According to realists, statesmen think and act in the national interest defined as the preservation of security of the struggle for power. In their relationships with other states, they must at times pursue courses of action that would be legally or morally wrong if applied to domestic politics or to private individuals.

Political realists see their elevation of national interests over ethical ideals as being amoral rather than immoral. In this they are part of a continuous tradition which understood Machiavelli to be saying that politics is beyond or above morality. Politics is located in a separate autonomous realm of power, free from the ethical constraints and limitations of the moral realm. This implies that moral considerations, impulses and principles are irrelevant in politics and that moral praise or blame is inappropriately applied to political behaviour. Political imperatives are simply technical imperatives or prudential demands which take priority over moral requirements. Political judgements are reduced to what is rationally required given the realities of political power and every state's concern with preserving and furthering their own interests. Like Machiavelli, political realists claim to be studying the world as it is, rather than how we would like it to be.

The realist justification of lying and other immoral means as amoral and politically necessary has been, and is, most obvious in debates about international affairs. Realists argue that the use of deceit is justified because it is required to defend national or strategic interests against enemies or rivals. But, *realpolitik* arguments have also been used to justify government deception of its own citizens whether by outright lies, propaganda, the withholding or distorting of information, secrecy or silence. Justification for government dissimulation here too is given on grounds of reasons of state. Domestic deception involving military and intelligence operations, sensitive national defence information, secret operations and negotiations regarding foreign policy are justified in terms of national security interests. Evasion, subterfuge, manipulation and cover-ups in relation to government's business relationships and commercial interests, their agricultural, health and environment, economic and social policies are justified under the all-embracing umbrella of the national interests. *Realpolitik* is justified because the government's obligation is to further national interests, not to be morally conscientious.

There are, however, others who take the view that this kind of defence of government dissimulation is inadequate. They attempt to strengthen the realist case by arguing that lying in politics is not just necessary, nor is it amoral. On occasion, it is the morally right thing to do. Utilitarians justify acts of deception by the good consequences they promote, so that prudential calculation is not just rational, it is also moral. It is not just rationally required, it is also morally justified.

A moral defence of lying

The realist defence of political means based on the autonomy of politics is then supplanted by claims that political imperatives are part of morality. There is a specific morality appropriate to practical politics that is different from a morality of absolute principle. The difference is not a contrast between expediency and principle, the amoral, immoral and the moral, but a contrast between one type of morality and another. The morality appropriate to political life is not based on abstract ideals, but is a utilitarian or consequentialist morality whereby actions are judged according to the good consequences they promote. According to this view politics is not divorced from ethics. Politically necessary actions decided by prudent evaluation of the political consequences to which they are likely to lead are themselves overwhelming moral considerations.

If the aim is to maximise good consequences, then justifiable political means exclude no class of actions as wrong in themselves independently of the good consequences that result. All other moral considerations are subordinate to this. Consequentialism then morally sanctions actions normally classed as immoral or unjust because the use of fraud, force, lies and violence can have beneficial political consequences, and this is what counts morally.

The case for consequentialism in political life rests on the claim that it would sometimes be wrong for politicians to refuse on moral grounds to disregard ethical norms and standards that are adhered to outside politics. It would be irresponsible to act out of pure motives of individual conscience or in accordance with absolute principles if doing so is contrary to the general welfare of society, the national interests or the common good. In practical politics it is necessary to adopt a consequentialist ethic when ends that are judged to be good cannot be achieved without recourse to means which if judged according to the principles of alternative moral traditions would be impermissible. Adherence to moral principles in these circumstances would make the end unrealisable.

The case against moral absolutism is not just that its practice is incompatible with political success, but that acting out of pure motives can bring about worse consequences than acting immorally. Sometimes it is a lesser evil to perform an act that is normally and prima facie wrong. Moral absolutists would disagree. For Kant it is wrong to tell a lie, even if it is to prevent a greater evil. We have an unconditional duty to tell the truth in all circumstances. In his notorious example, Kant argues that if a would-be murderer asks whether our friend who he is intending to kill has taken refuge in our house, we should tell the truth and reveal his whereabouts rather than lie to protect our friend. If the murderer kills our friend, the responsibility for the harm caused is his, not ours. We have done nothing blameworthy because the murderer is responsible for his own actions. If we tell a lie to prevent the murderer's wrong, then we are responsible for any harm that results. Kant believed that lying always harms mankind generally and is destructive of human dignity. According to this position, it is wrong to do the lesser evil and tell a lie because we are responsible for the bad consequences of our actions. It is not wrong to fail to prevent the greater evil (the murder) because we are not responsible for the bad consequences of our omissions.

This view, however, operates with a narrow understanding of what we can be held to be responsible for. It depends on accepting that we are responsible for our actions, but not for our failures to act. In contemporary literature this position is defended in the Acts and Omissions doctrine. This states that a failure to perform an act with certain foreseen consequences is morally less bad than to perform an act with the same foreseen consequences. Consequentialists reject this doctrine and argue that certain omissions are as blameworthy as certain acts and sometimes more so because those who fail to act, whatever their good intentions, are causally responsible for the harm they could have prevented. We are morally culpable when we refuse to tell a lie to prevent a murder no matter how much others are to blame for the actual deed. In this way consequentialists argue that if any action which employs violent, cruel, duplicitous or otherwise immoral means is the only way to achieve a good end, then those who fail to act will be responsible for maintaining the status quo or for allowing worse consequences to continue.

According to realists and consequentialists, it is illusory to think that good ends can be achieved by adhering to absolute moral principles. Utilitarian justifications for war or revolutionary violence are often underpinned by these kinds of arguments. Idealism is not only incompatible with achieving the common good, preserving freedom, ending institutional violence or liberating humanity, but can itself be immoral. Failure to resist force with force, violence with violence, lies with lies will involve allowing the present evils to continue or to worse consequences, increasing human suffering. In these circumstances abstaining for so-called immoral reasons is self-deceiving, self-indulgent and morally wrong.

If in the political sphere actions are rightly judged by their consequences, it follows that the morally right thing to do in politics is what unproblematically leads to good consequences. There is no conflict with or between other moral principles when calculating the best means to achieve political goals. Political consequentialism justifies the apparent immorality of the means to secure these. These means are not immoral or amoral, but a different kind of moral practice.

Lying and dirty hands in politics

The condemnations and justifications for lying in politics considered so far tend to ignore the moral problems in political action. Those who condemn lying as immoral and hold that we have a duty to tell the truth in all circumstances, suggest that it is possible in politics to keep to moral principles and that when this is done, regardless of the consequences or political costs, no moral problems arise. Those who see lying as an amoral practice dismiss moral problems as irrelevant considerations. Straightforward consequentialism dissolves any moral problems by theoretical fiat. But others who justify consequentialism in politics recognise that there is a conflict between this and other ethical standpoints which gives rise to complex moral dilemmas. They recognise that keeping to moral principles can in itself be morally problematic and that a consequentialist morality is appropriate to the political sphere. However, they do not fully endorse the utilitarian view that there are no moral problems as long as good ends are achieved. They acknowledge that competing moral principles are not so easily jettisoned and moral conflicts not so easily smoothed away.

This was implicitly recognised by Machiavelli who, though he justified all political means for reasons of state, also said that it cannot be called good to lie, cheat, murder, be cruel or faithless. In telling the prince to learn how not to be good Machiavelli implies that there are actions which are judged to be bad whether or not they lead to good consequences. These actions may be condemned on various grounds: because they clash with Christian, traditional or Kantian ethics, or with any kind of moral absolutism or idealism; because they are contrary to the word of God, universal reason, the dictates of conscience or personal integrity, or because they violate conceptions of justice, fairness or rights.

Machiavelli, like many Marxist and revolutionary thinkers following him, thought that these moral considerations should not restrict the use of means which would lead to a better, more humane future, but they do not deny the contradiction of achieving moral ends through moral means. Trotsky advocated lying and violence to achieve revolutionary ends, but he also said:

> Nevertheless do lying and violence in themselves warrant condemnation? Of course, as does the class society which generates them. A society without contradictions will naturally be a society without lies and violence. However there is no bridge to that society save by revolutionary, that is violent means … from the point of view of 'eternal truths' revolution is of course anti-moral. But this means idealist morality is counter revolutionary, that is in the service of the exploiters. (Trotsky, 1973: 46)

It seems then, that lies and violence in politics are both right and wrong. Right when they achieve good ends, wrong because the means used are incompatible with other ethical ideals. This apparent contradiction implicit in Machiavelli and revolutionary thinkers is made explicit in modern discussions of the dilemma of 'dirty hands' which highlights the paradox of actions which are morally justifiable, but despite this morally wrong. Walzer in his discussion of this paradox argues that 'a particular act of government may be exactly the right thing to do in utilitarian terms and yet leave the man who does it guilty of a moral wrong' (Walzer, 1973: 161).

From a consequentialist perspective which evaluates actions from an impersonal point of view in terms of outcomes, particular acts of torture, deception and killing may be justified. At the same time though, they may be condemned from a deontological or absolutist stance which justifies actions from the perspective of the moral agent. Walzer, like all political realists, argues against the possibility and desirability of a morality of absolute principle in politics. If politicians never violated a moral rule and kept their hands clean, they would fail to do the right thing in utilitarian terms and also fail to live up to the responsibilities and duties of office. Against a deontologist or absolutist, Walzer suggests that we would 'not want to be governed by men who consistently adopted that position' (Walzer, 1973: 162). Politicians cannot do good in politics unless they are prepared to use the necessary means for 'no one succeeds in politics without getting their hands dirty' (Walzer, 1973: 164).

Walzer accepts that consequentialism is necessary in politics but resists the conclusion that prudential calculation exhausts the content of moral judgement. The politician who breaks moral rules in order to achieve a good end is nevertheless guilty of a moral crime. The truly moral politician is one who knows he or she has done something wrong and accepts this moral burden while being prepared to get his or her hands dirty to do the right thing. Bernard Williams takes a similar view, arguing for the necessity of consequentialism in politics and at the same time acknowledging the wrongness of the actions involved. He writes: 'it is a predictable and probable hazard of public life that there will be these situations in which something morally disagreeable is clearly required. To refuse on moral grounds ever to do anything of that sort is more than likely to mean that we cannot even pursue the moral ends of politics' (Williams, 1978: 62). However, Williams also argues that despite the good consequences of immoral acts, the moral disagreeableness of those acts is not thereby cancelled or annulled. Although the moral justification for a political act is consequentialist, there is a moral remainder, an 'uncancelled moral disagreeableness', a moral cost involved.

If utilitarian or consequentialist morality predominates and is correctly applied to political actions, as Walzer and Williams argue, then it is unclear why the politician who has done the right thing, all things considered, should be guilty of a moral crime. Guilt implies that he or she has done something wrong. Feelings or charges of guilt are inappropriate because the politician who has acted to promote good consequences is innocent according to the utilitarian account. For Williams and Walzer, this is precisely what is wrong with utilitarian thinking. Both want to argue that feelings of guilt and moral unease are a sign of sensitivity to moral costs despite the fact that the right thing has been done in the circumstances. Williams argues that the notion of moral costs indicates a subtlety and a complexity in ordinary moral thinking that is absent from straightforward utilitarian calculation. Utilitarianism leaves no room for moral as opposed to other costs. Success in achieving political aims may justify politicians lying, misleading and bullying, but no political end can cause deception and force to cease to be morally wrong. Although we may value the outcome of such actions, it does not follow that we value how they were achieved. For Walzer, it is the guilt involved in the violation of other values, the acknowledgement that a moral wrong has been done that is a crucial feature of moral life and of our ordinary moral intuitions.

According to these views, judgements we make about political means are both consequentialist, that is end-orientated, and action- or agent-orientated. What is the significance of this agent orientation and these moral costs, though, if at the same time as acknowledging them, consequentialism is endorsed as both necessary and right in politics? The problem facing Williams and Walzer is to show how to pursue political ends using consequentialist calculation while at the same time setting limits on the use of morally permissible means. The notion of moral costs must have some practical implications for curbing the immoral behaviour of politicians over and above a simple acknowledgment that sometimes what they do is wrong.

Moral costs and the limits on permissible means

Walzer tries to show the implications of acknowledging that a moral wrong has been done by discussing three views of moral costs: Machiavellian, Weberian and Camus', in *Just Assassins*. According to Walzer, the Machiavellian view of the political actor who must do terrible things, simply throws away morality for the good results that will be achieved. Moral costs and immoral means are subject only to prudential control. For Weber in *Politics as a Vocation* (Gerth and Mills, 1946: 77–128), the good man with dirty hands is a tragic hero who is horribly aware that he is doing bad in order to achieve good and that in doing so he surrenders his soul. The moral costs here are measured by the tragic hero's capacity for suffering. In these two traditions the moral costs are simply set aside, or acknowledged within the confines of the individual's conscience.

In *Just Assassins* (Camus, 1965), Camus' good men with dirty hands are assassins who, having killed, are prepared to die and will die by execution. Execution is self-punishment and expiation of the moral costs involved in achieving their just ends. Hands are washed clean on the scaffold. For Walzer, this is the most attractive view of the moral costs involved in consequentialist action. Although there is no executioner waiting in the wings to administer punishment, this scenario requires us to imagine a punishment that fits the crime and so to examine the nature of the crime. This refers us back to the moral code which has been violated. If we could enforce moral sanctions against the politician, then we could, 'honour the man who did bad in order to do good, and at the same time we could punish him. We could honour him for the good he has done, and we could punish him for the bad he has done' (Walzer, 1973: 179).

Walzer is right in finding the first two views inadequate in that they simply set aside moral standards and moral costs. But surely the third view too is an inadequate acknowledgement of the moral costs of doing wrong. Walzer writes as if the problem of dirty hands was simply a matter of trying to discover some form of social recognition and public sanction for the necessary wrong that politicians do. This approach does not tackle the problem of ascribing responsibility for political decisions. It implies that it is relatively straightforward to pin the blame on particular individuals and ignores the fact that political outcomes are the product of the actions of many people, and that the nature of policy making often obscures who should be held accountable. Nor does it tackle the problems involved in constituting an authority to give out the honours and to enforce the appropriate punishments. Even if these problems were addressed, Walzer's claim that politicians should feel guilty and be punished for breaking a moral rule fits uncomfortably with his view of the inevitable use of immoral means to achieve good ends and that the politician did what he had to do in the circumstances. This dual judgement pulls in opposite directions and each aspect threatens the other. If the politician who breaks a moral rule acted rightly on the whole, as Walzer claims, then there is no reason for him or her to feel guilty or be punished. If he or she should feel guilty and deserves punishment, then there are grounds for thinking that breaking a moral rule is unjustified and that the politician acted wrongly. Moreover, it is difficult to make sense of the idea that we should both honour and condemn the politician for the same deed, or to see what it would actually mean to simultaneously punish politicians for the use of immoral means and at the same time reward them for the ends these achieved.

The notion of punishing the politician for the immoral means inevitably used, like the other two views of moral costs, focuses too much on the man with dirty hands. If we think that it is important for politicians to achieve the outcomes politics values, then there could be grounds for guilt and punishment when politicians fail to achieve them through careless miscalculation, when they are guilty of official misconduct or when they act to further their own interests. But if they act in accordance with the duties of public office to pursue public interests and promote shared values, then it would seem disingenuous for citizens or authors who are supportive of these ends to punish the politician who has to do the evil on their behalf and for their benefit. It would seem wrong to lay the blame at the politician's door, the one who did the deed, if we think these deeds are necessary and on the whole justified.

Walzer's views focus too much on the politician with dirty hands in another way. They seem to sanction his or her immoral actions as long as he or she is punished for them after the event. All three views of guilt and moral costs overlook the significance of the moral wrong done to the victims of immoral means. These are the dirty consequences of dirty hands – the fact that people have been wronged, innocents killed, tortured, deceived and betrayed, their rights violated. These moral costs are not annulled, cancelled out or compensated for by simply acknowledging them and punishing the perpetrator of the crimes. It is not as if they had never been done. Walzer's attempt to find a place for acknowledging moral costs fails because neither the guilt nor the punishment of politicians has a place in morally justifying immoral actions. If moral costs are only counted after the event in the private or public guilt or suffering of politicians, then it is difficult to see how this can have much effect as a moral constraint on the means to achieve desirable ends. It removes considering moral costs from the heart of the dilemma and includes them only in the post-mortem. It suggests that the use of immoral means is justified as long as they are acknowledged as being immoral. *Post hoc* acknowledgement of moral costs has practical purchase in limiting them only in so far as punishing politicians has deterrent effects, making them and others reluctant to use them or indeed reluctant to even become politicians. In these cases politicians would not be abiding by the rules or refusing to engage in political activity out of any moral motivation but out of fear of punishment. This kind of constraint on means could hardly be described as a recognition of the wrongness of the action, of a moral cost, but only as a recognition of a personal cost.

The only way in which recognition of moral costs could provide restrictions on immoral means here is if the guilt of politicians, rather than the fear of bad consequences for themselves, prevented them from using immoral means in the future. Williams argues that if politicians find certain actions morally disagreeable then this is not only a correct reaction to the moral costs, but is also a socially useful habit. Only those who are reluctant to break moral rules and who are sensitive to moral costs will have a chance of abiding by the rules when the consequences do not justify breaking them.

However, this conclusion only puts limits on permissible means when the consequences *do not* justify breaking them, and in this Williams's position is no different from the utilitarian who would not justify actions when costs outweigh benefits. Williams's point, though, was that utilitarians pay no attention to moral as opposed to utility costs. He argues that we need politicians who will hold on to the idea that there are actions which remain morally disagreeable even when politically justified. This attention to the moral costs of actions and the moral dispositions we would like politicians to have may mean that politicians who are aware of them are more likely to hold on to their integrity or be guided by a sense of duty; they will be disinclined to use immoral means, will consider alternatives and will calculate carefully, giving moral objections the right weight when confronted with political dilemmas. But attention to the moral reluctance of politicians still gives us no criteria for determining what are permissible means to justified ends. Williams says that it is probable, indeed virtually certain, that politicians will find themselves involved in what he calls 'morally disagreeable activities' if they are to promote the moral ends of politics, or they are to pre-empt opposition to worthy projects. Where political activity involves bargaining and the expression of conflicting interests, politicians might be involved in 'such things as lying, or at least concealment and the making of misleading statements, breaking promises, special pleading, temporary coalition with the distasteful, sacrifice of the interests of worthy persons to those of unworthy persons, and ... coercion up to blackmail' for defensive, pre-emptive or other worthwhile reasons (1978: 58). In these circumstances it seems that recognition of moral costs does nothing to prevent their sacrifice.

Other writers on the problem of dirty hands are also vague about the limits on permissible means. Nagel (1978) begins promisingly with the assertion that there is no reason to think that individuals in public roles are released from moral requirements or that in politics the end justifies the means. He claims that in political life there must be a balance between action and outcome-centred morality. Agent restrictions do apply in public life, but because politics is concerned with results the restrictions are weaker, warranting coercive, manipulative and obstructive methods not allowable for private individuals. Again greater lassitude about means is allowable, given that within 'appropriate limits' political decisions should be consequentialist. What these appropriate limits are is never fully explained.

For Nagel, the only limits on agent-centred restrictions in public life seem to come from the special obligation that public officials have to treat people in the relevant population equally and therefore from the requirement of impartiality. According to Nagel, morality's impersonal aspects are more prominent in the assessment of public policy and action than in the assessment of individual action. Politicians must be impartial and leave no room for the personal attachments and inclinations that shape individual's lives. Means which involve self-indulgence, favouritism, partiality, nepotism and patronage are thereby ruled out in political life. This balance of outcome and action-orientated morality justifies the design of public institutions whose officials can do what would be unsuitable in private life. Attempts to limit incidences of dirty hands are to be achieved by a tighter specification of the moral rules which govern institutions and offices, some of them in terms of consequences and some in terms of impartiality. According to Nagel's argument then, the only restrictions on means is the requirement that they are impartial.

Similarly, Hampshire (1978) in his slippery discussion on the limits to immoral means leans heavily towards justifying consequentialism in politics. Political ends justify the withholding of scruples that in private life would prohibit using people as means to ends and also from using force and deceit. He does not actually say what restrictions there should be on these means. He only says that responsible politicians have duties of careful calculation and that this should be 'tempered by ordinary moral decencies', that there should be a blend 'between rational policy making on one side and natural feelings and reflective intuitions of right and wrong on the other' (Hampshire, 1978: 51).

It seems, then, that all those who want to argue that a Machiavellian or realist approach in politics is both right and wrong, right because of the end result the action produces, and wrong from the perspective of the moral agent, end up endorsing a political morality whereby moral rules, principles and dispositions give way to consequentialist calculation. Acknowledging the wrong that is done cannot have any moral significance if this moral sense, these reflective intuitions of right and wrong, are ultimately overridden by utility considerations. One of the reasons for the difficulty of finding a significant place for ordinary morality in politics is the general belief that consequentialism is appropriate to the political realm. If this is so, then ordinary moral principles and decencies are bound to play a subsidiary role.

The distinction between public and private morality

To show that consequentialism is appropriate to the public realm, these writers have to make a sharp distinction between the public and the private and show that there is something special and different about politics and public life that separate them from private life. Although they recognise that dirty hands are a general and familiar feature of both public and private life, the considerations that are said to magnify the problems in politics tend to obscure the significance of this continuity for the justification of a separate morality appropriate to the political sphere.

The following contrasts between the public and private supposedly justify making concessions to the immoral behaviour of politicians. (1) The moral dilemmas associated with the necessity to lie, manipulate, betray, cheat, steal and kill arise more frequently in public life and in the execution of public policies than they do in private life. Violence and force are always a prospect in politics and in the normal run of things do not occur in private life. (2) Political actors are responsible for policies which have greater and more enduring consequences that effect a greater number of people than the actions of private individuals. (3) In modern democratic politics, actors in political life are representatives of and accountable to the people. They have obligations and duties attached to their representative roles which require them to serve the interests of and explain and justify their policies to those they represent. Therefore politician's actions ought to be assessed in a different way. (4) The impersonality required for public life implies a heightened concern with results and a stricter requirement of impartiality in the morality appropriate to it.

What is morally special about the political realm, then, is the extent and frequency of moral dilemmas, the far-reaching consequences of political decisions, the assumption of a political role which carries added responsibilities and the requirements of impartiality. These are said to lead to a bias towards consequentialist morality in politics and the justifiable employment of means that in private life would be prohibited. Two observations on these conclusions immediately occur. One, that some of these considerations which supposedly mark out politics as a special realm do not in fact do so, and two, those that do could just as easily prohibit consequentialism as endorse it.

On the first point, it is not necessarily or inevitably the case that moral dilemmas occur more frequently in politics than they do in private life. As Coady points out, politics may be relatively bland and stable presenting few moral crises, whereas private life may be riven with agonising conflicts, 'like the decisions facing a mother in an impoverished, crime dominated urban ghetto, or those confronting and inmate of a concentration camp' (Coady, 1991: 376). Life and death decisions, particularly at the beginning and end of life in choices to be made about abortion or euthanasia are not unusual moral problems for private individuals. Nor is it unusual to use means–end calculation to resolve these dilemmas. Less dramatically, it is not necessarily true that occasions to lie and manipulate others occur less frequently in non-state institutions or even in the mundane business of ordinary living, nor that private individuals show any inclination to abide by absolute principles when faced with these opportunities. The moral conflicts and the problem of means–end calculation is not unique to politics. Rightly or wrongly, consequentialist calculation is an intimate feature of our daily lives; in all the small lies we tell and in the promises we break, we constantly act as if the end justifies the means.

The supposed difference between the private and public aspects of social roles does not give any credibility to the idea that political actions in particular should be judged by consequentialist criteria. Jones (1984), for example, argues that if we condemn politician's betrayal of trust, dishonesty or lack of integrity then we are illegitimately assimilating public roles to private roles and mistakenly judging politicians as if they were our close associates, spouses, friends or children. The representative role of the politician which requires them to act in the interests of those they represent justifies political lies when they promote good consequences, whereas justifications in private life are not principally consequentialist, but governed by more complex and disparate values such as love, fairness, friendship and integrity (see also Hampshire, 1978).

In relation to both political and private instances of lying, however, there is often a continuity of consequentialist justification in both. Political lies are thought to be justified when they achieve good consequences. Similarly with private lies. Those benevolent falsehoods not meant to injure anyone, but to produce benefits or to protect or further the interests of others are the lies we condone or forgive. We condemn the lies told by politicians to citizens and by private individuals to each other when either they cause harm (as some would argue is inevitably the case even with well-intentioned lies), or when they are not told for benevolent purposes or when they are told to cover up other forms of wrongdoing. We condemn and condone both public and private lying in the same way and with the same kinds of arguments.

Similarly, Nagel's argument that it is the emphasis on impartiality in politics which justifies a bias towards consequentialism is not convincing. It is true that politicians' representative role requires them to treat people as equals and to be impartial and that this rules out nepotism, patronage and personal gain. It is also true that private individuals are widely thought of as justified when they are partial in the sense that they favour the interests of their colleagues, clients, patients, family and friends over the interests of strangers. It is not obvious, though, that this shows any significant difference in the moral considerations that underpin and apply to political and private life.

Politicians' specific duties derived from their representative role are parallel to private individuals' special obligations in that they come from their assigned roles as mother, father, friend etc., which legitimate the preferential treatment of associates and intimates. But fundamentally partial relationships are not permissible in personal relations for exactly the same reasons as we condemn them in political ones. We condemn exploitation in and of personal relationships for private profit just as we condemn politicians exploiting their political position for private gain, because this signifies that those who do so are not fulfilling the obligations they have to others by virtue of their social roles. Both condemnations are derived from the same moral considerations, the special duties and responsibilities we have to consider, protect or even promote the interests of others. We condemn the partiality of politicians for the same reasons we condemn partiality in personal relationships. The differences between them are merely differences in scale. The arguments from the frequency of moral dilemmas, the differences between public and private roles and the requirement of impartiality do not suggest that consequentialist morality is uniquely appropriate to political activity.

In relation to the second point, made earlier, some of the considerations that make political activity different from private activity provide good reasons for avoiding the use of immoral means rather than for thinking that they are justified. Even if it is the case that moral conflict arises more frequently in politics than in personal relations, immoral means are not obviously justified by reference to the frequency of moral dilemmas or to the possibility of the use or threat of violence or force which is constantly present in political life. If it is true that danger is ever-present and that conflict is more frequent in politics, then this could be all the more reason for adhering to moral principles rather than a justification for overriding them. The frequency of moral conflict and the greater possibility of violence and force do not automatically licence fewer moral restraints or legitimate methods excluded for private individuals. The greater prevalence of lies, violence and force cannot on its own justify the general habit of performing such deeds or even for thinking that they are always necessary. Similarly, though political decisions may have more important and far reaching consequences that effect larger numbers of people than personal decisions, this might lead us to suppose that political actors and policy makers should be more cautious and more reluctant to employ immoral means or to depart from moral standards than actors in private life. This is especially so given the difficulty of predicting the long-range consequences of political choices and the fact that the consequences of personal choices are likely to be more circumscribed and therefore easier to determine.

Nor does it follow that the politicians' representative role justifies a bias towards consequentialism. The claim that in a modern democratic society public officials are representatives of the people and accountable to them, and it is this which justifies assessing actions on consequentialist grounds, raises special problems for the use of democratic dirty hands. In this respect, the most difficult means to justify are those which involve concealment, deceit, secrecy and manipulation.

If politicians deceive their citizens, these acts by virtue of their secrecy and public ignorance of them cannot meet the criteria of accountability because they cannot be made public. The justification of lies and deceit on consequentialist grounds seems to violate democratic principles rather than being compatible with the fact that in a modern democratic society politicians are representative of, and accountable to, the people. The politician's role would seem to prohibit the use of such means rather than endorse them.

So far we have outlined arguments for justifying lies and deceit in politics which in various ways are modifications and embellishments of Machiavelli's arguments that in the political sphere good consequences outweigh the use of immoral means. All these justifications rest on debatable differences between the public and the private sphere and do not necessarily show that consequentialist justification is uniquely appropriate to political activity or that politics is above, beyond or exempt from the moral order. It cannot be denied, though, that consequentialist calculation of a Machiavellian kind is descriptive of political activity.

We can agree that the methods advocated by Machiavelli are depressingly familiar in the conduct of political affairs. Political practice is littered with countless examples which testify to the widespread use of Machiavellian techniques. Politicians follow in Machiavelli's footsteps when they sanction violence to defend their power positions, when they resort to fraud and force to eliminate opposition, when they break their promises, when they manipulate the sentiments of their citizens, when they deceive them though propaganda, lies and silence, when they justify these methods in the name of the national interests or the public good. Whether or not the use of means which involve concealment, deceit, secrecy and manipulation are necessary, rationally required, appropriate, inevitable or justified in a democratic society is the subject of the next chapter.

2
Democratic Dirty Hands

Maureen Ramsay

Secrecy, lies and deception

The last chapter explored and criticised the idea that politics involves, or even requires, a transcendence or violation of ordinary morality, and questioned the assumption that there is something special about politics that justifies applying different evaluative criteria to political actions. This chapter will enlarge on the problems involved in attempting to justify secrecy and deception on consequentialist grounds in a democratic political order. It will first be argued that even if consequentialism is the appropriate morality for politics, it is particularly difficult to justify secrecy and lies in politics on consequentialist grounds because consequentialist considerations themselves often rule out the use of deception for political ends. Second, it will be argued that problems of justification are particularly acute in relation to secrecy and lies in a democratic political order. The chapter will conclude by suggesting that rather than looking for justifications for secrecy and lies, we should critically examine the political contexts in which they arise. We will begin by examining the consequentialist case for deception in politics.

The 'just' lie

Public officials, political realists and those who concede to their claims justify lies and deception on consequentialist grounds. They claim that these means produce substantial benefits. Democratic accountability is justifiably suspended when national security, the national interest or its analogue, the public interest, is to be protected or promoted. When national security is at stake, lies, secrecy, propaganda, misinformation and disinformation to both hostile foreigners and to the government's own citizens is thought to be justified. It has even been argued by a former assistant secretary for public affairs that when national security is at stake, the government has not only the right, but also a duty, a positive obligation to lie (*Saturday Evening Post*, 18 November 1967). This is because military secrets cannot be revealed, information on the possession and development of new weapons must be kept secret, because decisions for planning and escalating war, for the employment of intelligence agents or under-cover surveillance cannot be announced in advance, because diplomatic negotiations with foreign governments must be protected from preliminary disclosure, since prior knowledge of these would defeat the purposes for which they were employed and threaten national security. In order to protect national security and to prevent sensitive information benefiting the 'enemy', governments justify misleading their adversaries and deceiving their own citizens.

Similarly with domestic affairs, secrecy and lies are justified because they are necessary to protect a public interest. In relation to secrecy, it is argued that public knowledge about economic decisions or policies such as alterations in the value of sterling or resources, plans for devaluation of information about the extent of debt cannot be disclosed without harm to the economy. Access to information about crime control would hamper law enforcement and criminal investigations. Commercial confidentiality is necessary to avoid industrial sabotage and to prevent competitive markets from being disadvantaged. Secrecy in policy deliberations of government and other bodies is justified because private debate is necessary for a candid exchange of views and because it produces more rational policies free from public pressure.

In relation to lying, it cannot be predicted what range of issues may be thought to be in the public interest. They may range from lies told about unemployment and crime figures, to lies told about trading arms to hostile foreigners, to lies told about the causes and effects of disease and epidemic. The common denominator for these justifications is that true information might cause internal resistance, sabotaging important and worthwhile political projects. Such lies are told when governments regard the electorate as frightened, irrational, volatile or ignorant of political realities and so unwilling or unable to support policies which are in the public interest.

These defences of lying are not, but could be defended as, a 'just lie' theory, analogous to a just war theory, which does not push immoral means beyond the scope of moral judgements by merely defending them as necessary for success. Just as in the idea of a just war, ethics requires necessary discrimination between legitimate and illegitimate uses of force, so the idea of a just lie could be said to require a distinction between legitimate and illegitimate uses of deception. Like orthodox thinking about the morality of war, originally codified by Aquinas, wars are just when they are undertaken for a just cause and when they are prosecuted by just means. The justice of a lie then, would depend on the cause or end for which it was undertaken, on whether there were other means available, whether the harm caused by the lie does not outweigh the good achieved and on whether there is a reasonable chance of success in achieving the end through these means.

According to a 'just lie' theory, secrecy and deception would first have to be justified according to whether they were undertaken to secure some just cause, some vital objective, some national or public interest. In order to reconcile secrecy and deception with democracy it would have to be argued further that these means are justified because politicians are acting in our name and in our interests and because of this it can be assumed that in a hypothetical situation of foreknowledge the public would consent to the deception in advance. If it could be assumed that the pubic would give prior consent to the deception, then governments could mislead without violating democratic principles. But actual instances of government lying are not so easily justified by referring to the justice of the end, nor are they so readily made compatible with democracy.

It cannot be assumed that consensus exists on the question of what constitutes a just end, or that there is agreement on what is a national or a public interest and how much value should be attached to it. Nor can it be assumed that citizens would have consented to, or approved of, either the deception or the ends to be achieved had they known about them in advance in some counterfactual situation. Those who argue that politicians are justified in the use of immoral means seem to take it for granted that politicians represent the general interests and that they act with good judgement. As has been argued, justification for lying and secrecy and indeed any other immoral means depends on whether the ends to be achieved do represent the general interest, whether they are in the national and public interest, and on whether judgements about the necessity, efficacy and proportionality of the means are sound and likely to be shared. If justification for the use of immoral means depends in the first instance on judgements about the worth or value of the ends they achieve, then it is clear that some political ends are too contestable for their pursuit to be justified with reference to universally shared ends. In theory it is easy to say that one of the criteria for a just lie is that it is undertaken for a just cause – in the pursuit of ends that are in the national or the public interest. But, as we will show in detail, once we move from a abstract definitions, the concepts of the national and the public interest prove to be too amorphous to provide clear criteria to justify government secrecy and deception.

The national interest

At an abstract level of generality, national interests are the vital objectives or values ascribed to a nation which transcend the interests of individuals or private groups. What these vital objectives are, though, is subject to different and controversial interpretations. From a realist perspective, national interests are defined in terms of power. The most prominent exponent of this view, Morgenthau, writes 'the main signpost that helps political realism to find its way through the landscape of international politics, is the concept of interests defined in terms of power' (Morgenthau, 1967: 5). This equation of national interests with power is based on the realist assumption that in an anarchical international system self-seeking states must necessarily struggle for power to preserve their independence. The necessity for power politics in inter-state relations justifies the sacrifice of other values, the violation of promises, lies and aggression. In much political discussion of international relations, power is sought not as an end in itself, but as a means to achieving security. National interests then shift from being defined in terms of power to being equated with national security through power. But the concept of national security itself has no generally accepted meaning. It is defined either too narrowly or too broadly and so fails to provide any clear standard by which to justify government deception.

If national security is defined narrowly as defence against military attack (Almond, 1956: 371) or as the preservation of physical integrity and territory (Brown, 1983: 4), then the equation of national interests with security not only fails to cover other vital national objectives, but could also only legitimate lies, deception and secrecy in a very limited number of foreign policy contexts.

If national security is defined more broadly to include vital interests in addition to physical survival, such as economic prosperity and the integrity of a society's normative order (George and Keohane,

1980: 222–5), then other problems arise with using national security as the criterion by which to justify legitimate deception. These problems centre around finding agreement on an operational meaning for these national goals. Only a highly restricted meaning could be agreed upon. All would agree that vital national interests are involved when there is a direct and acute attack on the physical survival of citizens, when basic democratic institutions and values are fundamentally and severely threatened, when there is immanent danger of national collapse or economic ruin. Beyond this it is debatable what level and degree of security, democracy and prosperity constitute vital national interests. Moreover, once national interests encompass a range of objectives there will be different opinions on, and different value judgements made about, which has priority, which is the most vital, which justifies the sacrifice of other values.

In theory there may not be a difficulty on agreeing on ends which constitute a just cause which are in the national interests, such as the preservation of law and order, national security, democracy, freedom, peace and economic prosperity. In practice, though, the scope of these ends can be so widely interpreted that almost any policy could come within their boundaries and any means be said to serve them. The looseness of the concept gives opportunities to politicians to use deceit for private gain, to stay in power, to cover up their mistakes or to implement policies which advance class or business interests in the guise of actions to protect the national interests. Politicians are able to appeal to and rationalise these personal and partial interests as necessary for the common good.

The danger of opening up opportunities for politicians to pursue self-seeking ends masquerading as national interests is inherent in some alternative definitions of the term. Instead of defining national interests in relation to vital national goals, some writers define national interests inductively by examining what state actors say and do, so that national interests are defined in terms of the concrete interests of governing institutions, (Huntingdon, 1968: 24, Beard, 1966: 6). Krasner (1978) argues similarly that national interests are directly defined by government objectives, as these are induced from the statements and behaviour of central decision-makers. These kinds of definitions reflect the fact that the actual practices of government policy makers are not informed by any specific or formal definition of the national interest or national security as conceptually distinct from whatever the interests of the government in power happen to be. This was made clear in the Official Secrets Act trial of Clive Ponting when the courts decided that what constitutes national interests and national security are matters for the government of the day to determine:

> Interest of the State…mean the policies of the State…the policies laid down for it by the recognised organs of Government and authority.
> We have general elections in this country. The majority party in the House of Commons forms the Government. If it loses majority support it ceases to do so, but for the time being, it *is* the government, and its policies are those of the State. (*R. v. Ponting* 1985)

Definitions and practices which identify national interests with what governments say and do though are only descriptive of government objectives. They cannot provide criteria to judge whether or not their ends or the means they employ to achieve them are justifiable or even capable of universal assent. They imply that governments can never act contrary to the national interests if they consistently pursue what they define as general societal goals. Given these problems with defining the national interests, the concept over and above a narrow definition cannot provide a universally or generally agreed upon goal which justifies particular acts of government deception. If justifications of secrecy and deception depend on judgements about the value or worth of the ends they achieve, then it is clear that the meaning of 'national interests' is too contestable for their pursuit to be justified by reference to generally accepted goals.

The public interest

Similar problems of definition arise in relation to the concept of the public interests. At an abstract general level, the public interest refers to the interests of the whole political community rather than the interests of elites or minorities. According to Cassinelli this means that 'the ethical value in the standard of the public interest applies to every member of the political community' and that the public interest is 'consistent with a political situation that is beneficial to everyone' (1962: 46). But, like the concept of national interests, there is no consensus on how the public interest ought to be defined (see Schubert 1962; Sorauf 1957, 1962 for an examination of the various meanings attributed to the term). The concept of the public interest is frequently criticised as ambiguous and vague and its validity as a goal which policy ought to pursue and its use as a justification for government deception is therefore brought into question.

The kinds of societal goals and values that ought to be embodied in the public interest are difficult to determine even at an abstract general level except perhaps in times of national emergency, wars, economic or natural disasters. In these circumstances it may sometimes be clear what the basic common interests of conflicting groups are. In other circumstances, what kinds of goals and values make up the public interest are more difficult to determine. Because of the concept's vagueness, what is in the public interest can be stretched to include everything that is good and desirable in society, everything that ought to be achieved in politics. This not only reduces the concept's meaningfulness, but exacerbates the problem of operationalising societal goals in any way that could be agreed upon. There is no agreement on what combination of circumstances, what kind of policies or social arrangements, what degree and level of goods, services and material welfare would maximise the public interest. Still less is there agreement on what priorities ought to be when there is a conflict between the setting, and achievement of, various goals.

Not only is there disagreement on what the public interest is, but there is also no consensus on how it should be measured or who should decide how the public interest is to be determined. For some Benthamite liberals and utilitarians, the public interests are empirically identifiable interests, whatever the public happen to want or prefer, measured by aggregating the sum of individual preferences. Here it is assumed that individuals can never be wrong about their interests and that they can have no interests which are antagonistic to those of the community. For other liberals, public interests are identified in decisions which result from democratic political processes because of the opportunities these give for diverse interests to influence government decisions. Here it is assumed that democratic processes give equal opportunities for participation and influence, and that any policy that results from such procedures will be compatible with the public interest.

Like the concept of national interests, the public interest too has been said to be determined by government fiat, defined in terms of the concrete interests of government institutions, identified with, and identical to, the policy decisions of public officials. This denies the fact that governments may make mistakes in determining the public interest or that they are ever motivated by personal or partial goals. Idealists identify public interests with the best interests or enlightened self-interest of the public whether they know it or not. This definition is often used as a justification for government paternalistic action in general, and government deception in particular. Citizens are said to be deceived for their own good, so that governments can pursue the public interest unhindered by public opinion. It is assumed that the public are deficient in some respect, that they do not know their own interests, that they are unable to grasp the implications of decisions, that they will misconstrue the rationale for government policies. The public interest then is determined by those with superior knowledge, understanding, rationality or political skill. As such it is hostile to the demonstrable wants and preferences of the public and antithetical to democratic choice and accountability.

These differences in defining and identifying the public interest mean that there is no unified or consistent theory of the public interest. Sorauf has argued that 'not only do scholars disagree on the definition of the public interest, they disagree as well about whether they are trying to define a goal, a process or a myth' (1962: 185). This lack of consensus weakens the concept as an analytic and justificatory tool for assessing the morality of political policy. The general looseness and vagueness of the term, like the term 'the national interest', gives politicians opportunities to appeal to the public interests as a rationalisation for the pursuit of particular group interests or for their own self-seeking goals. It enables politicians to appeal to and use the public interest as a unifying strategy to make unpalatable policy decisions more acceptable. As Bailey writes: 'There is perhaps no better example in all language of the utility of myth than the phrase "the public interest". It is balm for the official conscience. It is oil on the troubled waters of public discontent. It is one of society's most effective analgesics' (Bailey, 1962: 97).

Just means

On a 'just lie' theory, lies in pursuit of ends that are in the national or public interests are justified, but in practice it is difficult to establish a generally accepted just cause which would legitimate or excuse government deceit. The difficulty in establishing agreement on what is a just cause would seem to make consequentialist justification of lies and deception particularly problematic in politics. But, even if a just cause could be found, lying to achieve a good political end would have to satisfy other criteria to be deemed a justified or 'just' lie. Pursuing the just war analogy, these criteria involve the justice of the means. Means involving secrecy and deception would have to be the only alternative to achieving the good end, the harm incurred must not outweigh the good to be attained and there must be a reasonable chance of success in achieving this end through these means. If just means must satisfy these criteria, then it would seem that even fewer political lies could be justified on these grounds. Secrecy and deception are rarely the only alternatives, the overall harm caused by the lie frequently outweighs the good intended and the deception often has counterproductive effects. Even on straightforward consequentialist criteria, the use of secrecy and deception is rarely legitimate simply because the costs and harms incurred outweigh the supposed benefits.

In politics, as opposed to private life, these familiar problems with means–end calculation are intensified because of the added likelihood of distorted judgements, discrimination, ideological bias, error and self-deception involved in politician's judgements about the necessity, appropriateness and utility of the means they use to further national or public interests. As a result, they may overestimate the benefits to be gained, underestimate the costs involved or overlook alternative solutions to the problem. Added to this is the practical difficulty magnified in politics of predicting long term consequences and the efficacy of the means to meet them.

Costs and harms which outweigh benefits

Even if secrecy and deception could be justified to protect a vital interest, the costs in terms of the toll they take on democratic principles alone could be said to outweigh their benefits. The use of concealment, deceit, secrecy and manipulation even to achieve good political ends has serious implications for the vitality of democracy. This is because these means contradict the basic principles of democratic society based on accountability, participation, consent and representation.

Deceit and secrecy by government officials offends against the fundamental constitutional principle of accountability (Friedrich, 1972: 177–80). The withholding or distorting of information or the spread of false information means that citizens cannot collectively decide whether to support or reject public policies. Concealment, deceit, secrecy and manipulation prevent citizens making judgements about the acceptability of moral costs or the rightness or wrongness of government actions and decisions. Official decisions cannot be sanctioned or censored by the democratic process. If the decision involves a moral cost or a moral wrong, then that decision becomes even harder to justify without democratic legitimation. Not informing the public, or misleading them, shields policy makers from the judgements of the public and avoids accountability for acts for which there is no democratic consensus.

Accountability is seriously undermined by government secrecy and deception. Sometimes it is argued that accountability is meaningless unless there is a public right to know, a legal right to government information. (see Madison's letter to W. T. Barry in Padova 1953 for a classic exposition of this view). Without accurate information it is not possible to hold public officials to account. Without the right to know, the way is open for governments to withhold, distort and manipulate information for their own ends. The idea that politicians can justifiably withhold information from the public, even if this is to achieve worthwhile and agreed-upon political goals, renders the requirement of accountability meaningless.

Government deception and secrecy undermine democracy in that lack of information about the decisions and actions of political leaders hampers public participation, which is an essential and fundamental requirement of democratic politics. Within the liberal tradition, following Bentham and Mill, access to information is considered important because it gives opportunities for free and open discussion and creates active and involved citizens. An uninformed public would be unable, unwilling or incompetent to perform what the operation of representative government requires. Political participation is thought to be important not just because the logic of representative government requires it, but because participatory government is itself an agent for bringing about political education and for developing independent thought and political judgement. Mill also believed that democratic debate in a free society requires access to information and freedom of thought and expression as conditions for overthrowing dangerous and erroneous ideas. According to Mill, the silencing of discussion and the suppression of ideas assumes the infallibility of government decisions. Different ideas must be openly debated and exposed to contradiction and refutation, rather than suppressed.

Information is important not just because if the public does not know what is going on, then they cannot participate in deliberations, but also because if they do not participate, governments need not be responsive to their demands. This threatens the notion of democracy as popular government based on consent. The very distinction between a democratic and a non-democratic government is that in the former politicians rule by the consent of the people. If governments deceive their citizens, then they act without consent and politicians avoid persuading citizens of the rightness of their actions through the democratic process. If governments act without consent, then they violate one of the conditions for justifying decisions in a democratic political order.

Government secrecy and deception also contradicts the democratic principle of representation (see Shils, 1956; Rourke, 1966; Friedrich, 1972; Galnor, 1977). When politicians lie or withhold information, they fail to discharge their obligations to explain and justify their policies to those they represent. Moreover, the logic of representation would seen to demand that information about government deliberations and decisions is available to ensure that politicians act on behalf of their citizens, in accordance with their wishes, desires and opinions or in pursuit of their welfare, needs and interests. It would seem then that secrecy and deception are incompatible with democracy because they violate the democratic principles of accountability, participation, consent and representation.

Some would also argue that secrecy in government deliberations has other unacceptable costs. Because information is only available to a small number of people, this limits debate and hinders communication between those who need to know the facts in order to ensure that sound decisions are made. It also narrows the range of perspectives and opinions brought to bear on solving problems, restricts consideration of all the implications of a course of action and prevents criticism and dissenting views from being heard. It is widely accepted that secrecy results both in bad decision making and that secrecy itself is used to cover up bias in the decision-making process, mistakes, inefficiency, waste, policy failures as well as corruption and other forms of injustice.

Secrecy and lies in politics can have yet other long-term consequences that outweigh their supposed benefits. One, because the habitual use of these means can corrupt and spread, leading to a decline in the standards of public life. Politicians can become so used to making moral excuses that they become insensitive to the truth. Deceit and manipulation may become the first resort of politicians whenever they decide that a particular case requires it and whenever they can convince themselves that as a result people would be better off. In the process of lying politicians can lose sight of the truth and come to believe their own lies (see Arendt, 1972: 31–4, for a discussion of the connection between deception and self-deception in relation to the Pentagon Papers).

Political deceits are often counterproductive. Even when they are genuinely employed as a tactic to further a good end, they may rebound and have detrimental effects once they are discovered and brought to light. They may cause further lies to be necessary and lead to retaliation by opponents. Equally damaging is the cynicism, disrespect and distrust of politicians once deceptions are uncovered. The harm done by the 'credibility gap' created by the lies told by the Johnson and Nixon administrations undermined public confidence in these presidents and in the political system generally. Recent scandals regarding 'cash for questions' and lobbying in Britain by exposing the vulnerability of government institutions to corruption eroded confidence in British parliamentary procedure and faith in the integrity of British democracy.

Political lies can be unsuccessful instrumentally and defeat the purposes for which they were intended. Telling lies about policy or withholding information can work against the national and public interests. Vital interests are often best served by disclosure and open debate. Of course, if lies and deceit are counterproductive or unsuccessful, if they create more harm than good, then political consequentialism would not endorse them. Utilitarian considerations themselves provide restrictions on lies and deceit for technical, instrumental reasons. Similarly according to the notion of a 'just lie', lying in politics could not be justified when this has bad or counterproductive effects. What this discussion shows though, is that even if we accept that lying in politics is justified on consequentialist grounds or that the notion of a just lie is tenable, this very acceptance rules out much lying in both foreign and domestic affairs.

Alternatives to lying – situating the problem

Those who advocate consequentialism in politics and claim that lies and other immoral means are necessary, too readily assume that it is not generally the case that lies and deceit will have bad overall consequences. At least they assume that there are political conjunctures when it is simply not possible to achieve the desired result without resort to these means, that some political ends and political situations are such that adherence to moral rules would be wrong, unreasonable or unrealistic. They take it for granted that the proper ends of politics can only be achieved by lies, deceit, fraud, force and strength; that lying is instrumentally necessary; that moral refusal will lead to political catastrophe.

But moral dilemmas where politicians must choose a lesser evil in order to avoid political catastrophe are not a standard ingredient of political life. Deceits to save innocent lives, end an unjust war, confound enemies or forestall attack are the product of extraordinary situations and not everyday political decisions. The costs of moral refusal are not frequently national ruin, vulnerability to enemies, threats to democracy or economic disaster. Even when and if lies and secrecy, the withholding and distorting of information, seem justified to prevent a greater evil, the arguments above suggest that when this is weighed against the special dangers of deception, there is little to support the idea that any overall benefit can be gained. Deceptive practices can be self-defeating, counterproductive and exert an unacceptable price in terms of other values central to the well-being of a democratic community.

The assumption that lying and immoral behaviour of all kinds is necessary in politics and that a consequentialist justification can be given takes place within a theoretical background which seems to presuppose a Machiavellian view of the world. This automatically excludes consideration of alternatives to Machiavellian techniques to achieve political ends, and also does not sufficiently distinguish the political situations in which the need for dirty hands, lies and deception occurs and does not examine the different situations which cause clashes between political imperatives and morality.

The political context

The need to transgress moral norms originally arose in a Machiavellian world where relations between states were anarchic, inherently conflictual and characterised by the struggle for power. In the context of lawlessness, where there was no check on power, where states must rely on their own resources to protect their interests, morality is displaced. Modern versions of political realism assume this background situation still applies. Morality is thought to be justifiably overridden in relations between sovereign states to protect national or strategic interests.

The need to transgress moral norms also arises in the context of revolutionary justifications for lies and violence and from the perspective of individuals or groups subjected by states that have oppressed citizenship and politics (see O'Neill, 1990). From the point of view of those fighting for justice, when they have no other power to change things, abandoning moral principles to achieve liberatory ends has seemed to be justified. In these contexts of conflict where the political situation is already amoral or immoral, where the moral predicament arises because sovereign states are so powerful or because individuals are so powerless, the achieving of political ends has seemed to justify and necessitate lies and violence and other forms of immoral behaviour. In these circumstances there seems to be some plausibility in the claim that refusing to act immorally will defeat legitimate political ends, that idealism will allow a worse situation to result or an unjust situation to continue.

However, the context in which much twentieth-century lying takes place is neither one where sovereign states compete for power to protect their individual interests, nor one where victims of oppression resist injustice. Political deception does not take place in a realist context which assumes state sovereignty in a world of independent, autonomous, lawless and competing states. In a realist scenario where sovereign states each strive to secure or enhance their own power, relations between states are relations of enmity. Relations with other states are characterised by suspicion, mistrust, the anticipation of the threat of fraud, force and violence and instrumental calculation. Within this paradigm arguments for the practical necessity of immoral action, for the breaking of promises, for lies and violence can seem compelling. It is easy to see how they are thought to be inevitable and how alternative solutions to conflict are ruled out.

Justifications for lies and violence as rational and realistic responses to political problems are less compelling, however, when applied to political contexts which do not conform to the realist model. Notions of practical necessity and *raison d'état* are inappropriately applied in the context of relations between and within liberal democratic states. That is in the context not of competing hostile states, but in the context of complex interaction and interdependence between states. Here it could be supposed that mutual recognition, legitimation and common standards should dictate norms of inter-state behaviour and give rise to generalised principles of conduct. In these international contexts the Machiavellian discourse of conflict, confrontation, conquest, domination and prudential calculation between states is more fittingly replaced by the discourse of interdependence, co-operation, collaboration, reciprocity and conciliation among states. Alternative solutions to secrecy and lies are opened up because they are implicit in the relationships between and within liberal democratic states, the principles which govern them and the values they share.

In domestic affairs debates about political morality take place in our societies in the context of a democratic, not an oppressive, political order. In both international and domestic affairs, the background situation is not necessarily or automatically characterised by conflict, suspicion, hostility, the anticipation of force and violence or domination and suppression. In these circumstances, claims that political ends necessitate immoral means are not so justifiable. The regulative ideals which acknowledge the interdependency of nations and which are supposed to preserve the balance of power between them would seem to undercut and replace arguments for the inevitability and necessity of fraud, force, lies and violence. Similarly, justifications for lies and deception within liberal democratic states can be undercut because these violate the democratic principles of accountability, participation, consent and representation. Secrecy and deception offend against citizens' right to know, which gives substance to the notion of democratic accountability, and which is a condition for effective participation and a means of ensuring that government actions represent the interests of their citizens. Secrecy and lies break the conditions on which political power is checked and controlled. By insulating governments from popular control, the powerful are able to maintain their monopoly of power. They violate the freedom from political power that is itself a condition for the existence of a democratic political order.

The point here is that arguments for the necessity, inevitability and justification of lies and deceit tend to ignore these different political contexts and the different power relations within them. Clarifying and distinguishing these contexts is important because arguments for the inevitability and necessity for the use of immoral means may be more defensible in genuine Machiavellian or oppressive contexts than they are in the context of dealings between and within liberal democratic states.

In another way too, those who argue that the end can justify the means in politics blur the context in which particular deceptions occur. The very project of justification, the weighing up of the pros and cons of various means and ends, the very process of calculation diverts attention away from the conditions in democratic contexts which allow politicians to lie with such consummate ease and which cause secrecy and deception to be necessary. They obscure the fact that many instances of government lying are not defensible on consequentialist grounds, nor are they justified in a democracy. Talk of political realism and political necessity disguises the fact that often the circumstances that supposedly justify deception are themselves immoral, and that what is wrong and morally unjustified is not simply the deception, nor that it was possible in a democratic system. What is wrong is the circumstances that called for the deception, the actions and policies that the lying attempted to cover up.

We need to critically examine the conditions that enable lying to be possible, and the circumstances that require lying to be necessary, rather than merely accepting that deception in politics is inevitable and trying to find criteria to justify its use.

The next chapter will attempt to explain how lying is possible in politics and why it seems to have emerged in particular contexts, in contexts that are democratic and that rarely provide any special justification. The analysis given here will be applied in subsequent chapters to show that the examples of political deception discussed in this book could not be justified on consequentialist grounds, even if means–end calculation is justified and appropriate to politics.

3
Explanations: The Political Context

Maureen Ramsay

Explanations for political deception are of two types. Those which identify the mechanisms and institutional practices which enable governments to withhold or distort information, and those which explain the causes of secrecy and deception. The first set of explanations reveal how lying is possible within different political contexts. These examine how executive dominated constitutions, doctrines of ministerial responsibility and executive privilege, absence of Freedom of Information legislation, laws prohibiting disclosure, classification systems, national security bureaucracy, elitism in national security policy making and secret intelligence operations, government control of information channels, ineffective mechanisms of accountability, poor safeguards for civil rights and the culture of secrecy and paternalism variously contribute to different governments' power to lie.

Consideration of these issues has frequently led to demands for reform to improve public access to official information, for a Bill of Rights to enhance aspects of citizenship and open government, for safeguards on freedom of speech, for freedom of the media to report on matters of public interest and for restructuring a framework of state power within which public bodies are compelled to promote the public interest.

If these reforms were in place, and some do exist in different countries, governments may indeed find it harder to lie or to withhold information. In theory governments would be more accountable to the public and citizens would be empowered to make a contribution to the political process. But these reforms alone would not address the problem of why governments lie or what causes the need for deception.

The causes of government deception

Although there are numerous empirical studies of particular examples of government secrecy and lies, systematic theories which analyse the causes of government deception are few. To the extent that general explanations can be deduced from the existing literature, they can be divided into four types.

The first is broadly a 'reason of state' explanation. It is implicit in realist justifications for secrecy and lies and is widely promoted by governments themselves. It suggests that deception in foreign and domestic affairs is explained as well as justified by the need to promote the national or the public interest.

The second is explanations in terms of the intrinsic nature of power or authority. Government deceptions are explained either as manifestations of the balancing act between the process of wielding state power and the preservation of democratic values, or similarly, as the outcome of the conflict between political authority and the requirements of democratic government.

The third is bureaucratic explanations which suggest not only that governments are able to deceive because of various aspects of bureaucratic functioning, but that the operating procedures of bureaucratic agencies and the relations between them generate government secrecy and deception.

The fourth set of explanations revolve around the need to thwart dissent within government and/or within the population. These, however, explain this need as an expression of the self-interest of policy makers or as serving the purpose of protecting privilege, selective interests and the concentration of power in private hands.

'Reasons of state' explanations

There is no explicitly articulated explanation for government secrecy and lies in terms of reasons of state. However, implicit in realist perspectives and public officials' defences of official secrecy are explanations which coincide with their justifications. According to this view, secrecy and deception can be both explained and justified with reference to the common good, national security, the national or the public interest.

Government secrecy and deception are justified and also explained by the need to protect sensitive information from foreign powers and external enemies or rivals; by the need to mislead their own citizens in order to ensure elite control over foreign policy. Leaders should not be prevented from taking effective decisions in the best interests of their citizens through fear of public disapproval. Morgenthau (1967:142–3), noting the conflict between the requirements of good foreign policy and the preferences of public opinion, suggests that 'the novel weapon of propaganda' be used to manipulate public opinion. Leaders must 'by devious means gain popular support for policies whose true nature they conceal from the public'. Realist explanations could be extended to deceiving citizens about domestic affairs as well as about foreign policy. It could be assumed that the government misleads the public in order to promote their best interests. Secrecy and deception then are explained by the government's fear of resistance from an uninformed, irrational, volatile or otherwise deficient public, who, it is implied, do not know, or who will mistakenly identify, their true interests.

Justifications for secrecy and deception in the national or public interest were criticised in the last chapter on the normative grounds that they were elitist, paternalistic and antithetical to democratic values. Explanations for any particular act of deception have to be assessed empirically. The adequacy of national or public interest explanations for any particular act depends on whether or not there is a demonstrable need to deceive hostile foreigners or fear that citizens will irrationally oppose policies that are in the public interest. But, more fundamentally, the plausibility of these explanations depends on whether or not particular actions of government were motivated by a concern for the national or public interest. This can be difficult to assess for two reasons. The ambiguity, vagueness and elasticity of the terms 'national and public interest' means that almost any deceptive action could be explained with reference to them. This together with the tendency to equate national and public interests with the interests of the government in power makes it difficult to explain government action in any other terms. The explanation becomes irrefutable. The only way to refute such explanations would be to challenge the definitions themselves and then demonstrate empirically in particular cases that deception cannot be explained as a result of a concern for the national or public interest. The country contexts and individual cases in this book will attempt to make this assessment.

The second difficulty arises from the problem of assessing the motivations of politicians. Politicians may claim to be motivated by a concern for the national or public interest. If they are, their beliefs about, or desires to promote, these interests explain their secrecy and deception in the sense that they show these actions to be appropriate, intelligible, reasonable or rational in the light of their political beliefs and desires. But these stated beliefs and desires may not be the politicians' 'real' reasons for deception. Their given reasons may not explain the deception. They may rationalise and make intelligible their actions in terms of the general interest while being motivated by private or partial concerns. Moreover, their actual motives may be only partially relevant to explaining the prevalence of lying in politics. Assessing explanations which assume that politicians act in the general interests involves challenging their stated motivations, questioning the adequacy of explanations in terms of motives and providing evidence for alternative causes for the pervasive phenomena of political deception.

Power and authority explanations

(a) The ambiguity about the use of state power in democracies

These explanations focus on the nature of power and the structure of authority in liberal democracies. Markovits and Silverstein (1988) explain political scandals which characteristically involve secrecy and lies, with reference to the ambiguity or 'schizophrenia' about the use of state power that is inherent in liberal democracies. They claim that political scandals are manifestations of the balancing act between incompatible ingredients of liberal democracy.

The liberal element defends the freedom of the individual against the power of the state. Liberals seek to counteract the private, secretive and exclusive nature of state power with the public, open, inclusive nature of due process, defined by strict rules, procedures, the creation of checks and balances, and public scrutiny of the exercise of state power. This liberal suspicion of coercion by the state may clash with the democratic element because the democratic tradition champions participation and equality often at the expense of individual freedom from state compulsion. The essence of democratic thought is to capture and employ state power to benefit the community, to enhance social welfare or to promote national security.

According to Markovits and Silverstein, political scandals are a product of the inherent tension between a liberal ethic which fears state power and which celebrates process as a means to limit and control it, and a democratic statist philosophy which demands effective state power to further the common good. Political scandals involve a violation of process, a betrayal of public trust, an abuse of accountability and of the very processes that legitimate the liberal democratic state, that ensure that the state is democratically controlled. But scandals are often perpetrated in the name of more effective use of state power. If the state is constrained by the rule of law, by procedural checks and balances, it may be unable to compete effectively or to protect its citizens from foreign threat. They argue that this is why fears for national security so often trigger political scandals. They arise out of attempts to circumvent checks and balances in order to act decisively to protect national security. In the eyes of those involved in such scandals, this legitimates the violation of process and justifies attempts to conceal the violation of process.

Markovits and Silverstein's arguments, then, suggest that secrecy and deception are a product of the ambiguity between the need to promote the national interests or the common good unhampered by rules of procedure, that is, between the requirements of governing or statecraft and the morality of liberalism which seeks to limit state power. Their views, however, do not explain the difference between those deceptions which arise when the morality of liberalism (due process) conflicts with the effective use of state power (in terms of promoting democratic values to further the common good), and other deceptions which arise when the morality of liberalism conflicts with the abuse of state power in the sense that the ends pursued promote partial, self or selective interests. The difference between the two and why they occur remains a fact to be explained, a fact that cannot simply be explained with reference to the intrinsic, contradictory nature of state power in liberal democracies.

Their arguments, however, could explain how both types of deception are possible in actual democracies: secrecy and deception occur when politicians' use or abuse of state power is insufficiently checked and controlled. This would explain how lying occurs, but would leave unexplained the reasons and causes of different acts of political deception.

(b) The structure of political authority

Robertson (1982) explains the degree of secrecy in different political systems as a result of different structures of political authority. His views could be extended and applied to other forms of political deception. According to Robertson, it is the structure of authority which creates an interest in secrecy or disclosure, and the ability or lack of it to further that interest. Levels of secrecy are affected by two factors, the degree to which the civil service or administration is the direct responsibility of elected representatives, and the extent to which that responsibility is undivided and hierarchical.

In the US, where the constitution separates the executive from the legislature, and where no single body has the monopoly of authority to make political decisions, levels of official secrecy should in theory be lower than in a system where one body has sole political responsibility and authority. The tendency for the President to become dominant or 'imperial' accounts for the increase in deception and secrecy up to and during the war in Vietnam.

In Britain, high levels of secrecy are the outcome of the centralised and politically hegemonic position of the elected executive arm of government which requires a clearly identifiable group of elected representatives to take broad responsibility for all the actions of state. In such a system, secrecy will be widespread because there is a strong incentive for elected representatives to control the dissemination of information. No information is politically neutral. Disclosing or withholding information has consequences for politicians' ability to exercise control and for their political survival. The political decisions they make reflect their competence and authority and their ability to make judgements. How these are viewed in turn affects their reputation and popularity. Providing, withholding or distorting information is part of the struggle for political power.

According to this view, explanations for secrecy and lies in politics are found in the structure of political authority, and within that, the interests politicians have in maintaining political power and control. Their desire for control motivates secrecy. Robertson concludes that in his view the reason for government secrecy: 'is based on the desire on the part of governments and politicians to preserve an area of autonomy, to protect the point at which politics comes to rest from the infinite demands to which it is subject and to protect the political process from arbitrariness and collapse' (Robertson 1982:194).

Those who make decisions seek to protect themselves from the constant accusation that a particular decision is not the correct or rational one. Robertson's arguments have resonance with those of Markovits and Silverstein, suggesting that there is a basic conflict between democratic government (understood as popular government) and political authority. That is, there is a conflict between democratic governments' obligation to act in the general interest, between democratic demands to de-centralise power, between democratic principles of accountability, between participation in the decision-making process, and, the kind of political authority that is needed for strong, effective decisive government. He claims that 'the boundaries between strong, effective and decisive government are maintained by secrecy'. In a pluralist democracy political judgments are inevitably opposed by some people, the government 'know that they will not satisfy every member of the electorate, but that must not prevent them from taking decisions' (Robertson 1982:183).

Like Markovits and Silverstein, Robertson does not explain the difference between secrecy and deception to carry out the common good unhampered by due process or democratic control, and deception that arises from other motivations and for other reasons. The arguments of both are similar to realist explanations in so far as secrecy and deception are explained by the need for strong, decisive government action, implicitly assuming this is always to further the common good. Like realist explanations, power and authority explanations assume that politics is an arena for the exercise of effective leadership and it is these leaders who interpret the common good. In doing so they ignore what is at issue in explaining different kinds of political deceptions. They ignore the question of whether the interests that politicians promote by disregarding process, the interests they have in effectively exercising power and in preserving autonomy are always identical to the public interest. They can ignore this question partly because they tend to assume that the public interest, decided by popular control of the decision-making process, as an expression of people's choices and preferences is fundamentally incompatible with the effective exercise of political power in the public interest. This is why they can explain secrecy and deception as intrinsic to the very process of wielding power, and to the nature of political authority.

(c)   Bureaucratic politics and bureaucratic rivalry

The bureaucratic politics explanation sees government secrecy as the outcome of the operating procedures, codes, rules and conventions that are characteristic of bureaucracies. According to this view the bureaucratic tendency to withhold information is irrational in that it is not informed by either national or personal interest motivations, but is simply the result of adherence to bureaucratic practices. This perspective implies that withholding or concealing information is arbitrary in its purpose and sub-optimal in its outcome (Allison 1971), though it can be systematic in the sense that information may be concealed because it is routinely concealed (see Gibbs 1995:215, 225, note 2). Whether or not bureaucratic norms and structures cause or reinforce secrecy is an empirical question which has to be assessed in relation to specific examples.

Explanations of government secrecy in terms of bureaucratic rivalry take as their starting point Weber's contention that bureaucracies operate 'to increase the superiority of the professionally informed by keeping their knowledge and intentions secret' (see Weber's 'Bureaucracy' in Gerth and Mills 1946:233). It seems to be generally accepted that bureaucracies have an interest in secrecy because individual bureaucracies are motivated by the desire to increase their influence and power in relation to each other (see Goodin 1980:50; Destler 1974:66). Secrecy insulates them from control and enables them to pursue their interests without restraint from other government agencies and organisations. Government secrecy is explained with reference to the motivations of officials to increase their influence, and in terms of competition between, and even within, various bureaucratic agencies, sub-agencies and personalities. The prime target of secrecy is not foreign rivals, enemies or the unenlightened general public, but other competing government officials, agencies or departments. These explanations suggest that officials conceal information for reasons only accidentally related to national or public interest objectives.

The assumption that bureaucracies are motivated by power does not explain why bureaucrats want to increase their power and influence, unless it is accepted as given or is the case that the desire for power is a brute fact about bureaucratic personalities. Otherwise bureaucratic rivalry does not explain what interests bureaucracies promote when they compete to increase their power over other agencies. Bureaucratic explanations imply that it is their interest in power and influence *per se*, and do not differentiate between the personal interests bureaucrats have in enhancing the mystique and superiority of their profession, the parochial interests of their own agencies and the personal rivalries between them and the interests that pressure groups bring to bear on particular agencies. Nor do they distinguish between their own political, partisan or ideological interests and the interests other government agencies would oppose as a result of their own self-interest or for tactical or moral reasons. Competition for power between bureaucracies may be simply endemic, the result of bureaucratic practices or personalities, and this may explain some instances of government secrecy. But in other cases competition remains a fact to be further explained, to show why bureaucracies need to shield information from other government agencies, or from more general government scrutiny.

Furthermore, bureaucratic perspectives do not explain, and collapse the distinction between, government secrecy where bureaucratic operations have escaped control by politicians, where professional administrators manipulate and deceive those with legitimate authority, and government secrecy where politicians as well as bureaucrats have a vested interest in secrecy. Explanations in terms of bureaucratic functioning and rivalry fail to fully explain why government secrecy occurs, and do not consider the possibility that bureaucratic operations themselves may reflect these reasons, being a symptom rather than a cause.

(d) Thwarting dissent

Nincic (1992) writes about foreign policy, but his arguments could be applied to deception in relation to domestic affairs. He suggests that a significant portion of existing secrecy and lies can be plausibly explained by either the need to thwart dissent within government or within the general population. Political deceits are motivated by a concern that other government units would oppose a preferred course of action or are intended to insulate policy makers from the judgments of the public when policy and the public's contextual beliefs and normative convictions are incompatible. He writes:

> Insulating policy makers from the judgments of the public and Congress when actual policy collides with official pronouncements or with the nation's expressed preferences or tacit values seems to have been the basis for much of the deception that has come to light in recent decades. Its frequent purpose is simply to avoid democratic accountability for acts that democratic consensus would punish. (Nincic 1992:148)

Chomsky and Herman agree that governments deceive and manipulate public opinion in order to thwart dissent and to 'manufacture consent' amongst those sections of the population who would otherwise oppose government actions and policies because these are immoral and indefensible. Their 'propaganda model' explains how in a democratic society with an independent privately owned media, those in power set the agenda for what information is offered, emphasised or suppressed and how it is viewed, as well as offering an explanation of why in liberal democracies systematic deception occurs. (Chomsky 1989, 1992; Herman 1986; Herman and Chomsky 1988). The propaganda model focuses on the inequalities of wealth and power, the way different social strata are involved in the policy making process, the effects on the media and the media's role in screening unsavoury events and policy goals from public discussion. It describes the filters by which information is managed in the US as a general model for western liberal democracy:

> It traces the routes by which money and power are able to filter out the news fit to print, marginalize dissent, and allow the government and dominant private interests to get their message across to the public. The essential ingredients of our propaganda model, or set of news 'filters', fall under the following headings: (1) the size, concentrated ownership, owner wealth, and profit orientation of the dominant mass-media firms; (2) advertising as the primary income source of the mass media; (3) the reliance of the media on information provided by government, business, and 'experts' funded and approved by these primary sources and agents of power; (4) 'flak' as a means of disciplining the media; and (5) 'anti-communism' as a national religion and control mechanism. These elements interact with and reinforce one another. The raw material of news must pass through successive filters, leaving only the cleansed residue fit to print. They fix the premises of discourse and interpretation, and the definition of what is newsworthy in the first place, and they explain the basis and operations of what amounts to propaganda campaigns. (Chomsky and Herman 1988:2)

The media serves the societal purpose of 'protecting privilege from the threat of public understanding and participation' (Chomsky 1989:14) and of training 'the minds of the people to a virtuous attachment to their government' and to the arrangements of the social, economic and political order more generally (Chomsky 1989:13). Herman and Chomsky offer a view of the political sociology of the American 'public' divided into three circles: the power-holders, who cross cut the fields of politics and corporate business, the broader middle class with whom they share the same essential economic and social interests, and the masses of the population whose interests are opposed to theirs and largely ignored. The last group are not the subject of news manipulation; they are kept marginalised by diversions such as sport and the entertainment business and media. The inner group have to be kept informed and need a flow of accurate news. The middle group are in fact the 'opinion leaders...who are the prime targets of the manufacture of consent' (Chomsky 1989:47). They are educated and want to be informed, and some of them have moral consciences which can make them withdraw their normally passive support for the actions of the powerholders. This repugnance has been most likely to emerge with regard to certain ruthless foreign policy operations, and could be seen especially in the case of Vietnam. It would be all the more common, according to Herman and Chomsky, if they were really aware of some of the government's adventures and actual foreign policy aims.

It is generally thought that the propaganda model offers too deterministic a view of how the media operates, that it is totalising and pessimistic, seeing the media as essentially manipulative and capable only of supporting the status quo (see, for example, Schlesinger 1989: 295–302). Herman and Chomsky do admit that the media is 'not monolithic' and point to the alternative media, grass roots information sources and public scepticism as limits to media effectiveness (Herman 1986:172–3). Despite this, Herman and Chomsky tend to overemphasise the media's ideological function and undertheorise media opposition and resistance to specific policies and to mainstream accounts; its challenge to the dominant ideology; the media's investigative capabilities and its significance in uncovering government secrets and lies.

If the propaganda model doesn't fully explain the conditions under which oppositional voices can be heard, it does begin to provide an embryonic explanation of why in liberal democracies social, political and institutional forces combine to thwart opposition. With regard to foreign affairs, which are Chomsky's main concern, he, like political realists, locates the explanation for government deception in the elite control of foreign policy. Realists, however, imply that governing élites manage and withhold information from the public in order to promote national security and national interests more effectively, or to pursue some goal that would be generally approved, such as freedom, self-determination, equality, human rights or democracy itself.

Chomsky argues that US foreign policy needs to be hidden precisely because it is not informed by national security, a concern for national interests or generally approved goals, but because it is an expression of the private interests that govern America. US foreign policy reflects the concentration of privilege that requires the state to create and maintain an international order that will foster arrangements which entrench privilege and is part of a project developed during and after World War II to construct a global system which the US could dominate and in which US corporate and business interests could thrive. For this reason the containment of the Soviet Union was a dominant theme in US foreign policy since the US became a global power after the Second World War. For Herman and Chomsky, US foreign policy and the need for manufacturing consent in relation to it is an elaboration in a particular context of the reasons why government lying occurs in capitalist democracies. The function of government is to serve the interests of those who hold power, to enable them to maintain their own economic and political hegemony. It is this social reality which needs to be hidden from the general population in order to protect the interests of the powerful from dissent from below. According to this view there is a pervasive pattern to be discerned in acts of political deception. Patterns of deceit in both domestic and foreign affairs are explained by their function in relation to established power and the needs of major power groups. The purpose of political deceit is to inculcate and defend the economic, social and political agenda of private groups that dominate society and the state. Systematic lies are required to mobilise and maintain support for these special interests.

Like power theorists, Chomsky sees secrecy and deception as rooted in the tension between the nature of power and democratic politics. Power theorists explain secrecy and lies as the product of the contradiction between power/authority and democratic control *per se*. Chomsky sees secrecy and lies as the product of the basic contradiction not between power itself, but the concentration of power and decision making in private hands and the democratic ideal that people rule in principle; between the reality of social and economic inequality at the core of capitalist society and the notion of political equality at the heart of democracy. Chomsky argues that in existing democracies the tension between private interests and public interests is resolved in favour of the former, through propaganda, secrecy and lies which function to eliminate public interference, and to deflect public challenges to private interests, power and authority.

Conclusions

No single theory need necessarily explain all government deceptions. It is not contradictory to explain some political deceits with reference to national security or the public interest, to explain others at the level of the realities of power or as resulting from bureaucratic politics and to explain yet others by the need to foreclose dissent within government or the general population for actions and policies which cannot be justified in the national or public interest. Moreover, some explanations may be specific to a particular structure of power and authority. Neither are all the theories discussed here mutually exclusive. Some acts of secrecy and deception may be better explained in terms of both the need to protect national interests and by aspects of bureaucratic politics, others by both bureaucratic rivalry and the need to protect selective interests, and others by the structure of political power and authority and the indefensible nature of the event or the activity being lied about. Equally, the mix of factors in several national cases might be similar and might well owe something to the particular political system.

But if we are trying to explain why governments share a tendency to lie and to withhold information in general, there must be adjudication between competing perspectives. Each differs in prioritising the main causal factor in secrecy and deception, the motivations of those who withhold and distort information, the principle target of secrecy, the extent to which secrecy and deception is accidental, systematic or endemic in liberal democracies, and over the range of issues that secrecy and deception potentially encompasses. Which factors most plausibly explain government deception in general, and in particular within two political contexts – the US and UK – where much deception actually takes place, will be examined below. The record of these two countries will be briefly explored to identify what might be seen as systematic patterns, and will be analysed to identify what particular mix of theoretical and contextual factors might be given most explanatory weight in the two polities.

4
Explanations: Deception in the US Political System

Lionel Cliffe

Lying and secrecy are not exactly new phenomena in US politics. However, many observers feel that they have become more prevalent in the last half century. Certainly some major examples surfaced in this period which, moreover, became notorious: first, because they exposed hidden activities to public scrutiny; second, because they excluded not just the public from knowledge about policy, but also some of those supposedly in power.

Most cases arose in the area of foreign policy, although as Nincic (1992: 125) points out: 'Woodrow Wilson's admonition that government should be "all outside and no inside" has never adequately characterised U.S. external affairs.' It is admittedly hard to assemble statistical evidence that would establish the increase empirically. But the several major, infamous cases in this period do begin to make a *prima facie* case and will be briefly reviewed here.

However, it is possible to document the change in popular awareness of government's truthfulness. In the view of the director of a politics survey centre (quoted by Wise, 1973), in the 1960s there was a 'massive erosion of the trust the American people have in their government'. Several surveys seemed to confirm a shift from about two-thirds of people in the early 1960s stating they had a high degree of confidence in the federal government to one-third by the end of the decade. Gallop polls in 1971 showed that 69 per cent of the public felt that the Nixon administration was not telling them enough about Vietnam, percentages slightly higher than voiced about the Johnson administration. The term 'credibility gap' entered political discourse and was openly discussed by politicians: Nixon even made an issue of it in his 1968 campaign. Lying had thus become a political problem; indeed, it had become a problem for those in power, for their legitimacy had been eroded. Wise (1973) argues that this period marked a political watershed in another sense: from a 'past (where) policies were generally formed by government officials to respond to events, or to anticipated events and crises. Today we have reached the point where *events* are shaped to fit policies'.

This section will first explore some of the earlier instances, prior to the two major US case studies in Chapters 6 and 7, where there seem to have been such a shaping of events. It will also review the various possible explanations for both reactive and pro-active lying and the apparent increase in the phenomenon, seeking to identify what factors in the US political system explain that tendency. In so doing, light will be shed on some aspects of the working of the political system as a whole. It will show in particular how it became commonplace for the US government to commit acts overseas which it has not admitted, has covered up or explicitly denied, or about which it has spun some false story. It will also show how such secrecy and outright lies have, more fundamentally, obscured overall policy and the foreign policy making process from public scrutiny.

Covert operations and US foreign policy in the cold war

This is not the place for a full-blown discussion of US foreign policy in the post-World War II period, but some review of experiences can illustrate the pattern of lying and the extent to which it became systemic, particularly in what can be considered the formative years under Presidents Eisenhower and Kennedy, whose images were far from mendacious. The core of foreign policy was of course 'anti-communism', the defence of the free world – the 'national religion' of Chomsky and Herman's propaganda model. That aim was probably accepted by the vast majority of American citizens, and perhaps only needed regular reinforcement. It became in fact the slogan by which all foreign policy activities were justified. Apart from the philosophical issue, seldom raised, as to whether that was an adequate argument, the policy-makers frequently ran into a problem of massaging the perception of some foreign arena so as to match the image that intervention was indeed in defence of the free world, let alone of the US homeland thousands of miles away.

The policy makers' problem became acute as the US did in fact intervene in what were often internal affairs of other countries. Intervention to support counter-insurgency could at least be passed off as legally valid as it was 'requested' by a foreign government, however unrepresentative or repressive. But intervention to overthrow regimes was more difficult to justify as that clearly transcended American democratic ideals as well as the sovereignty principle of international law. One way to get over such difficulties was the growing tendency to ensure that such interventions remained 'covert'.

Instances of intervention against existing regimes occurred with coups-*cum*-uprisings manufactured by the CIA: for instance, against the economic nationalism of Mossadeq's government in Iran in 1953; against the radical, elected government of Guatemala in 1954. It supported military coups: in Indonesia in 1965 (where it had some complicity in the subsequent assassination of half a million suspected communist party cadres and supporters), and in Brazil in 1964. Senate investigations (reported on in the book by the Counsel to the Select Committee on Intelligence, the Church Committee – Treverton, 1987) were later to reveal intervention in coups in Sudan in 1956, in Ghana in 1966, and against the government of President Allende in Chile in 1973, as well as involvement in events in the Congo in 1960s. Other findings of the Church Committee concerned 'alleged assassination plots' (US Senate, 1975): 'solid evidence of a plot to assassinate Patrice Lumumba'; 'American officials encouraged or were privy to coup plots which resulted in the deaths of Trujillo (Dominican Republic), Diem (South Vietnam), and Schneider' (Chilean General loyal to constitution); 'concrete evidence of at least eight plots to assassinate Fidel Castro from 1960 to 1965'. It was revealed even later that among the CIA's counter-insurgency role in 'allied' regimes was the 'shopping' of Nelson Mandela in 1956.

During the 1950s and 1960s the CIA was also involved in large-scale programmes of assistance in counter-insurgency to regimes, many of them extremely repressive, in Laos, Nicaragua, Guatemala, Colombia, El Salvador and Bolivia, where their agents had a hand in the killing of Che Guevara and the suppression of the rebellion in which he was involved. One major action was the training of, and logistical support for, the 1500 Cuban exiles who attempted the disastrous invasion of the country at the Bay of Pigs in 1961; indeed the CIA instigated the whole episode, although this was denied by the Ambassador to the UN, Adlai Stevenson, noted for his integrity: 'no US personnel or government airplanes' had participated (quoted in Wise, 1973: 53). The CIA even dissimulated in the committee to inquire into this mis-adventure: (then CIA Director) 'Allen Dulles marched an endless column of men in and out of the committee rooms who had either nothing or very little to do with the real Bay of Pigs operation' (Prouty, 1973: 125).

Most such activities remained clandestine until the 1970s, but, if necessary, were justified in terms of the anti-Communist crusade. However, the realities were often more complex. Most of the governments overthrown were at best 'radical' in their domestic social programmes, 'nationalist' in terms of their control over their economic resources, and/or 'neutral' in cold war terms rather than communist or revolutionary. Those who were targets for assassination were leaders of such regimes, or in some cases of 'allied' regimes (Diem, Trujillo) who presumably had become expendable embarrassments. This evidence has lead some analysts to suggest that cold war anti-communism was simply a propaganda cloak for an underlying strategy that was as much, or even primarily, targeted against independent stances in the Third World (Kolko, 1988). Chomsky (1989) gives a prominent place in his explanations to a process of creating 'illusions' by targeting certain regimes and their leaders, usually 'but not always' tarring them with the 'communist' brush, a 'demonisation' that would justify intervention for 'containment' purposes. Certainly many of the kinds of policies and the specific tactics illustrated above do have the potential, in Chomsky's terms, to worry the consciences of the educated politically-active middle class who are the main targets of the propaganda model. That is why these kinds of activities have to remain 'covert'.

It was, of course, these kinds of lies about the war in Indochina, discussed in the next section, which not only amplified this practice, but also triggered the scrutiny of an array of activities over the previous two decades by the Senate investigations (the Church Committee) in 1975.

The war in Indochina

Critics of government activities in connection with Vietnam contended that the American people had been lied to consistently about the war: Lyndon Johnson's assurance that he sought no wider war while he was actually planning one, the false reporting of the Gulf of Tonkin incident, Richard Nixon's hinting that he had a plan to end the war if he was elected. Some were willing to ascribe the embarrassingly optimistic official forecasts of imminent victory (all the upbeat talk about 'turning the corner' or 'home by Christmas' or 'the light at the end of the tunnel') to mere ineptitude, sheer ignorance of the situation in the field. Others, however, saw these predictions as part of a policy of conscious deception, knowing attempts to beguile and mislead. Inflated official estimates of enemy dead, hiding American casualty figures from the public, secret bombing of Laos and Cambodia that lasted for months, the clandestine activities of the CIA and the FBI in spying on the free citizenry of the United States, the use of provocateurs and infiltrators, the attempts to control the media or to intimidate the peace movement – all indicated a government, according to the antiwar critics, that had turned away from established ethical practices and traditional constitutional guarantees. (Levy, 1991: 62–3)

US involvement in Vietnam in the 1960s, and what was said officially about it, marked a stage where government deception became endemic. In the early 1960s the Kennedy and then Johnson Administrations were involved in what was still essentially a covert operation: the US military supplied 'advisers', who were not supposed to be involved in combat, and arms to the government of South Vietnam. These were operations orchestrated by the CIA. Like earlier covert operations, their character, scale and intent were the subject of denials and misinformation.

In fact, dirty tricks activities against North Vietnam date back to 1954 when the Geneva agreement was signed to end the 'First' Indochina War for independence from France, dividing the country into two zones, in what was supposed to be a temporary arrangement to facilitate demobilisation leading to a country-wide election within two years. The US backed sabotage and terrorist operations with the South Vietnam authorities against the North, keeping them secret so as to be able to refute charges that it was violating the Geneva accords. Indeed, the historian of the Vietnam War, Karnow (1984), suggests that this marked the origin of a 'practice of dissimulation, loftily termed the "principle of plausible denial" … still pursued today to shroud undercover operations that may create diplomatic complications'. But the deception went deeper, for it sought to obfuscate the very nature of the war and of US policy in the eyes of the American public. The two zones were presented as two independent states, and the setting up and survival of anti-Communist South Vietnam, against the provisions of Geneva, was pursued by Washington. The war when it grew, first as an insurgency within the South (as the leaked Pentagon Papers, see below, were to confirm), could be passed off as an international act of aggression from the North, (the evidence for which the Pentagon Papers found 'not wholly compelling' – Sheehan, 1971: 67), rather than a civil war. This labelling was a major issue in foreign policy in the early 1960s, and the Administration's interpretation justified the military support to South Vietnam – although the scale of it, the fact that the number of advisers had reached 12 000 by 1963, and that helicopter and plane pilots and others among them were engaged in combat missions, were covered up. The increased involvement also enabled a mushrooming of the South Vietnamese forces from 100 000 to 270 000 in the early 1960s.

During this build-up in 1961–3, US policy makers became more convinced that the regime of President Diem, with its propensity for corruption and repression of non-communist opposition, was itself an impediment to successful counter-insurgency. Some US officials began to urge his removal; Ambassador Henry Cabot Lodge in an August 1963 cable said: 'We are launched on a course from which there is no respectable turning back: the overthrow of the Diem government' (Pentagon Papers, reproduced in Sheehan, 1971: 197). The US government became aware of plans for a coup by the generals at the beginning of 1963, and President Kennedy instructed US Ambassador Lodge in Saigon:

> If you should conclude that there is not clearly a high prospect of success, you should communicate this doubt to the generals in a way calculated to persuade them to desist at least until chances are better … But once a coup under responsible leadership has begun … it is in the interests of the U.S. government that it should succeed.
> (Quoted from the Pentagon papers by Karnow, 1984)

The US did not participate directly in the eventual coup which lead to Diem's murder in November 1963, but knew about it and had indicated their general approval, while ensuring that any involvement could be 'plausibly denied', by the withholding of aid to Diem's government, widely interpreted as a signal, as well as specific messages transmitted to the Generals.

The major escalation came with the introduction of US ground troops in the South and the initiation of bombing raids on North Vietnam. These events occurred in 1964, a few months before Lyndon Johnson was to win a landslide victory as the 'peace candidate'. The President used two naval incidents in August in the Gulf of Tonkin, off North Vietnam, and the reports that two US ships had come under unprovoked attack to get Congress to approve the Tonkin Resolution, within days giving him authorisation for sending troops and for bombing – and almost unlimited other powers to take all necessary measures to prevent further aggression, without a formal declaration of war. The actual Tonkin Incidents turned out to be quite different from reports: the USS Maddox which was 'under attack', was challenged seemingly by North Vietnamese patrol boats, two of which were sunk, but on return to base it had received one bullet-hole in this act of unprovoked aggression! Its role in supporting regular covert incursions by South Vietnamese boats and its presence in North Vietnamese and not international waters was denied by Secretary of Defense, Robert McNamara. He testified before a secret session of the House and Senate Foreign Relations Committees on 6 August 1964 that: 'our Navy played absolutely no part in, was not associated with, was not aware of, any South Vietnamese actions, if there were any ... The Maddox was operating in international waters, was carrying out a routine patrol of the type that we carry out around the world at all times' (Sheehan, 1971: 265). But the second incident two days later most likely never occurred at all: the Maddox's captain was later to admit 'there was no actual visual sightings' merely blips on the radar more likely to be a result of freak weather than enemy attack. On this spurious evidence the House of Representatives passed the Resolution unanimously and the Senate with only two votes against. The influential chairperson of the Senate Foreign Relations Committee, Senator Fulbright, who was persuaded to ferry the Resolution through Congress, was later to complain bitterly about being duped. What cast further doubt on the story was the later revelations that the South Vietnamese naval raids were not so much designed to pressure the North to stop its support for the NLF in the South, but as acts of provocation; that a scenario which envisaged a bombing campaign against the North and other escalations to really pressurise the Hanoi Government and that some incident could be used to trigger this process and to get war powers from an (until then) reluctant Congress, had been put before President Johnson in May 1964. These and other major doubts about the Incidents that sanctioned prosecution of the war were finally brought out (Senate Foreign Relations Committee, 1968). In his book on Vietnam 30 years later, McNamara rejects the assertion of critics 'that a cloak of deception surrounded the entire Tonkin Gulf affair ... that the administration coveted congressional support for war in Indochina, drafted a resolution authorising it, provoked an incident to justify support for it, and presented false statements to enlist such support' (McNamara, 1995: 139). However, he does admit that Fulbright and other Congressional leaders had been misled by assurances that Congress would be fully consulted on the use of the powers they were persuaded to grant. In the event, President Johnson increased US troop deployments from 16 000 to 500 000 without any approval from the legislature.

The Resolution led to the introduction of US combat troops on the ground, and their number grew inexorably until there were 500 000 in 1968. The progress of this war was also the subject of an up-beat spin by a plethora of army information personnel. Kolko (1986) describes this pattern:

> The daily announcement of body counts personified the extent to which sanctioned slaughter would go, but as most knew then, and openly admitted later, the emphasis on inflated numbers bore no relationship to who was winning the war. The Pentagon's Systems Analysis experts routinely discounted such figures. Meanwhile they simply horrified ever-larger sectors of American and world opinion.

The military PRs' ability to present their own version of the progress of the war became constrained as some members of the massive press corps that US involvement in the war had spawned developed their own sources and made their own observations. In future wars, part of the strategy, learning from the very structured access the media was given to the British war in the Falklands/Malvinas, was the very careful orchestration of reporters' access to war (see Hoffman, 1991, on Panama). But the picture of a war gradually being won, with images of GIs being ferried to villages for the hard, patient graft of 'search-and-destroy' missions, seen directly on US television, was shattered by the NLF–North Vietnamese offensive at the lunar new year, Tet, in 1968. Major towns and cities and not just villages, even the 'impregnable' US Embassy in down-town Saigon, were simultaneously under attack – and screened to an American audience. Although it did not have the effects intended by its generals, the Tet offensive did have the unintended consequence of decisively shifting public opinion in the US against the war.

Given the interlinking of counter-insurgency and pacification efforts through an emphasis 'centring on the military and technical means for physically controlling the population' (Kolko, 1986: 131), it became inevitable that military operations by US and South Vietnam troops would often be directed against the villagers. One such episode at the village of My Lai, where 450 ordinary – many old – men, women and children were murdered, later became a *cause célèbre* and the officer in charge of the detachment was court-martialled. But that only occurred after a cover-up; at earlier moments, 'the My Lai operation was briefed for visitors as one of our successful operations', according to Colonel Henderson, who was acquitted of charges in 1971 of covering up the massacre (quoted in Wise, 1973). A full acknowledgement by the US army of the brutality could be said to have waited until the whistle-blowers who reported the incident were finally honoured in 1998.

The overall upshot of specific deceptions, even if it sometimes involved self-deception, of the origins, character and progress of the Vietnam war was that there was no questioning of the overall strategy of its conduct, a strategy whose 'assumptions were deeply flawed'. McNamara (1995: 210) was to admit 30 years on: 'We did not force the Vietcong and the North Vietnamese Army to fight on our terms. We did not wage an effective anti-guerrilla war against them. And bombing did not reduce the infiltration of men and supplies into the South below required levels or weaken the North's will to continue the conflict.' His account of the decision-making process brings out how any alternative approach was not so much rejected as never seriously considered. Arguably the general mis-information and exclusion of genuine political accountability – until the protests had crescendoed by the end of the 1960s – helped to perpetuate the pursuing of an unrealistic and tragically brutal policy.

1964 had seen the beginnings of another escalation of tremendous proportions elsewhere in Indochina which was never approved by, nor notified to, Congress and was kept completely from the American public. From the point of view of powerholders anxious to keep their barbaric acts from public scrutiny, this perhaps represented the most successful example of hiding the facts of the whole Indochina wars. In that year the US Air Force began the systematic bombing of two areas in neighbouring Laos. On the few occasions when justifications were made, or the bombing was ever referred to publicly, it was cited as part of the effort to interrupt the flow of war supplies along the Ho Chi Minh Trail along the border areas of Laos and Cambodia from North Vietnam to the insurgent forces in South Vietnam. This explanation might cover some of the bombing in the South of Laos, but not that in the Plain of Jars in the North of the country, which received the heaviest bombardments. Saturation bombing was designed to reduce the population directly or to make life there untenable, rather than to attack specific military targets. These tactics corresponded to 'forced draft urbanisation' (to force peasants to flee to towns where they would not be available to give sustenance to guerrillas and the revolution), advocated by expert adviser Harvard Professor Samuel Huntington, which were those used in NLF-controlled areas of South Vietnam. In northern Laos the bombing went on from 1964 to 1971 before Congress was informed that it was happening. Casualties were estimated at 30 000 deaths a year, with one and a half million people being made refugees. Up to that time, according to a former USAF reconnaissance expert 'The Rules of Engagement were strictly adhered to from 1966 to 1968 (that forbade attacks on civilian targets) but for all practical purposes after ... March 1969 they appear to have been discarded and are only cited to placate Congressmen in Washington' (quoted in Littauer and Uphoff, 1972: 83–4). Thus while administration officials continued to insist that no civilian targets have been hit except as a regrettable result of what in later wars came to be called 'collateral damage', the scale of the bombing and types of weapons, and the massive destruction of people, their farms and homes and the environment suggests that the bombing campaign was in fact a deliberate onslaught against the people.

These several events and dimensions of the war which were the subject of cover-ups, secrecy or dissembling are but a selection (for thorough documentation see Prados, 1986) which indicate the endemic character of the lying that went on. They also eliminate one common justification for falsification in time of war: confusion of the enemy. The Laotian peasants knew they were being bombed, killed and hurt, as did civilians in North Vietnam, or peasants in 'pacified' villages in South Vietnam. The truth about the various episodes and strategies was being kept from the public at home in the USA. The lies were to cover the overall character of the war, and the underlying policies. This imperative became a major dimension of government policy as opposition to the war mounted to an enormous scale through 1967, up to the invasion of Cambodia in 1970. The systematic falsification of what was happening was the biggest single element in the 'credibility gap' that Richard Nixon was referring to in his 1968 election campaign. But far from reducing it, his own record and his eventually being forced into resignation for lying massively widened it, as we shall explore below. The contrast between his public stance on Vietnam and his actions contributed to the process. He presented himself as the 'peace candidate' in the 1968 campaign, and he did gradually reduce US troop levels, but only by escalating the air war and the high-tech electronic battlefield, and funding a vast increase in the size of the South Vietnamese army to over a million. All in the end to no avail: a consistent lie of all administrations was that a war was being won that finally lost in 1973.

Before tracing how this and other patterns of institutionalised falsification infected other areas of US political life and policy-making, especially around Watergate, one further legacy of the mistrust of government generated by the war must be noted. There grew up a 'Vietnam Syndrome', a great reluctance on the part of politicians and public to commit the US to action, and particularly to commit ground troops, in any situation that offered the prospect of a 'slippery slope' of increasing and irreversible involvement in a possibly unwinnable foreign war. That sentiment and the implied argument was to remain a factor in foreign policy making for the next thirty years, and did decisively constrain some overseas adventures and affect the reaction of Congress and public to them. The resulting policy calculations took various forms, some very pragmatic ones that lead to the use of proxy troops where possible. But the Vietnam syndrome also had a more idealistic strand, corresponding rather precisely to the moral repugnance of certain sections of that body of informed opinion that ordinarily had interests basically the same as those that governments tended to further, which Chomsky's model (Herman and Chomsky, 1988) envisages. Conversely, some argue that government orchestration of perceptions was precisely targeted to overcome the constraint on foreign involvements of the Vietnam syndrome.

The domestication of covert politics and Watergate

Before probing further the implications of the Vietnam syndrome and other legacies of the war for the working of the whole political system and government relations with the public it is necessary to consider parallel trends in the covert politics associated with foreign interventions that were afoot within the country. By the late 1960s the CIA was beginning to exceed its mandate and operate against what it considered 'subversive' elements at home. Far more widespread were the activities of the Federal Bureau of Investigation (FBI). Its long-serving director, J. Edgar Hoover, had seen it as part of his role to be vigilant against the 'menace of communism', but in the 1960s began an orchestrated campaign of harassment, infiltration, use of agents provocateur, and participation in assassination of activists, targeting not only the US Communist Party against which an operation had been running since 1956, but others on the left like the Socialist Workers Party (Blackstock, 1988), elements of the black power and civil rights movements such as the Black Panther Party and Martin Luther King's organisation and the American Indian Movement (both documented in Churchill and Van der Wall, 1988), and what was broadly termed the 'New Left' – the student radical movement and the anti-war movement, plus the Puerto Rico independence movement and the

Ku Klux Klan. These counter-intelligence operations were referred to by their official acronym, COINTELPRO.

In general, the COINTELPRO operations exceeded the FBI's legal powers which allowed for a level of intelligence gathering for internal security purposes but not the pro-active, aggressive acts that were described by a Senate investigation (US, 1976) as 'misdirect, discredit, disrupt and otherwise neutralise' specific individuals and groups. The specific operations had not, seemingly, been approved by any other executive authority, let alone the legislature. These revelations moved Senator Church to refer to COINTELPRO as 'one of the sordid operations in American law enforcement' (Churchill and Van der Wall, 1988: 62), and House majority leader, Hale Boggs, to talk about 'when the FBI adopts the tactics of the Soviet Union and Hitler's Gestapo' (Congressional Record, 1971: 9470). The questionable legal nature of the operations and the fact that the tactics would be viewed as abhorrent meant that, of course, they were kept secret, and denied when the tip of the iceberg began to appear.

Other analysts point to another factor making these kinds of operations possible: Hoover's files gave him the ability to blackmail other powerholders, and thus provided the basis for considerable autonomy. Epstein (1991) in fact takes this argument a stage further suggesting that the autonomy of security agencies and their ability to exert leverage meant that: 'presidential power is severely mitigated, if not entirely counter-balanced, by the ability of officials in key agencies to disclose secrets and private evaluations to the public that could severely damage the image of the president (p. 1).' He builds on this observation, and a great deal of documentary evidence, notably from Egil Krogh, Jr., on Nixon's White House staff dealing with law enforcement and convicted over the 'Watergate' operations, to suggest that Nixon was so concerned by the disparate structure of these bureaucracies and their uncontrolled character that he set in motion the 'Plumbers' project. He further argues that this was more than just a team that sought to plug 'leaks', and which undertook a variety of covert political activities, culminating dramatically in the Watergate burglary and the array of other operations disclosed with it, but sought to set up new structures that 'would have so radically changed the balance of power within the government that it would have been tantamount to an American *coup d'état*':

Nixon, realising that he securely controlled only the office of the president, methodically moved to destroy the informal system of leaks and independent fiefdoms. ... a series of new offices were set up, by executive order, ... which, it was hoped, would provide the president with investigative agencies having the potential and the wherewithal and personnel to assume the function of the 'Plumbers' on a far grander scale. (p.2)

He further posits that this scenario was legitimised by the need for a massive campaign to halt the 'drugs epidemic'. That proposition, and the misconception of the problem of drugs and of the problems of crime and deprivation in the inner cities that it purportedly 'caused', will be explored in the chapter on the 'War on Drugs'. The fate of the project was sealed with the exposure of Watergate-related activities. How far it offers evidence of an explanation of government deception in terms of a 'secret state within the state' will be explored below. Here we should simply note that it suggests that rather than an integrated, homogenous power beyond any possibility of democratic control the FBI and the CIA and other intelligence agencies could be seen as several, uncoordinated 'security states'. Indeed, a central goal of Nixon's project was to call them to heel and bring them together.

One of the first operations of Nixon's plumbers, a year before Watergate itself, involved a further legacy of the Indochina Wars: the Pentagon Papers. This collection of thousands of documents with commentary, which encompassed 13 volumes when published as a Senate Paper (Gravel, 1972), was commissioned by McNamara in 1967, who says he was concerned about the costs and wanted to help future historians explain 'why this failure?' (McNamara, 1995: 280). It does indeed reveal much of the policy process, its rationale and what government's own reports documented was happening as opposed to what press releases said. But it became a *cause célèbre* in the US when it was leaked to the *New York Times* by one of the researchers who had worked on it, Daniel Ellsberg. Although it dealt primarily with events up to 1968, before his election, President Nixon reacted by trying every legal channel to block publication, and when Senator Gravel read it into the Congressional record and the Supreme Court sanctioned publication he sought to have the leakers punished. The White House plumbers were revealed by the Watergate inquiries as responsible for a 1971 break-in of Ellsberg's psychiatrist's office, and the FBI had bugged his phone since 1969. The break-in was no doubt seeking evidence against Ellsberg and Anthony Russo who were in fact indicted on charges of conspiracy, espionage and theft of government property (although not for passing the Papers to the press), the first ever case in the USA of criminal prosecution of people associated with the leak of classified information. This crucial test case raised a range of basic issues about presidential power (Kincaid, 1992): the charge of 'theft' raised the question of who owns information in a democracy; the charge of 'espionage' for releasing material to American readers through American newspapers implied, quipped Russo, that the Nixon Administration regarded the American people as its enemy! Unfortunately no judicial precedent on these constitutional issues was established, as the case was thrown out by the judge after dragging on for ten months, on the grounds of 'improper government conduct' when the burglary became known.

The burglary and planned bugging of the Democratic Party headquarters was in fact only one of many dirty tricks organised around the 1972 election. The plumbers and their like tried to use black propaganda against the candidature of Ed Muskie, the Democratic candidate they feared the most; they spread false stories about the opposition, sent false mail and press statements purporting to come from the Democrats, announced that meetings were cancelled. The one member of the Senate Committee that was eventually set up to investigate Watergate who could claim some independence from either party's machine, Lowell Weicker, said at the outset of the investigation that these people 'almost stole America' (quoted in Wise, 1973: xiv).

Even if the actual burglary of the Democratic party headquarters was but one of a range of events labelled 'Watergate', it assumed great significance because it led to the investigation which eventually unravelled the involvement of senior government personnel in that, and other, illegal political activity and their cover-up, and in turn the resignation of President Nixon. That process of investigation is also revealing. It offers a window through which not only specific political activities but also the nature of politics at that time can be publicly viewed. It is also cited by those who retain confidence in the self-correcting ability of the US political system as an example of how abuse was rooted out and reversed. Specifically, it is pointed out that the media did act as a 'fourth estate', and that indeed its critical, investigative role was reasserted through the Watergate experience; and that the division of powers allowed the Legislature to hold the Executive to account, and thereby clawed back some of the war powers of an imperial presidency and checked the application of the questionable doctrine of 'executive privilege'. Critics argue against such complacency, pointing out that far from the media or the Congress performing their watch-dog roles, only a few newspapers, notably the *Washington Post*, and a very hesitant, late-in-the-day Senate Committee took part; that there was virtually no challenge until well after Nixon's re-election over five months after the break-in; that the Democratic Party and most professional politicians in Congress were most reluctant to press issues (Karp, 1973); and that break-ins and other illegal acts against political groups outside the main stream, like that into the Socialist Workers Party as a COINTELPRO operation, which was found illegal, attracted no interest [which comparison Chomsky (1989) offers as a test for his propaganda model]. In fact the *Washington Post* journalists' own account (Bernstein and Woodward, 1974) demonstrates how their investigation might have petered out at several moments, and how it depended on the crucial pointers from within the system provided by 'Deep Throat'.

A key role, and one that could not have been anticipated, was in fact played by the court of Judge Sirica, which in January 1973 set out to try the five burglars and Howard Hunt and Gordon Liddy who had stage-managed it – supposedly the only ones involved in this 'maverick' operation. He became convinced and angered by an apparent collusion between defence and prosecution, especially when the plea was changed to 'guilty' – later to be shown as a result of a pay-off for silence, with covert funds from the re-election kitty – so he widened the investigation by recalling the grand jury that had first investigated the burglars' involvement and set a high bail for Liddy and McCord, the only one of the defendants who had not pleaded guilty. At the prospect of severe punishment, McCord implicated others in the White House and indicated that the defendants had been pressured into confessing, and confessing they were the only ones in the know. These and subsequent revelations finally prompted the Senate into appointing in mid-1973 an investigative committee under Sam Ervin, and the Attorney General, Richard Kleindienst, who had succeeded John Mitchell, into appointing a Special Prosecutor, Archibald Cox. In the succeeding months, the circle of those involved not just in CREEP, but also in the White House, widened. Some of Nixon's closest advisers were forced to resign, the range of related activities, the scale of the cover-up, and the degree of the President's knowledge of, and complicity in, the events also widened. A crucial and almost accidental revelation was of the tapes made by Nixon of every conversation in his office. But Nixon fought a rear-guard action. He sacked the Special Prosecutor he had himself appointed, after the Attorney General refused to – an act which was arguably illegal and which for some had the profoundest constitutional implications (Kassop, 1992). (It was this action which provoked Congress into passing legislation for an Independent Counsel to give more legislative control – an office that was to come into play over Iran–Contra and over Clinton's affairs.) He refused to let go of the tapes and managed to lose some strategic minutes from them when finally forced to give them up by Judge Sirica's sub-poenas and the Ervin Committee. It was not until August 1974 that pressures from the Senate Committee, proposals for his impeachment and a groundswell of public protest finally forced Nixon to resign.

The release in 1996, after a long legal battle, of many more hours of tapes finally 'provide[d] a massive, overwhelming record of Nixon's involvement and his instigation of obstruction of justice and abuse of power ... [and] expose[d] a level of culpability far greater than imagined twenty five years ago' (Kutler, 1998: xv).

The Vietnam syndrome and the Watergate legacy

By the mid-1970s the combined effect of the revelations about Watergate, the withdrawal after defeat in Vietnam and the consequent exposure of posturing about the war, and the investigations about covert action culminating in the Church Committee, had changed the political climate somewhat (see Silverstein, 1988). Covert operations were less likely to be concealed and foreign adventures, whether covert or not, were less likely to be endorsed by a Congress more jealous of guarding its powers against an encroaching presidency and a suspicious public – although this did not amount to a complete sea change. It was agreed that covert actions had to be reported to a congressional oversight committee. Congress did, for instance, pass the Clark Amendment soon after the outbreak of the so-called 'civil war' in Angola in 1975 under which covert or overt military assistance to any movement opposing the Angola government was prohibited (Wright, 1997). But this was locking the stable door after the horse had bolted, as there had been a CIA operation to back two of the three contesting movements, and collusion with the apartheid regime in South Africa which had invaded Angola – even though this was denied by Secretary of State Kissinger it was later confirmed by the whistle-blowing account by the CIA's director of operations (Stockwell: 1978).

Successive US administrations continued to provide indirect succour to the rebel movement in Angola, and even sought to repeal the Clark amendment, until the early 1990s (Wright, 1997). A similar scenario of

covert support being maintained in the teeth of congressional pro-
hibitions was also played out in relation to US support of the right-
wing *contra* rebels in Nicaragua (see chapter on Iran–Contra). In this
latter case the dissembling was made even more 'deniable', and more
direct control by the Reagan Administration was ensured – no doubt
having learned from Nixon's exposure – by locating the covert actions
not in the CIA but in a semi-official unit of the National Security
Council with direct access to the White House, but able to operate with
little scrutiny. The Vietnam syndrome perhaps operated to prevent any
commitment of US troops to Angola or Central America, but did not
inhibit overt military invasions of Grenada in 1983 and Panama in
1989. These were respectively justified in terms of a response to the
overthrow and killing of the President Maurice Bishop, and the 'arrest'
of President Noriega as a drug trafficker. However, the killings and
destruction were more widespread than would seem to be warranted by
these excuses, especially in Panama, and both interventions were followed by the installation of regimes through a political process orchestrated by the US. It is noteworthy that the suffering imposed, and
evidence that might reveal the real policy objectives, was largely successfully 'managed' by the military carefully controlling the access of
media reporters; they were kept out of each country for some days
(Hoffman, 1991), learning perhaps the advantages from the British
military control of the media in the Falklands campaign, and in
marked contrast to the open access in Vietnam.

Explanations

This rapid survey has concentrated on deceits over foreign policy and
comparable patterns of 'covert politics' at home. A similar though less
dramatic portfolio of cases could be assembled about economic policy
if space allowed. It would tend to show how policy matters that affect
ordinary people are often settled on the quiet without 'ever really
being treated as a "public issue"' – as Grieder (1992: 66) commented
about one of the most notorious of such cases, the Savings and Loan
scandal of the 1980s. Explanations should therefore not be confined
solely to the foreign policy area.

There are few systematic attempts to provide an overall explanation
of these several types of cases and of the prevalence of lying in the
US political system. Even Chomsky's propaganda model is stronger
on the means rather than the reasons. However, in the considerable
literature on these separate incidents, explanations abound, often

implicitly – including examples of the four levels and types of explanation considered in Chapter 3.

However, one additional level of explanation of the apparent acceleration of deceit under certain administrations is, of course, in terms of the personalities involved. As Wise (1973) remarked, 'there was a certain inevitability that the term "credibility gap" should have been born during the Johnson administration'. Wise characterises him as 'complex and immensely secretive' and sees a 'frequent gulf between his words and reality'. Similarly, Karnow (1984: 319): 'Lyndon Baines Johnson, a consummate politician, was a kaleidoscopic personality... cruel and kind, violent and gentle, petty, generous, cunning, naive, crude, candid, and *frankly dishonest*' (emphasis added). These characteristics have been memorably brought out in Caro's (1990) biography. Richard Nixon had a similar image even before coming to the White House. President Harry Truman's verdict on Nixon was: 'He can lie out of both sides of his mouth at the same time, and even if he caught himself telling the truth, he'd lie just to keep his hand in.'

Nevertheless, when elected in 1968, Nixon explicitly addressed the 'credibility gap' which he, correctly, saw as a real problem of governance that he had inherited. A special appointee to a new post of Communications Director for the Executive, Herbert Klein, promised that 'truth will become the hallmark of the Nixon administration' (quoted in Wise, 1973: 21). Despite this commitment, it chalked up its full share of distortions about the war in Indochina that Nixon was elected to end: about the policy goal behind the invasion of Cambodia (not just to interdict 'communist' Vietnamese troops but to support the military government of Cambodia) and the degree of continuing engagement there (denial that US air raids were to support invading South Vietnamese troops), surpassing the Johnson administration's total of bombing sorties into Vietnam in its first three years.

Nixon was also to become infamous for the plethora of dirty tricks in domestic politics known collectively as 'Watergate', his denial of them, and his obligatory resignation after lying to congressional and judicial inquiries. But he was also involved in attempts to control official information flows, not just individual acts of lying. He sought to shape the whole process of government control over information in a systematic struggle to keep the press, and to some extent the electronic news media, in line. Wise (1973) gives details and quotes the conclusion of a report by the American Civil Liberties Union to the effect that: 'Attacks on the press by officers of the government have become so widespread and all-pervasive that they constitute a massive federal-level attempt to subvert the letter and spirit of the First Amendment'. More subtle measures were efforts to squeeze and manipulate the White House press pool.

However, while noting these trends and acknowledging that there were two successive incumbents who were notorious for deception, it would be too simple to explain lying and information control as facets of Richard Nixon or Lyndon Johnson, just as any reliance on the personality of the chief executive as the predominant factor in explaining any policies of US administrations would be an over-simplification. Ronald Reagan, for instance, had a very different image: rather than retreating into secrecy, he was the 'great communicator'. But that did not prevent a gross level of personal dishonesty in his administration: apart from the senior officials prosecuted for conspiracy to defraud as part of the Iran–Contra episode which is the focus of Chapter 6, some 225 Reagan appointees faced charges of ethical or criminal wrongdoing during 1981 to 1988 (Ross, 1989), including the administrator of NASA, the Commissioner of the Food and Drug Administration, the Deputy Secretary and an Assistant Secretary of Commerce. Many of these misdemeanours related to incumbents using their political position for gain for themselves, friends and business associates. That game is, of course, as old as politics, but how far it is curbed or finds room to spread do characterise different administrations and times, and some of the resulting institutional tendencies will be explored below.

Nixon himself gave it as his opinion that his problems in being believed were mainly to do with the Vietnam war, and that once people realised he was bringing it to an end, 'I think the credibility gap will rapidly disappear. It is events that cause the credibility gap, not the fact that a President deliberately lies or misleads the people' (quoted in Wise, 1973: 74). This conclusion is obviously self-serving, but the stress on 'events' as a causal factor is not to be dismissed. Indeed, in noting that there was a 'certain inevitability' about the emergence of the credibility gap under Johnson, Wise (1973: 32) recognises the significance of the context: 'it was a case where the man and the times fused'. However, it has also to be remembered that these policy-makers were initiating, or at least influencing, events, although the record we will explore shows that they were not above orchestrating not only the way that events were perceived but also actually constructing certain happenings the main purpose of which was to manipulate public opinion.

One set of explanations for the growing phenomenon of government lying does focus on 'events'. These give particular emphasis to the US foreign role as superpower in the period since the 1940s. One version of this argument is offered by one element in the 'propaganda model' put forward by Herman and Chomsky (1988). This perception of the 'problem' of managing information about foreign affairs from governments' point of view is broadly consistent with that of establishment analysts who operate from a *real-politik* viewpoint: 'that democratic foreign policy suffers from having to accommodate the sentiments of the public and its representatives, sentiments that are grounded in a combination of factual ignorance and emotive drives that clash with the tenets by which international affairs are best managed', as Nincic (1992: 153) characterises it.

In his path-breaking work on government lying, Wise (1973) also stressed the foreign 'events' that shape the pattern but saw them interacting with and in turn shaping institutional factors:

> To sum up, America's vastly expanded international role, the growth of a powerful national security bureaucracy, government control of information channels, the establishment of a system of official secrecy, the communications explosion, elitism in national security policy-making, and secret intelligence operations have all contributed to government lying and the erosion of public trust. (Wise, 1973: 32)

Of course one justification for dissimulation or secrecy is that the American public has to be lied to in order to mislead hostile foreigners. For instance, Nincic (1992: 125) quotes a deputy under-secretary at the State Department at the time of the controversy over the leak of the Pentagon Papers (see section on Vietnam above): 'Perhaps, if we could talk only to the American people, we could tell a lot of secrets, but … other people listen in.' Apart from questions about the validity of that as a justification in a democratic society, this kind of statement is factually incorrect. As several writers on covert operations point out, the screening is from the very American people Mr Macomber referred to. An exposé of CIA activities by an ex-USAF Colonel (Prouty, 1973: 448) shows how 'an unwitting Congressman or reporter' would not be told of the many CIA personnel assigned on 'temporary duty' to a Military Assistance mission, but that:

> All of this is a game. The secrecy can't mean a thing to the host country. They know exactly how many are there and it makes no difference how many are Army, Army temporary duty or Army cover. By the same token, the Soviet embassy, as all other embassies,

will know exactly how many Army men are there … The only people these devices fool are Americans. American reporters, American Congressmen, American government specialists, and of course the American public.

Wise (1973: 502) made the same kind of observation: 'When Lyndon Johnson issued his National Security Action Memorandum of 6 April 1965, which ordered that the commitment of American combat troops in Vietnam be kept a secret, his actions were patently not designed to fool Hanoi or the Viet Cong, who would find out quickly enough who was shooting at them; it was designed to conceal the facts from the American electorate.' And in similar vein, Nincic (1992), in arguing that the issue of 'legitimate deception', of deceiving Americans to mislead foreigners, does not apply to many cases of prevarication:

> Whatever one might think of the rationale for President Nixon's clandestine bombings of Cambodia in 1970, his attempts to mislead Americans on this score had little to do with deceiving adversaries (the bombing was no secret to the Viet Cong, to the Vietnamese, or to any of their allies). When President Kennedy initially concealed, in October 1962, the discovery of Soviet missiles in Cuba, it was plainly not with the aim of hiding their presence from the Soviet Union.

Karnow (1983: 363) in referring to 'covert American agents helping the Saigon government to carry on clandestine activities against North Vietnam' ever since the 1954 Geneva agreements partitioning Vietnam, points to another specific reason for dissembling about Indochina: 'to refute charges of violating the accords. The practice of dissimulation, loftily termed "the principle of plausible denial", is still pursued today to shroud undercover operations that may create diplomatic complications.' However, that kind of diplomatic consideration would apply in a limited number of similar foreign policy areas, Central America for instance.

As we saw, the custom when covert operations surfaced was to justify them in terms of the anti-Communist crusade. However, the realities of which people had to be convinced if this argument were to be used were often more complex. Most of the governments overthrown in the 1960s and 1970s were at best 'radical' in their domestic social programmes, 'nationalist' in terms of their control over their economic resources, and/or 'neutral' in cold war terms rather than communist or revolutionary. Those who were targets for assassination were leaders of such regimes, or in some cases of 'allied' regimes (Diem, Trujillo) who presumably had become expendable embarrassments. This evidence has lead some analysts to suggest that cold war anti-communism was simply a propaganda cloak for an underlying strategy that was as much or even primarily targeted against independent stances in the Third World (Kolko, 1988). Chomsky (1989) gives a prominent place in his explanations to a process of creating 'illusions' by targeting certain regimes and their leaders, usually tarring them with the 'communist' brush, a 'demonisation' that would justify intervention for 'containment' purposes. Certainly many of the kinds of policies and the specific tactics illustrated above do have the potential, in Chomsky's terms, to worry the consciences of the educated politically-active middle class who are the main targets of the propaganda model. That is why these kinds of activities have to remain 'covert'.

Reviewing these various attempts at explanations suggests that the increasing foreign involvements do indeed provide the main contextual framework, but that a more specific imperative for cover-ups and plausible denials is to avoid criticism – by the international community on occasions, but primarily by the American public – and thus answerability for actions that are dubious, unethical or illegal. The Church Committee pointed to a related outcome of such patterns of covert operations becoming systemic which added up to a more fundamental trend. These many foreign adventures had led to the 'institutionalising of clandestine services'. Writers like Wise (1973: 500) had already pointed to:

> The deception in Vietnam was symptomatic. The emergence of the United States as a world power during and after World War II proportionately increased the opportunities, the temptations, and the capacity of the government to lie. The expansion of American power resulted in the growth of a vast national security establishment and an often unchecked intelligence bureaucracy. Covert operations of the CIA required official lies to protect them, and the standard in such cases became not truth, but whether the government's actions were 'plausibly deniable'. In other words, whether the government's lies were *convincing*.

However, a similar bureaucratic evolution can arguably be said to have occurred in domestic affairs. Critics of Hoover's FBI getting out of hand with COINTELPRO also point to the emergence of a 'state within the state', or a Security State (e.g. Keller, 1989). He argues that the FBI in the period from the 1950s to 1971, when there was 'an almost total absence of control over its activities' (p. 15), corresponded to this model, where the goals and methods were not necessarily the same as those of the political elite and main decision-makers, although its main function was to eliminate the 'enemies of the state'. The FBI's undertaking of unauthorised hostile 'counter-intelligence' against groups, plus its being funded, like the CIA, through a pro forma appropriations process, thereby removing its actions from the knowledge, let alone scrutiny, of the legislative and judicial branches of government furthered the prospect of a security state. But Keller argues that these developments that ran counter to the tenets of the liberal state could only have been allowed to happen by the liberal establishment with state acquiescence – which was given because it was expedient to have this heightened level of internal intelligence when threats to internal order were apparent, and to have these functions done at arms-length.

The perspective derived from Nixon's reputedly wider aims of his plumbers' project puts a greater emphasis on inter-bureaucratic rivalries and on the constraints to complete secret unanswerability than does the Herman–Chomsky model. However, both views would locate explanations of government lying not only in the perceived imperatives of an interventionist foreign policy but also in those institutional structures and their reshaping that Wise (1973) detected. These structural explanations would seem to be more sustainable than one located in the venality of individuals, whether Johnson, Nixon or Hoover. They also run counter to the argument used in several cases once the cat starts to come out of the bag, that various underlings were 'out of control'.

In concluding this discussion of the kinds of calculations that might lay behind the deceptions about US foreign military adventures, some weight probably needs to be attached to the self-perceptions (and mis-perceptions) of those in power. One particular contradiction that arises between the imperatives of brutal intervention and alliances with repressive regimes and tyrants, and the need to think well of one's self and to identify with the cause of freedom, has been well captured in this quote:

> In brief, American-style liberalism encumbered itself with the dilemmas of being an international policeman, of subsidising repressive and hated Third World societies, yet of being unwilling because of the ideological legacies of past centuries to perceive itself candidly

in terms of its real functions and roles. This intense, and even pathological desire, to appear unsoiled to itself and to have those under its yoke esteem it continued throughout the Vietnam War and was a peculiar attribute of the United States' sustenance of police states everywhere. (Kolko, 1986: 239–40)

His argument comes close to those like Cohen and Rogers (1991) who are sympathetic to Chomsky's explanations, but who feel that his emphasis on the informed middle classes with conscience as the target for deception underplays the extent to which power-holders are themselves carried away by their own ideological sloganeering and come to believe it in part – and the consequent need to fool themselves. Such views depart from Chomsky's stress on the pursuance of the interests of a class that transcends politics and business as the central explanatory factor. They suggest the perceptions of how best to pursue an interest can vary – and that power-holders could get carried away by the 'religion of anti-communism' that is one crucial link in the propaganda model. It is also not self-evident what particular interests are at play in foreign policy agenda.

Analysts who have focused more on the arena of domestic politics and conduct of the economy, however, come back to the emphasis on interests – not simply the broad interests of a class but the specific interests pursued by politicians. Grieder (1992), for instance, suggests that a mutation has occurred in the American political system that has changed the nature of representation itself. It was noted above how administration officials have used their position for private gain for themselves and clients, and how this seemed to peak under Reagan. The same tendency has always been present in the way that representatives in Congress have always conducted themselves, seeking to get personal gain and win political backing from vested interests. But it is suggested that the intensification and near generality of this phenomenon has reached a level where it 'has assumed a different purpose – taking care of clients, not the larger public interest' (Grieder, 1992: 61). He goes on to argue that one outcome of this pattern is to generate a pervasive mood, not anything as concrete as a policy or executive order or a conspiracy, toward obfuscation: 'Since most everyone is engaged in this enterprise, both legislators and the Executive Branch agencies, a mutual interest arises among them – how to manage things so that all of them will be able to elude public accountability' (p. 61).

5
Explanations: Secrecy and Deception in the British Political Context

Lionel Cliffe

There is no shortage of suggestions about what particularities of the British political system might amplify those more general tendencies towards deception and secrecy rooted in the nature of power or of 'elite democracy' that were considered earlier. Some of these special characteristics that are offered to explain *how* government manages to promote and get away with dissimulation will be reviewed, then an attempt will be made to identify those imperatives that might explain *why* there has been this tendency in British official politics. A review of some of the more significant cases will help to explain how those patterns have been changing. This account will also provide a backdrop to the most recent and notorious cases explored in the case-study chapters, which have combined to give an impression that deceit is an endemic aspect of contemporary British politics. This perception has also become widespread among the general public, so that in the 1990s the UK was experiencing what the US had gone through in the 1970s – a credibility gap which was in turn generating apathy and the beginnings of a crisis of legitimacy. For instance, a 1993 survey reported that 77 percent of those asked the question: 'does the government tell the truth?' answered 'no', and 60 percent admitted that they did 'not trust the government' (*Observer*, 19 December 1993).

Mechanisms of secrecy and deception

In explaining these recent trends towards public distrust it will be argued that the basis for government lying in Britain is less a product of particular developments in the last few decades than in the US, and owes more to long-standing features of 'a constitutional and political system which, traditionally, has been characterised by an adherence to official secrecy' (Pyper, 1995: 144). These have generated theses about a 'secret state' (Thurlow, 1994; Dorril, 1993; Gill, 1994; Rogers, 1997) similar to those put forward with respect to the US, which highlight in the same way the centrality of the security services and their obsessive secrecy and obfuscation, and consequent unaccountability. But some analysts (e.g. Michael, 1982) use such labels to refer to the whole British central government structure, which they see as infused with a restrictive 'need-to-know' formula, not just to the centrality of the intelligence agencies. Indeed, the late cabinet minister, Richard Crossman, famously referred to secrecy as the quintessential 'British disease'. The recent Scott Inquiry into arms for Iraq echoed some of the same sentiments in its conclusion about ministerial accountability, which the Report defines as 'the duty to give Parliament, including its Select Committees, and the public as full information as possible about the policies, decisions and actions of the Government, and not to deceive or mislead Parliament and the public' and then points to 'example after example has come to light of an apparent failure by Ministers to discharge that obligation' (Scott, 1996: K8.1, p. 1799). Civil servants also share the view that those in power and who have the overview know best, and there is no need to inform either colleagues, politicians or the public.

The secret nature of the state is seen as a reflection of the characteristics of governmental structure and not just of bureaucratic culture (Robertson, 1982). Like all governments, issues that can be plausibly labelled 'matters of national security' are ring-fenced against public scrutiny as far as possible. But the British government has a greater range of legal weapons to enforce such closures than most democracies. Evidence in any court case can be suppressed by administrative fiat in the form of a 'Public Interest Immunity Certificate' – notoriously used at the trial of company bosses of Matrix Churchill over the arms to Iraq issue. A similar attempt to use PIICs was made in a 1995 case against another arms exporter, Ordtec, but quashed by the judge. Censorship of any topic from being aired in the press operates through the 'D–Notice' system under which a nominally independent committee of civil servants and, conveniently, of journalists themselves 'guides' editors on what matters should be restricted – an arrangement which Hooper (1988) considers would not even be *legal* in the US. But most draconian is the Official Secrets Act. Such legislation dates back to the 1880s, but an Act of 1911 was the tool used until a revised law of 1989. It had contained in Section 1 severe powers against any betrayal of the nation's secrets to a foreign power, but the infamous Section 2 allowed the prosecution of anyone – journalists and those who listen to and propagate the stories as well as any officials themselves – who divulge official information *not necessarily involving national security.*

This latter provision has been widely used to prosecute whistle-blowers, authors and investigative journalists, but the pervasive threat of it and even its rather vague formulation, plus the arbitrary way it has been invoked, has created an overall climate where certain actions and actors, even certain opinions, can be seen as a threat to the state. Rogers (1997: 4) goes on to argue such use of the Act and other state instruments allow 'policy-makers ... to control the parameters of political discourse through defining and invoking national security in ways that serve to target and discredit groups and individuals', and she makes the further point that this sanctioning often extends to 'activities that they consider detrimental *to their own interests'* (emphasis added). She sees these 'interests' as essentially those of class, although she offers a more differentiated view of how the 'political centre' works, conceptualising it as a set of interacting élites. Rusbridger's (1991) book on the 'pointlessness of so much of the work of intelligence services everywhere reaches a similar conclusion about the operation of this secret part of the state, which seeks to 'claim that those who disagree with government policy are dangerous subversives who must be treated as enemies of the state – which automatically provides a limitless supply of suspects'. However, his analysis identifies the 'interests' that dictate this labelling as those of the bureaucratic structures of the intelligence agencies who act 'in order to justify their ever-increasing budgets (by) continually inventing all manner of windmills to tilt at'. This consideration, he argues, that they have to bid for their share of the public purse, poses a dilemma for intelligence services (and, by extension, to some degree to other government bodies). They would prefer to keep everything buttoned up and secret but at the same time need to give the impression that their work is essential, has to be maintained at an increasing level (something of a problem in the post-cold war era), and that they do it effectively, which in turn means giving the public a glimpse of 'successful' operations or policies (real or created) or dis-information. This is achieved by judicious *leaks,* what Richard Norton-Taylor, an investigative journalist specialising in unveiling secrecy, calls 'designer leaks'. But these pose a further dilemma: allowing those leaks which are instrumental, while keeping the clamp on leaks that would be really revealing.

There were in fact some important, potential test cases in the 1980s. Cathy Massiter, a junior employee of MI5, resigned to make public her evidence that MI5 was breaching its own guidelines by tapping telephones without warrant and 'keeping dossiers on people and organisations that were neither subversive nor a threat to the state but merely disagreed with government policies' (Rusbridger, 1991: 208). In 1997, a former MI6 officer, Richard Tomlinson, served a six-month prison sentence for sending an outline of a projected book on the security services to an Australian publisher. In the 1980s, Sarah Tisdall, a junior Foreign Office official, leaked documents revealing the manner in which missiles were being deployed at the nuclear weapons base used by the US Air Force at Greenham Common, which she felt showed how the Defence Secretary, Michael Heseltine, was misleading the public. Rusbridger (1991) contrasts her prosecution under OSA and long sentence with that of another cabinet minister, Leon Brittan, who leaked letters about the controversial issue in 1986 of how to rescue the only British helicopter manufacturer, Westland – actions which lead to Heseltine's resignation. He concludes: 'secrecy is used to the advantage of the government in power. It leaks when convenient and then prosecutes others for doing the same.' (206) This contradiction was blatantly brought out by Prime Minister Thatcher's press secretary, Sir Bernard Ingham (1991), in his autobiography: 'I must tell you that I – and I am sure my colleagues – have never regarded the Official Secrets Act as a constraint on any operations. Indeed, I regard myself as licensed to break the law as and when I judge necessary.'

Clive Ponting (1985), a senior Ministry of Defence official, was another whistle-blower brought to trial in 1985 for leaking documents to a back-bench MP which revealed how Parliament was being misled over the sinking of the Argentine battleship, the *Belgrano*. He was acquitted, despite clear instructions from the judge that he had broken the law, by a jury that accepted his justification that he was putting the record straight 'in the public interest' – morally valid, perhaps, but not according to some interpretations of the law. That case directly stimulated the first amendment to OSA in 80 years. Despite rhetoric at the time about promoting 'open government', the main substantive change in the new 1989 OSA was to remove any ambiguity about the possibility of offering a 'public interest' defence, and thereby effectively sent out a warning signal to future whistle-blowers. These cases and apparent victories for the press and the principle of openness in fact 'led to a tightening rather than a loosening of state control of information' (Rogers, 1997: 108).

One can argue that another legacy of the British state, one that is seldom acknowledged by analysts, also contributes to a climate where deception is commonplace but also tolerated: the mythical or fictitious nature of the governmental system. We refer here to a pervasive rhetorical cloud within which much of the reality of political structures are shrouded (Harden and Lewis, 1986). First among the many examples that could be cited, and central to them, is the myth of the 'British Constitution'. This unwritten set of precedents and selected laws is the basis for showing that the rule of law operates in the UK, and is not simply arbitrary. Yet what set of laws, rules of procedure of Parliament and Cabinet, and precedents it can be said to include is ultimately untestable by a judicial or any other independent arbitration. What it constitutes, and how it is interpreted, is a matter of 'tradition'. All traditions are just collective memory, and thus selective, in this instance by those in power in the past, thus giving an authoritarian and conservative bias. And yet it is justified as 'flexible' – which, of course, means it can be easily changed – by decision of Parliament. The reality behind that bit of convoluted rhetoric is that no law can be proclaimed 'unconstitutional'; individual rights can be curtailed by the whim of any governing party with a large majority in a compliant Parliament – as occurred on several occasions, the last in August 1998 with the passing of 'state of emergency' regulations, originally justified in relation to Northern Ireland, but applied to the whole country. Other mythical trappings relate to the role of the monarch, in whose name much is justified: it is the 'Queen in Parliament' that is 'sovereign'; each new session of Parliament opens with the 'Queen's Speech', a term that refers not to an intervention by the titular, non-partisan head of state, but to a highly partisan policy statement written by the Prime Minister and performed by a ventriloquist's dummy. A system termed a *'parliamentary* democracy' has one of the least independent legislatures in the established democracies. These and other traditional deceptions act as a hall of mirrors. Small wonder that the public are confused about what is going on at any one moment in time.

Locating the imperatives for deception

Turning now to consideration not of the mechanisms that enable deceit and obfuscation, but analytical issues of why it occurs, another central element in the British 'constitution' provides both some explanation and also a justification. The British system of government is based on several related precepts that govern the respective roles of elected political officials and civil servants and their relationship.

The notions of the collective responsibility of Cabinet, and the accountability (to Parliament) of individual ministers are used to justify the non-revelation of Cabinet records and papers on the one hand, and the 'confidentiality' of the policy and other papers whereby civil servants offer advice to ministers on the other. These 'principles' not only serve to exclude large areas of decision-making from public, and even parliamentary, scrutiny, they have also been used as an argument against any freedom of information legislation, or of a constitutional principle of a 'right to know'. In practice, and because the unwritten nature of the constitution does not allow due process, the so-called 'principle' of ministerial responsibility, under which the political head should take the heat for whatever shortcomings there are in his/her department, has not prevented several important instances whereby individual civil servants have been left to carry the can in official investigations (see Pyper, 1995: 14–15). On his retirement as Head of the Civil Service, Sir Robin Butler talked publicly about 'a breakdown of government accountability', and pointed out that obsessive secrecy itself generated a paranoia about leaks which in turn encouraged further secrecy of decision-making. He points to a number of hurried cover-ups and reactive statements and decisions being made in this climate, including the first scientists' report dismissing the human risk from BSE, which he called a 'time bomb' (*Guardian*, 5 January 1998).

Scrutiny of some significant actual cases of official lying suggests, however, that they are not all simply examples of obsessive secrecy reaction by politicians or bureaucrats, nor of some mystical lack of clarity, nor that the explanations all lie in an unchanging pattern inherent in the governmental structure. Past experiences suggest that governments have not simply been reluctant to volunteer the facts, but that they have not been adverse to 'manufacturing' them. A Labour administration was guilty of constructing an elaborate charade when it responded to the 'unilateral declaration of independence' (UDI) of the white, racist government in the self-governing colony of Rhodesia in 1964 by imposing sanctions, which Prime Minister Harold Wilson claimed would bring the UDI government back to legality in 'days not years'. Fourteen years later the Report of an official inquiry (the Bingham Commission, 1978) into how oil continued to be supplied to Rhodesia, despite UN-backed sanctions and a Royal Navy patrol in the Mozambique Channel to intercept tanker deliveries to landlocked Rhodesia's nearest port, found that Rhodesia had arranged an oil swap with South Africa (Bailey, 1979). That avenue was an open secret to anyone with any knowledge of southern Africa, and must have been known to those in the British government. The government, however, was able to publicly remain ignorant because it contented itself with asking the technical question, are the sanction restrictions in place, instead of the practical policy-relevant one, 'if oil is getting there, from where does it come – and thus what can be done about this loophole?'. Moreover, if the Foreign Office knew oil was getting through and there was no strategy in place for stopping it, what conclusion could one draw about the purpose of the ships being deployed in the Indian Ocean, and the sanctions as a whole? They could only be part of a charade, a smoke screen to give the *appearance* to the British public that something was being done – and thus head off calls for an alternative policy of sending British troops to remove an illegal government (Cliffe, 1979). Such examples of elaborate 'spinning' of a fabricated scenario point to explanations that go beyond the instincts of a secretive bureaucracy or the distortion of the formal trappings of power. Some possible reasons include those that were proffered in the US case or variations on them: dubious foreign adventures that will not stand up to the scrutiny of those with a modicum of humanity might need to be covered up, or the need to cloud how far economic interests dictate domestic and foreign policies in a manner that is not in the interests of the majority or is not easily squared with 'ethical' concerns (to quote an adjective that the 1997 Labour government began to use about its foreign policy stance).

Some major instances of dissembling, like the Rhodesian sanctions cover-up, were indeed to do with questionable foreign involvements. When a British expeditionary force was sent to reclaim the Falkland Islands in the far South-west Atlantic from an Argentine take-over in 1983, there were parallel, elaborate constructions of a certain scenario around the major naval engagement of the (undeclared) war, the sinking of the Argentinean ship, the *Belgrano* (Gavshon and Rice, 1984). This sinking of a venerable second-hand battleship by a British submarine, in which 1100 sailors were killed, was the first engagement in which lives were lost and led to a major escalation of the conflict – at a moment when, it was finally, but not at the time, admitted, Peru was actively seeking a negotiated settlement. The justification for sinking the *Belgrano* was that it was 'part of a heavily armed surface attack group, was close to the Total Exclusion Group (the 200 mile circle around the islands wherein Britain had declared they would attack Argentinean ships) and was closing on elements of our Task Force, which was only hours away' and was attacked when spotted. (Statement by Defence Secretary John Nott to Parliament, 4 May 1982). It was eventually established that the attack occurred several hours (maybe 24) after the ship had been spotted – and followed, so that its trajectory *away* from TEZ could not be in doubt. These awkward facts were covered up, as otherwise Britain's action could be construed as in contravention of international law, because Britain claimed to be acting under the 'right of self-defence against armed attack' contained in Article 51 of the United Nations Charter, and Britain had never formally declared war on Argentina. The broader implications are that the British government, and especially the Navy (which had just been made the target of swingeing economic cuts – Ponting, 1985), were intent on an engagement and the use of maximum force, not the minimum which official statements claimed – a calculation that might owe something to the use of the war as a patriotic rallying point for a government that at the time was deeply unpopular. The whole incident has echoes of another 'manufactured' triggering of major escalation of conflict – the Tonkin Gulf incident in the Vietnam War.

Another example of British intervention that was covered up, but in this case by a secrecy which was unpenetrated, was the sending of Special Air Service (SAS) and other British military personnel to aid the Sultan's government in the Gulf state of Oman in its counter-insurgency against rebels there. However, the changing British power and presence in the non-European world since the Second World War, and particularly since the 'withdrawal from East of Suez' at the end of the 1960s, foreign adventures that the government wants to keep from the public, have been less frequently the kind of issue that has been covered up.

The one foreign dimension of policy that has become a frequent occasion for deception is the supply of arms overseas. Case-studies in depth in later chapters – arms to Iraq, the arms for aid deal to build the Pergau dam in Malaysia, – all involve arms sales. There is perhaps a certain inevitability about deceit in this area given the combination of the UK economy's reliance on arms exports, the industry remaining partly subject to public control, and the fact that dirty but well-resourced foreign governments are the best customers. Deals therefore have to be kept from that part of the public that has some interna-tional conscience. A further complication has emerged in recent years as it seems individual politicians have themselves got interests in the industry. The size and therefore general importance to the overall economy of the arms export sector can be easily indicated in figures: during the 1980s, the period during which our cases occurred, British exports of arms doubled from about £1 billion, and for most of this period it was the fourth largest exporter – indicating that the arms sector was relatively more important than in most other developed economies, except perhaps France. Even such figures are only estimates; they do not include illicit trade nor that in 'dual-use' equipment and technology (items like machine tools or radioactive materials or certain engineering designs, which were so much a part of the Scott inquiry). But a tendency to deceive cannot just be read off from the size of such indicators, for as Miller's (1996) study points out, apart from this correlation between the size of the arms trade and some possible links with government agencies and politicians, little has been known about the motives that drive arms exporting, or the underlying pattern of interests that are being pursued, or about the links between defence and the civilian trade. There is a tendency, she argues, for analyses to 'work backwards from outcome (exports) to motive (the perceived importance of the defence manufacturing base)' – and thence to explanation, if not justification for, deception. There is, rather, a need to understand the actual constellation of institutional forces so as to understand the political and economic calculations that operate in decision-making about the arms trade, and about how much should be revealed and what kept secret. Indeed, one reason why the Scott Report is important is that it offers a handy 'window on decision-makers' motives' (Miller, 1996: 2), albeit a partial one, given the limited terms of reference of the Inquiry and of the documents to which Justice Scott had access.

Even if questionable foreign interventions, operations and patterns of trade provide some of the most dramatic examples, official lying is certainly not confined to that area of government activity. We have seen how, in the USA, elaborate forms of deception in which security personnel or the services themselves were involved entered the domestic political agenda decisively with Watergate. There have certainly been parallels in British domestic politics. A notorious case of the 1920s, that had never been admitted in the public record to be the charade it was, concerns the 'Zinoviev Letter'. Official records released 75 years later (*Guardian*, 4 February 1999) finally confirmed that it was indeed a forgery, purporting to come from the Secretary of the Communist International in Moscow, and addressed fraternally to the Labour Party. It was conveniently 'leaked' to and used by Conservative Central Office to good effect in the 1924 election. Thurlow (1994) suggests that that episode was a throw back to an earlier 'die-hard' stance by Conservative leaders and the state establishment to tar the Labour Party as extremist; thereafter the approach was to bind them into the system as up-holders of British constitutionalism. But his work emphasises the extent to which there was consistently a general pattern of covert activity in domestic politics throughout this century. A range of political opinions and organisations continued to be treated not only as 'extremist' and beyond the pale but as enemies of the state – and continued to be the target of dis-information and dirty tricks. Of course this applied particularly to the Communist Party, those bodies thought to be or presented as allied to it, and others that could be tarred with the same brush throughout the cold war, without ever generating the public hysteria of McCarthyism.

However, the revelations in the notorious Peter Wright book, *Spycatcher* (1987), suggest a degree of panic in circles within the secret state, reminiscent of the die-hards of the 1920s, at the prospect of a Labour government led by elements they saw as embodiments of the communist threat. (A volume whose suppression the government pursued as far as an Australian court to stop publication there, at which the Head of the Civil Service admitted he had been 'economical with the truth'). Some of these security personnel perceived, or sought to portray, Prime Minister Harold Wilson as a Moscow agent (Wright, 1987; Leigh, 1988; Dorril and Ramsay, 1992) and may have had a hand in his eventual resignation. There has even been a suggestion that similar hidden forces were involved in the replacement of Edward Heath, a moderate, by the more militantly right-wing Margaret Thatcher as leader of the Conservative Party.

Evidence has gradually emerged of widespread surveillance of campaigning bodies like the Campaign for Nuclear Disarmament, the protests at the Greenham Common nuclear weapon air base, the Campaign for Civil Liberties, etc. – and there may have been instances of infiltration of them – reminiscent of, although not on the same scale as, the FBI's COINTELPRO. Militant trade unions were the target of both surveillance and infiltration and dirty tricks – especially the National Union of Mineworkers (NUM) which was seen as a particular enemy by Conservative leaders following its strike in 1974 which brought down the Government of Edward Heath, and its year-long strike against threatened pit closures as well as subsequent confrontations with the police and other organs of the state in 1984 (Milne, 1994).

One of the decisive areas of deception and security service activity has, of course, been Northern Ireland. Thurlow (1994) suggests that experience in dealing with security problems there directly led to 'the expansion of political surveillance to include radicals, socialists and trade unionists in the rest of the United Kingdom', and that

that was a trend as early as the 1920s which has continued until the present (see also Bunyan, 1977).

Our concerns are not just with secrecy but with lies, in the sense of passive denials and of manufacturing stories and generating perceptions. The occurrences of cases that are clearly not to do with issues of 'national security' points to the limits of that as a justification for lying. Two areas offer rich seams from which cases have emerged in recent years: those to do with the performance and management of the economy and the social effect on citizens, and others to do with environmental matters and environmental health. The first area became from the 1970s the one on which more than anything else people's satisfaction or dissatisfaction with government was based. This had emerged during a period when governments of both political parties took a major hand in seeking to manage the economy at a macro-level, and where national or local government was responsible in large part for provision of social welfare.

Changes began to occur from the late 1970s, partly as a result of aspects of what later came to be called 'globalisation', in particular the fact that a variety of economic and financial forces from the world economy made Keynesian economic management by the state increasingly impossible, and partly as a consequence of the deliberate embracing by most governments around the world, but especially of Thatcher's in the UK, of policies of state withdrawal from the economy. However, the language of electoral politics was one of appeal to economic well-being, real or perceived, even if government had little to do with it; the policy of economic liberalisation had in any event to be justified in such terms. During the 1980s a marked trend emerged for campaigning and educational groups, and then sections of the public, to define 'well-being' in terms of environmental health and not just economic prosperity and social security. This latter process put on the agenda another wide set of concerns by which government's performance would be judged and also, as we shall see, threw up a range of dramatic cases wherein government understated threats to the environment and to public health, or deliberately kept quiet or distorted the evidence that was made publicly available.

One area of economic obfuscation was in massaging performance indicators. For instance, in the 1980s, thirty changes were made in the official basis for calculating the rate of unemployment; the work force that were without work was narrowed by eliminating various categories from the job-seekers, like housewives, for instance (Perry, 1993; Tant, 1995). A similar game of mystification by numbers covered up some of the realities of privatisation, whereby public assets were often made available at knockdown prices to private individuals and corporate interests (Negrine, 1996). The National Audit Office published estimates that the taxpayer had been short-changed to the tune of £10 billion in the sale of state companies (*Observer*, 8 March 1998). The electric power grid was made over in 1995 as a gift to eight regional companies, whose assets are now valued at £5 billion. Rail privatisation alone involved £1.4 billion in fees and direct costs, apart from any undervaluation (*Guardian*, 3 August 1998). Environmental health has increasingly become another arena for official obfuscation and deception and of exposure by campaigning groups. The case-study of the handling of the BSE is a notable example.

Conclusions

The particular political context of the British political system does have features which would unduly encourage, justify and allow deception and lying. There has been a long legacy of a bureaucratic culture of excessive secrecy, buoyed up by a traditional vocabulary about the system that makes its working opaque. There has also been a long practice of employing security services to define parts of the political spectrum as beyond the pale of national security, and of even less legislative overseeing or other means of accountability than in the US or other democratic countries. This has given an apparent licence to act without any due process – as evidenced in the conduct of 'security' in Northern Ireland and in some apparent coups in the corridors of power. Secrecy is maintained by controls on the media and by official secrets legislation that is draconian by any international comparison, and which, in the guise of being relaxed, has closed loopholes for whistle-blowers.

The use of these means and more elaborate charades for secrecy and deception were used to cover up unsavoury, covert operations when Britain was a great power, but they still occasionally persist. They have been readily adaptable to what has become a major policy imperative in foreign policy, the export of arms, a factor in several notorious exposés of lying – as case-studies in this volume of arms to Iraq and Malaysia, testify. There has also been an overlap between the political calculations of those in government, of economic interests in the arms trade and the personal interests of some politicians or their relatives. A similar tendency to dissemble so as to confuse private interests with the public interest has been discernible in the last twenty years of economic liberalisation, privatisation and deregulation, with harmful effects on the material welfare of the majority as well as on public health.

Part II
Case-Studies

6
The Iran–Contra Affairs

Lionel Cliffe

These were no ordinary affairs. In retrospect, it will be seen that they threatened the constitutional foundations of the country. This is not a story and a warning for our days alone. If the story of the Iran-contra affairs is not fully known and understood, a similar usurpation of power by a small, strategically-placed group within the government may well recur before we are prepared to recognize what is happening. For this reason, I have felt that we cannot know too much about this case history of the thin line that separates the legitimate from the illegitimate exercise of power in our government.

(Draper, 1991: xi)

This quote insists on using 'Affairs' in the plural in contrast to more common usage that refers to an 'Iran–Contra Affair', arguing that there were two distinct operations: the sale of weaponry to Iran ('Irangate'), and the channeling of military support to the Contra rebels in Nicaragua ('Contragate'). The two were connected: they were both conducted mainly by the 'National Security Council staff', an institution that was itself part of the deception; and cash from the one exercise was used to finance the other. They were both not only ill-advised and later subject to widespread criticism, but they were also arguably contrary to specific laws passed by Congress, and were later to be exposed together in three distinct official investigations: a presidential commission of inquiry (the Tower Report, 1987); Congressional Committee investigations (Inouye and Hamilton, 1987); and an Independent Counsel appointed by the Attorney General, (Walsh, 1994). But Draper insists that the two operations had different origins, justifications and outcomes, which need to be separately specified.

The arms-to-Iran was the first bit of this convoluted set of covert operations to become unravelled publicly – by publication of allegations that this supply had been going on in the hope of securing the release of US and European hostages held in Lebanon. This was followed immediately by Attorney-General Meese admitting these sales had occurred and the profits had been channelled to the Contras. However, it was the Nicaraguan connection which had been developed first.

Contra-gate

The 1979 overthrow of the Samoza dictatorship in Nicaragua, a regime that had long been a US client, through a rebellion spearheaded by the Sandinista Front, posed a dilemma for US policy makers. The Carter administration reacted ambiguously: it was inclined to recognise the Sandinista regime and give aid, but was itself entering a more confrontational stance of 'rolling-back' perceived Soviet spheres of influence in what was seen as the 'Second Cold War' (Halliday, 1983). The Reagan administration immediately took a tougher line over Nicaragua, authorising the CIA to provide support and training for the Contras, the exiles engaging in an irregular armed insurrection against the Sandinista government and its army. It also authorised the Agency to undertake its own covert operations. Up to that point there had been little need for major deception: the Intelligence Committees of Congress were notified, as had become the requirement after the Church Committee investigations into covert operations, and they approved support to the Contras. Some element of dissembling occurred, however, as the President's 'Finding' of 1981, which was the instrument required in order to get the Committees' approval, was forwarded in December, after a National Security Decision Directive No. 17 authorising covert action had been signed by Reagan in November, and actions were already being implemented. The Finding asserted the aim of policy was merely to interdict the supposed flow of arms from Nicaragua to insurgents against military regimes in its northern neighbours, El Salvador and Honduras, rather than the overthrow of the Sandinista government which the Republican election platform had seemed to promise and which subsequent CIA actions seemed to be geared towards. Press reports of the apparent broader purpose of CIA actions in late 1982 led to Congress imposing a set of measures (the Boland I amendments), which initially forbade military support to the Contras 'for the purpose of overthrowing the Nicaraguan government'.

The lie to this formula about aims became clearer as the main beneficiary of aid was a break-away Sandinista leader, Eden Pastora, who led the most effective Contra faction. This, however, operated from Costa Rica, to the south, which was in no position to interrupt arms flows from the other end of the country. But the formula did provide a loophole allowing CIA operations and support for the Contras. One notable set of operations in 1984 involved the mining of the main Nicaraguan harbours. Concerned about such incidents and the consequent prospect of confrontation with the Soviets, who had had their shipping threatened, and of a Vietnam-type involvement, further restrictions were imposed by Congress. Boland II effectively precluded the use of funds available to agencies involved in intelligence activities for military aid, and similar amendments were renewed each fiscal year when the budget was approved – although Congress did not preclude civilian aid, and indeed voted to provide an amount which had risen to $100 million in 1984. The Reagan administration had, however, 'committed itself to backing the Contras at all costs. This policy could not be carried out without defying Congress. Open defiance was politically unfeasible. The only other way was to do it covertly' (Draper, 1991: 27).

It had, in particular, to seek ways, beyond even the usual deceits involved in covert operations, to circumvent Boland's ban on US agencies giving material support to the Contras. One answer was to transfer the operation to an institutional agency which could be said to be outside the ban, in that it was not technically one 'engaged in intelligence activities'. This was the National Security Council (NSC). The NSC was set up as a coordinating body which simply brought together the CIA, military intelligence, etc. However, a unit was established under the President's National Security Adviser (NSA), by Nixon which was directly under White House control – but it had been a body more for intelligence analysis (and perhaps plumbing duties) than intelligence-gathering or covert operations. It was this essentially amateur body with a direct chain of command from the President to NSA McFarlane, later replaced by Admiral Poindexter, to Oliver North, that thereafter orchestrated what North referred to his associates as 'running a war from his desk' (Hearings, Poindexter Testimony H 100–8: 51, quoted in Wroe, 1991: 14) – a term he explicitly denied in testimony to Congress. Another requirement was to find sources other than the federal budget of cash for the arms that were being supplied. Foreign governments and leaders with a right-wing agenda were 'solicited', without that word or the results ever being made public. And, of course, the use of the profits from Irangate were to become crucial.

This set of operations included the purchase and delivery of arms, eventually through drops within the country – these were organised by agents recruited by North, such as retired Air Force major general Richard Secord, but who remained 'private operators'. It also involved the provision of logistical support and military advisers – again on an officially 'private' basis but using personnel recruited through the NSA staff. These operations necessitated denials and deceits: none of this military support was happening, and insofar as it was, it was coming through a non-intelligence non-agency that was, it could always be claimed if it came out, outside the ban; any funding was coming through private well-wishers – not from US sources or other governments. These claims were blown in 1986 when a supply plane and one of its crew were captured in Nicaragua. Meanwhile, the Congressional ban on military support to the Contras was circumvented until 1986 when the renewal of the Boland Amendment did allow some military assistance; up to then the flow of arms and advice was being made possible in part from profits from the Iran arms supply, to which we will now turn.

Iran-gate

The Executive Summary of the joint Report of the House and Senate Committees investigating Iran–Contra starts by indicating what sparked off their inquiries:

> On November 3, 1986, *Al-Shiraa*, a Lebanese weekly, reported that the United States had secretly sold arms to Iran. Subsequent reports claimed that the purpose of the sales was to do with the release of American hostages in Lebanon. These reports seemed unbelievable. Few principles of U.S. policy were stated more forcefully by the Reagan Administration than refusing to traffic with terrorists or sell arms to the Government of the Ayatollah Khomeini of Iran.
>
> Although the Administration initially denied the reports, by mid-November it was clear that the accounts were true. (Inouye and Hamilton, 1987: xv)

Iran was another thorn in the side of the Reagan Administration – but not for the same ideological, cold war reasons as Nicaragua. To be sure, Iran had occasioned what had been very much a cold war involvement in the 1960s: the CIA had mounted a coup to install the Shah as absolute ruler displacing an elected, nationalistic government. The US continued to regard this regime as a close ally and key regional lynch-pin until it was overthrown in 1979, and eventually replaced by an Islamicist government which became virulently anti-American. Relations with Iran were at their worst in the early 1980s when US embassy staff were held as hostages. They were eventually released within hours of Reagan's inauguration – which sparked persistent speculation that there had been some prior 'deal' by the Reagan camp. Thereafter the new Administration simply avoided contact with the Iran government, presumably waiting until Khomeini's demise.

An arms embargo was imposed on Iran even before the Iran–Iraq war, by an executive order made by President Carter, a ban that was strengthened under the terms of the 1979 Export Administration Act which required Congress to be notified of any goods or technology to countries that 'repeatedly supported terrorism' – a label pinned on Iran in 1980. There were, of course, general laws requiring arms sales to be notified to Congress, both as part of general covert-action notification, and regular arms sales – although these had loopholes, later cited in defence of the covert Iran supplies. But up to 1985 the administration took energetic steps to dissuade other western governments from supplying arms. It rejected in 1984 a paper from NSC proposing a policy of trying to improve relations, for pragmatic reasons: to give support to elements in the army supposedly more pro-west, to avoid remaining cut off from a rich oil-producing country, to show a degree of neutrality in the Iran–Iraq war and perhaps to counter growing supply of arms and influence from the Soviet Union next door, to seek leverage to assist the release of western hostages being held in Lebanon by, reportedly, pro-Iranian groups. However, Reagan himself came to be more pre-occupied by the latter consideration, and that might have been the impetus for a change in stance in 1985 despite opposition by the Secretaries of State and for Defence, Schultz and Weinberger – who were later criticised by the Tower Report (see below; Tower, 1987) for failing to oppose the policy shift and ceding that policy area to NSC. Even before then, Israel had been supplying military equipment, which it was required by treaty obligations to inform the US about beforehand. Although no official notification was made, it is certain that some US officials were aware, and the Israelis seem to have proceeded on the basis of 'nods and winks' (*Congressional Quarterly*, 1987: 7).

In 1985 the Reagan White House went further and authorised stepped-up supplies by Israel of more sophisticated equipment: TOW anti-tank, and later Hawk anti-aircraft, missiles. It became more involved in November by stepping in at North's request to have the CIA make the delivery of some of the Hawks, by its 'proprietary airline'. However, Reagan forgot to give the prior approval or notify the Congressional oversight committees of this CIA involvement, as he was required to do by law. Poindexter was later to testify that Reagan signed the required Finding retrospectively on 5 December. He was also eventually to reveal that he conveniently destroyed that document a year later as it might prove 'politically embarassing' to the President if ever revealed (his testimony to the Congressional Joint Hearings, vol.8: 135).

This last transaction was a fiasco: only a few of the missiles reached their destination. The Iranians claimed they were inadequate in number and capabilities and demanded they be taken back. Not surprisingly, no hostages were released. Nevertheless Israel sent a further 500 of its US-supplied TOWs in the hope of inducing more US shipments, which were in fact sanctioned in early 1986 through another Finding of 17 January. This document contained an extraordinary provision, stating explicitly that Congress not be informed. A further method of distancing the White House and the CIA from any involvement was the stipulation that supply should be through 'third parties'. In the event this role was performed not by the Israeli government, although Israel was used as entrepot, but agents of the NSC team, former Air Force Major General Richard Secord, who had been the main conduit for Contra arms, and Manucher Ghorbanifar. The latter was an exiled Iranian international businessman, who claimed to have past involvements with the old Iranian secret police, SAVAK, and current ones with military and other personnel making up pro-western factions within Iran. He had been a CIA informer in the 1980s, but had failed lie-detector tests and proved generally unreliable and been side-lined. He was, notwithstanding, the chosen lynch-pin of the North team for negotiations as well as organising shipments. While broader strategic calculations influenced policy, the selective supply of weaponry was designed to give immediate leverage over hostage release – but that in turn required bargaining and bargainers. And Ghorbanifar was allotted the role as point of contact with the shadowy pro-Iranian groups in Lebanon who held the hostages. Eventually reliance on him proved disastrous and a second go-between, Albert Hakim, was used, who opened up what was referred to as a 'Second Channel' to Iranian officials.

These go-betweens were in fact picked out by North's NSC team, which took over responsibility for the operations more completely, not just to maintain the fiction of a distancing of the main agencies of US government, but because the CIA itself wanted out of seeming to be involved even in a facilitating role.

The unravelling

On 5 October 1986 a C-123 transport aircraft carrying ammunition to the Contras was shot down in northern Nicaragua and the one survivor of its crew of four, Eugene Hasenfus, was paraded in front of the media by the Sandinista government. 'Documents on board the airplane connected it to Southern Air Transport (SAT), a former CIA proprietary airline based in Miami' (Hamilton and Inouye, 1987: 287). An inquiry into SAT by the FBI was immediately ordered. Meanwhile, the immediate reaction of the Administration was a 'denial reflex' (Draper, 1991: 355). Thus Secretary of State Schultz: the airplane had been 'hired by private people ... (who) had no connection with the U.S. government at all' (*Washington Post*, 8 October 1986). President Reagan echoed the same words on the same day (Draper, 1991: 355). Assistant Secretary of State Abrams later testified to the Joint Hearings of Senate and House Committees that he was the one that gave those assurances to Schultz, assurances he repeated to the House Intelligence Committee on 14 October 1986:

> I will say that no American intelligence or Defense or any other kind of government officials was engaged in facilitating this flight or paying for it or directing it or anything like that, there is no U.S. government involvement, no government involvement, including anybody in the Embassies abroad. (Abrams to Hearings, Vol. 100–5: 65)

This and similar statements he was to admit at the Congressional hearings were 'completely honest and completely wrong' – the sophistry involved in the preliminary denials is revealed by the first part of this later claim; his disclaimer of knowledge of any government involvement, he later revealed, depended on him avoiding asking Oliver North outright whether he was involved in such actions.

Meanwhile Hasenfus admitted that arms were being supplied and said that he assumed his ultimate employer was the CIA. In part the later denials and the admissions about the NSC staff role were occasioned by that Agency ensuring that it distanced itself from events. On 14 October 1986, the Deputy Director denied CIA involvement in testimony to the House Intelligence Committee (*Congressional Quarterly*, 1987: A-28).

In early November the denials about the Contra arms supply were overtaken by another emergency. A Beirut magazine disclosed the secret trip made by National Security Adviser McFarlane to Teheran in May as one stage of the arms-hostage negotiations. The first reaction was one of denial. On 6 November Reagan told the press that the story of McFarlane's visit was 'without foundation' (even later when some disclosure was admitted he urged denial of a media report that McFarlane had visited because the story mentioned September 1985 not May 1986). But the next day administration officials admitted that in mid-1985 Reagan had approved contacts to improve relations with Iran and even that Israeli supply of old spares and weapons had been sanctioned, while obfuscating about any US arms shipments and whether the President had knowledge of the Israeli deal.

Within a week the White House strategy was changed to one that gave the appearance of coming clean. Internal documents reveal that the Watergate precedent of the damage caused to Nixon's presidency by a long process of keeping up denials only to have them eroded by media and congressional and judicial investigations was taken into account. On 13 November Reagan made the first admission to the public in a televised address that arms were in fact being supplied to Iran. A week later he authorised an inquiry into the Iran dealings conducted by Attorney General Meese, who began to conduct interviews with the main actors and to collect documents – this was the point at which Poindexter destroyed the only signed copy of the finding authorising CIA involvement to ship Hawks. Testimony by North and his secretary confirm that this was the day when they began to shred documents, despite Meese's request. Nevertheless, the following day Meese's investigators found an undated memo in North's office with a brief mention of the diversion of Iran arms sales proceeds to the Contra supply. From that moment the two distinct episodes, both beginning to unravel, become undissolubly linked in outside perceptions: 'Iran–Contra' emerges.

From then on the strategy for managing what the public should be allowed to know changes. Meese went public about the arms to Iran and the 'diversion' of funds and announced that Oliver North had been dismissed, Admiral Poindexter had been asked to resign, and the Justice Department and the FBI was looking into the question of illegality to see if prosecution should be considered. Three weeks later an Independent Counsel was applied for to pursue this latter possibility. In this last act of the NSC 'enterprise' there was still major obfuscation, and it was later revealed that documents were shredded or false copies substituted to cover tracks. But in the subsequent investigations and in the public media attention, there continued to be a denial that the President and the highest officials of state were involved. North and his immediate associates 'took the rap' but in admitting they had certainly lied tried to turn the tables on their accusers and cloaked themselves in the flag to justify the lying.

The investigations and their findings

The several official inquiries began with the Attorney-General's internal inquiry which it was later claimed merely sought to sort out inconsistencies in what different White House officials were saying, not search for any illegalities. The Republican Vice-Chairman of the Senate Iran–Contra Committee 'charged that Meese had "telegraphed" his moves to Poindexter and North' (*Congressional Quarterly*, 1987: 10), who thereby had a few days grace during which they shredded massive amounts of documents and falsified others. But it did turn up arguably the most telling document, the memo about diversion of funds. In the light of Meese's findings, and probably in the hope of heading off Congress setting up its own investigating committees, again with a backward look to Watergate, the President set up a Special Review Board with three elder statesman charged with reviewing the facts and reporting in two months. Its Report (Tower, 1987) unearthed a lot of internal documents that revealed much of what had occurred, and its conclusions, while in moderate language, were very critical of how the NSC team had been allowed to get away with their 'implementation' of policy. It indicted senior officials for not concerning themselves with what was being done and not asking the right questions that would have revealed it – blaming Reagan's 'management style'.

Congress had already set about its own investigations, initially through the Intelligence Committees of both Houses, holding closed-door and public hearings. During the latter, North and Poindexter pleaded the Fifth Amendment to the Constitution that protected them from self-incrimination. These led to the setting up of the two special committees which eventually produced a combined report (Inouye and Hamilton, 1987). Their investigations came up with further documentary evidence and their hearings in mid-1987 provided very dramatic testimony to an American TV audience, alerting it not only to the government's covert activities and deceptions, but also providing an opportunity for Oliver North to act out, and in some quarters received a hero's role for frankly admitting he lied in the national interest. But in an effort to reduce partisanship, the Committees' terms of reference were restricted to arms to Iran and to the Contra, leaving out related issues of the Contra's human rights record or suggestions that they were involved in drugs traffic, as well as any broader probing of the Administration's foreign policy. There was nevertheless a Minority Report by some, but not all, of the Republican Senators and Representatives which argued: 'there was no constitutional crisis, no systematic disrespect of the "rule of law", no grand conspiracy, and no Administration-wide dishonesty or cover-up'; there were 'just mistakes in judgement, nothing more' (Inouye and Hamilton, 1987: 437). They were intent on defending Reagan's record, and even the Executive's right to make foreign policy. They were at particular pains to remove any doubt that the President had any knowledge of the diversion – although doubts were all the Majority Report offered about Reagan's involvement. The Committees' leaders virtually ignored Reagan's role in the Iran–Contra affair' (*Congressional Quarterly*, 1987: 13).

Thus the various investigations tended to confirm the 'loose cannons' thesis: that the NSC team acted on their own, admittedly without proper over-sight, blaming the highest office-holder only for a lack of hands-on management style. There has been speculation that this was the ultimate cover-up, of plausible denial, based on North's evidence to the Congressional Committees that he had long seen in advance 'that there would come a time when you may have to have a political – I emphasize the word 'political' – fall-guy or scapegoat or whatever' (Volume 100–7: Pt I, p. 148 of Hearings, quoted in Draper, 1991: 535). However, the same source refers to CIA Director Casey's opinion that North was not senior enough and other heads might have to roll! In the event both North and Poindexter not only lost their jobs but eventually faced trial – but only for minor infringements of destroying and falsifying documents, and small financial accounting matters; there were no conspiracy charges. As Wroe (1991: 227) comments: 'Incredible as it seemed, the Iran–Contra operations – so wide-ranging, so misconceived and so mocking of the will of the Congress – boiled down to nothing but petty felonies'. One reason for the lack of serious charges, and for the two men winning appeals against con-viction, was that they had been granted immunity as bait to get them to testify to the Congressional Committees. The result was that they and other officials directly involved got off lightly; more basically the deniability of Presidential involvement was successfully maintained.

That in turn meant that Reagan got off lightly, politically if not legally, and the myth of out-of-control mavericks was preserved, although the fundamental issue remained one of management and implementation, not the flawed nature of the policies themselves. This success was, however, finally challenged in the Report of the Independent Counsel – although this took longer than the Starr Report, coming out in early 1994 – seven years after Walsh's confirmation in the role. His role was as a potential prosecutor, and having failed to provide a basis for further prosecutions, he was required to report on the reasons. In that Report, he did finally nail Reagan's involvement: 'He set the stage for the illegal activities of others by encouraging and, in general terms, ordering support of the Contras (despite a Congressional ban)... and in authorising the sale of arms to Iran in contravention of the U.S. embargo' (Walsh, 1994). Thus this Republican ex-judge, in his Report and his subsequent book (Walsh, 1997), did bring attention back to the mistaken *policies,* and went on to offer this conclusion of the political nature of the deceptions: 'The government problems presented by Iran–Contra are not those of rogue operations, but rather of executive branch efforts to evade congressional oversight.'

Finally, it should be noted that the whole process involved a cover-up of the involvement not only of Reagan but also of the CIA and, in particular, its Director, William Casey. As explained above, the Nicaraguan operations were initially those of the CIA; the Agency was also brought into the first arms shipments to Iran. But it was beyond dispute that the Boland Amendments applied to the CIA. Yet there is considerable evidence, not least North's testimony, that Casey himself remained informed and played an advisory role – albeit at a distance – while CIA operatives on the ground facilitated the NSC teams activities. This was successfully kept from serious scrutiny, and the full truth of involvement will forever remain a mystery because of the timeliness of Casey's death and the fact that he did not give testimony to the Hearings or the Independent Counsel.

Justifications

The Iran–Contra investigations were unusual in that there came a moment when the main actors ceased denying and proceeded to justify their lies – especially North at the Congressional Hearings and at his own trial. The analyst is thus offered a rare example of practitioners' explicit arguments. To be sure, he and Poindexter and those associated with them would always squirm in their answers to avoid the word itself. Thus Poindexter, denying putting out a cover story about Israel's direct involvement: 'and so to that extent we were withholding information. But there was never any effort on my part to mislead or deceive anybody' (Congressional Hearings Deposition in Vol. 20 of Appendix B). McFarlane, accused of lying to Congress about the Contras, said: 'It's very clear that I had withheld information ... [but] the assertion that I had wilfully lied to somebody is something I just couldn't accept' (North's trial transcript, p. 4799, quoted by Wroe, 1991). North, at his trial, explaining that traditional procedures of national security advisers in briefing Congress can not to be 'straightforward' said: 'You don't lie. You put your own interpretation on what the truth is.'

But North did make some admissions, with various justifications, many of them the classics familiar from the theoretical discussion in Chapter 2. He claims there is an inevitability in all such operations: 'There is great deceit – deception practised in the conduct of covert. They are at essence a lie. We make every effort to deceive the enemy as to our intent, our conduct, and to deny the association of the United States with those activities ... and that is not wrong '(Congressional Hearings Testimony, Vol. 100–7, Part I: 9–10). The justification of lying to the enemy is further elaborated elsewhere in his Testimony: 'Please. It was not right. It does not leave me with a good taste in my mouth. I want you to know lying does not come easy to me. I want you to know it does not come easy to anybody, but I think we all had to weigh in the balance the difference between lies and lives' (110–17, Part II: 107). (The 'lives' are presumably those of secret operatives working with, or the Contras themselves, or the American hostages in Beirut.)

Elsewhere they specifically said their aim was to protect the President – as in Poindexter's explanation of why he 'lost' the finding on Nicaragua. This is an Eichmanesque defence: 'only doing my duty'. But, as with all the justifications, it implicitly assumes that the policy itself, and the need to pursue it covertly, can be justified. Insofar as they offered any justification for those broader aims, it was some variation of the 'national security' or 'national interest'.

Explanations

Turning then to an examination of why these operations were pursued covertly, at one level the answer is straightforward: each involved actions that were proscribed by resolutions of Congress. As to why the

Administration sought to pursue them nevertheless, different answers have to be offered for the two Affairs. With regard to Nicaragua, the argument was relatively clear-cut. On the one hand, the Reagan Administration felt the overthrow of the Sandinista government was an imperative and saw the Contras as 'freedom fighters' who must be supported at all costs. On the other hand, many in Congress and broader sections of the public were not convinced that the US should support the overthrow of another government, either because of the questionable morality or propriety, or simply because of the Vietnam syndrome worry of getting involved in a morass from which it would be difficult to withdraw. The Democrat majority in Congress at first compromised and allowed civilian aid to the Contras, and then sought to tighten these curbs. The increasing degree of covertness, and the qualitative shift from a CIA to a NSC operation was first and foremost to get round the Boland Amendments. There was an irony in the fact that, coinciding with the November 1986 disclosures which ended the operations of NSC, a newly-elected Republican majority gave approval to military support to the Contras.

At another level, what has to be explained about the operations before that, is why support for the Contras was given such priority within the Reagan White House that these machinations were deemed worthwhile. Certainly the earlier justifications of interdicting Nicaraguan arms to Honduras had no validity; nor was the Sandinasta regime overtly Marxist, pro-Moscow or social revolutionary – though they were 'demonised' in the usual way as 'communist'. Nor did the Contras fit well the sobriquet of 'freedom fighters'; their social and political origins were narrow and their activities had been, and continued to be, steeped in corruption. The answer must lie in some mixture of ideological commitment, including the self-delusion noted at the end of Chapter 4, and the pursuance of a global cold-war strategy that had shifted from detente to 'roll-back'. As in Vietnam, Angola, Afghanistan and other places that experienced intervention, especially in the period of the 'Second Cold War' (Halliday, 1983) of the 1980s, the calculations had little to do with the country or region in question, but were about their symbolic significance within a globalist strategy.

Iran-gate had similarly to be kept from the knowledge of Congress, as this kind of action was proscribed on three counts: arms to 'terrorist states', requirements for notifying covert action and third party arms shipments, the general western consensus against bargaining with hostage-takers. Moreover, the operations involving Iran marked a shift from earlier policy. But again one has to ask why there seemed to be such an imperative for this policy change that made it worth ignoring these restrictions. Clearly cold war and globalist calculations were not the explanation. One immediate political calculation may have been the priority given to the possibility of the Reagan Administration gaining yet more kudos by appearing to deliver American hostages, after it had used Carter's failure so to do in the 1980 elections. Insofar as there were more pragmatic foreign relations calculations, they would have been rooted in the still persistent dilemma of whether to oppose Islamist regimes and movements or attempt to deal with the more 'moderate' elements in them – an ambiguity that is the greater where regimes sit on great mineral resources and revenues. That genuine policy dilemma was removed from any democratic debate by these Affairs.

Political impact

To the analyst and historian the potential implications of these events and the several investigations were immense. It had been shown once again that it was possible for an imperial presidency to undertake questionable covert operations overseas, despite more than a decade of efforts by Congress to impose checks on such freedom of policy making. In this case, the deception had involved a major change in the role of a governmental agency from the one prescribed and the creation of a new capability for initiating covert operations – all without due legislative process, or informing the public or its elected representatives (Canham-Clyne, 1992). Despite these blatant infringements and a relatively revealing Congressional investigation, Congress signally failed to bring forward any institutional or procedural proposals to tighten up on its oversight of the Executive to prevent any repetition – allowing itself to accept the 'loose cannon' explanation. It was only after both George Bush and Ronald Reagan had left office that the Independent Counsel provided evidence that they had both been involved, and finally gave the lie to 'the well-meaning mavericks getting out of hand' thesis.

The investigations did, however, yield an unparalleled volume of documentation, including the evidence and depositions given at the Congressional Hearings, as well as the Report itself, and the record of the Poindexter and North trials. Now publicly available, they repay study not only by historians but also by any concerned citizen who wants to be alerted to how security agencies and the White House can behave.

7
The 'War' on Drugs

Lionel Cliffe

> ... this war of lies, hypocrisy, and self-interest, which, like the Vietnam War is being fought with no intention of winning. The war itself is a fraud.
>
> (Michael Levine, ex-undercover agent: Levine, 1990)

In November 1989 President George Bush declared a 'war' on drugs and drug traffic. Many western governments followed suit and the UN set up its own International Drug Control Programme. There was therefore nothing covert about this operation. On the contrary, it was trumpeted from the rooftops. In what sense then does it warrant inclusion in a volume on lying? The above quote would put it in the realm of a 'charade': an elaborate campaign undertaken to give the appearance of tackling a problem. The policy itself and the claims made about it constitute the lie. This chapter will consider how far this interpretation is valid. As the case does not start with a denial, and the aim of the chapter is not to start by uncovering one, the structure will differ from others in the book. It will consider the nature of the policy proclaimed, which was only one of the strategy options available for tackling the problem, and discuss how the policy goal was affected by other agenda, and how implementation was affected by an earlier legacy of involvement of US agencies with drug trafficking.

The particular 'Andean strategy' that Bush's Administration developed had these components: a US-led coalition with governments in the region that attempted to suppress the supply of drugs derived from coca into the US by interrupting it at source, by joint operations of US enforcement agencies with local police or military either by destroying crops in the fields, or by disrupting the first stages in the chain of marketing and refinement in the countries of origin, or those that were crucial in the transit to the US. The announcement was followed almost immediately by dramatic action. In March 1990, 24000 US combat troops invaded Panama and whisked away its President, General Manuel Noriega, to face charges in Miami of being a 'drug lord'. More generally, there were major increases in budgets for military and police equipment and in training and other logistic and advisory support to certain Latin American governments. So too for the agencies that were to be charged with leading the war – the Drugs Enforcement Agency (DEA), naturally, but also the US Armed Services and the CIA.

This kind of campaign was presented as a praiseworthy effort to commit the necessary resources to attack at its roots what was becoming more and more seen as *the* national scourge. In a 1989 opinion poll, nearly two-thirds of American people considered drugs 'as the most important problem facing the country' (quoted in Scott and Marshall, 1991). But some critics suggest the campaigns are not directed at the most strategic targets. To put the significance even of the Panama invasion into perspective, for instance, it has been seen as 'only a strike against a downstream drug finance center and never approached the narcotics heartland of the Andes' (McCoy, 1991: 2). Certainly, a campaign involving US forces and massive resourcing of local forces did develop in the Andes themselves, but questions arise not only about the effectiveness and degree of commitment there, but also as to how far its aim of targeting the main source of drugs was fused with, and perhaps subordinated to, other goals in a 'narco-guerrilla' operation that had the hallmarks of earlier counterinsurgency intervention. Further doubt about the seriousness of commitment in Bush's war arose because a promised 'second front' which would attempt to root out the even more significant trade in heroin from the 'Golden Triangle' of South East Asia came to nought. Having filed a federal prosecution in 1990 against the self-proclaimed 'king of opium', Khun Sa, operating out of northern Burma, 'the gap between the attorney general's harsh accusations and impotent actions demonstrates the limitations of a global drug war still fighting its first battles' (McCoy, 1991: 2).

The legacy of past policies and practices

To further realise the limitations of the campaigns and the gap between rhetoric and reality, it is helpful to remember that Bush's was not the first all-out onslaught on drugs. President Reagan had declared a similar war in 1982. Before that, Richard Nixon had made the same kind of declaration – of a war on heroin – in June 1971, and it was he that set up the specialist Drug Enforcement Agency. Jimmy Carter had also shown his commitment to this cause, and had set up a White House Strategy Council on Drug Abuse. There was a strategy common to all these campaigns – in the Middle East, Latin America and South and South-east Asia – of persuading and aiding national governments to take action against suppliers, but also of fostering a US capability overseas for intelligence and intervention at arms length. This foreign outreach by US law enforcement was itself a tacit admission of a failure to curb the wholesale and retail drugs trade within the country itself, and to kill off demand by criminalising the use of drugs by consumers. The latter measure may have contributed to the continued growth of drugs trafficking by vastly inflating prices and hence profits – and thus may be one factor that contributed to the ineffectiveness of the 'wars'.

Developing this interventionist capability also raised doubts about the legitimacy of the operations, which were inevitably seen as infringements of local sovereignty. To put that intervention into perspective, one has merely to conjure up the likely response should Saudi Arabian anti-alcohol enforcement agencies post large teams at their US and British embassies, persuade those governments to reintroduce prohibition if they wanted to ensure continued oil supplies, and enlist the co-operation of local police in efforts to smash not only stills but distilleries in Kentucky or the Scottish Highlands! Would that kind of 'war' be justifiable?

The aims of these drug operations cut across and were confused in reality and in local people's minds with other interventionist policies that had been pursued throughout the cold war era. They also impinged upon a range of vested interests: the US military's response to the prospect of an additional role and funding; national governments and their militaries and intelligence services each with their own agendas. These crucially included the powerful interests involved in the drugs trade itself and their political leverage. The massive profits from what is an illegal activity has, of course, meant that the drugs trade is monopolised by organised crime, and also that the Mafiosi, warlords and cartels involved seek to reduce the legal constraints on their trade by courting political influence. But they also have the capacity to buy influence, buy politicians and even states. A 1994 UN Conference on Global Organized Crime estimated that the global trade in drugs could be valued at over $500 billion – greater than the oil trade (quoted in Castells, 1998). One Bolivian drug lord at one stage offered to pay off the whole national debt as part of considerations he was after.

Two consequences of their scale, financial power and considerable muscle need to be noted. First, another illegal activity, money laundering, is an accompanying and essential ingredient of their activities. Second: 'Besides the ability of criminals to bribe and/or intimidate police, judges and government officials, there is a more insidious and devastating penetration: *the corruption of democratic politics.*'(Castells, 1998: 203). From governments' point of view, cold war international political alliances and domestic political infiltration by organised crime have meant that backing corrupt political allies at home and abroad has often taken precedence over curbing the drugs trade. The convergence of these interests led to 'the secret collaboration of government intelligence services and parallel police throughout the world, and their use of criminals, particularly from drug networks, for political counter-subversion' (Scott, 1980:1). In such a context, as well as ambiguities of aims, inappropriateness of strategies and ineffective implementation, state structures tainted by organised crime would put on an image that was not a true reflection of the realities. These tendencies would be reinforced by the almost inevitable reliance of drug enforcement agencies on supposedly 'turned' drugs traffickers, mercenaries and former spies.

Drugs, covert operations and the CIA

The CIA Drug Connection is as Old as the Agency (headline, *International Herald Tribune*, 3 December 1993). In fact older. The Agency's precursor, the Office of Strategic Services (OSS) brought the US mafia on board to prepare for the invasion of Sicily in World War II. In the immediate postwar era they found the mafia in Italy and the Corsican gangs centred on Marseilles handy partners in curbing the considerable influence communist parties and their affiliated trade unions had acquired from their crucial role in the antifascist Resistance in Italy and France respectively. Turning a blind eye to their dominance of the international drugs traffic, which had been facilitated by their new-found political influence, seemed perhaps a small price to pay for keeping western Europe safe from godless communism. But the 'French-connection' in drugs which was established at that time was to be replicated on a global scale with the birth of the CIA – first in Asia (see McCoy, 1991).

In the aftermath of the liberation of China in 1949, the coming to power of the Communist Party of China, and the onset of the Korean

War, US intelligence agencies turned to existing OSS-established links with an alliance between dope-dealing gangs in Shanghai and other cities and the former governing Nationalist Party, the Kuomintang (KMT) – now both operating from exile – and sought to refocus their activities toward counterinsurgency. Two KMT armies fled to, and established their troops and their families, in the mountainous border areas south-west of China in the north of Burma. They were supplied arms by the CIA and were looked upon as a source of intelligence and even of insurgent raids into China, but always as a buffer against any Chinese encroachment. To play those roles they had to have some economic base, and so turned to opium cultivation. They also had to be independent of the control of the central government of Burma, which might crack down on their disruptive activities against China and on the opium trade – for the Rangoon government's attitude towards drugs was always ambivalent (Renard, 1996). Their efforts in both regards received a blind eye, and even at times tacit support, from the CIA throughout the 1950s and thereafter.

The same tactics were used in Laos in the 1960s when the CIA created a secret army among the Hmong, a mountain people near the northern border of Vietnam, to battle Laotian communists and interdict supplies to the war fronts in Vietnam along the famous Ho Chi Minh trail. In the first stages of the renewed escalation of the wars in Indochina, the CIA's role was central. It was the Agency that infiltrated the tens of thousands of 'military advisers' into Vietnam as well as training ethnically non-Vietnam tribes in areas controlled by the communist-led Government in North Vietnam. The CIA remained in charge of operations in Laos and Cambodia, at least until the invasion of the latter in 1970, and it, rather than the US military, dealt with the generals in Thailand (Prouty, 1973).

As the trade in opium from the Nationalist Chinese and other warlords in northern areas and the Shan states of Burma, north Thailand and in Laos, the infamous 'Golden triangle', grew, various clients of the CIA, and even the Agency itself, became complicit in the traffic. The opium grown in the Triangle was often partially refined into morphine and ferried out through northern Thailand, which became 'the region's main heroin entrepot' (McCoy, 1991: 413) – courtesy of and to the benefit of that country's ruling generals, themselves US protégés. Generals in the air force, that was so massively built up in South Vietnam by the US, were also useful middlemen. The Hmong commander, Vang Pao, and other tribal warlords were allowed to use flights returning south after arms deliveries to them from Saigon by the CIA's 'proprietary' Air America to ferry opium to global markets. Even though the CIA managed to convince the 1975 Senate investigation into its covert activities (the Church Committee) that it was not aware of its airlines being used to ferry drugs, it is now widely accepted that it occurred, and that it was known to occur. The trade in the 1950s and 1960s had been essentially to Asian outlets and much of it was in the hands of the Chiu Chau syndicate. But a great boost to the production of morphine, and eventually heroin, from Golden Triangle opium had come with the introduction of US ground troops into the Vietnam War in 1965, providing an enormous ready market close to hand. A great irony, too, as the widespread use of drugs – some units admitted 20 percent addiction rates (quoted in McCoy, 1991) – contributed significantly to the lack of effectiveness and loss of will of the US armed forces (Boyle, 1972). In 1969 the CIA's various covert operations clients opened up a network of laboratories for refining opium into heroin in the Golden Triangle (McCoy, 1991: 19) – allegedly at the initiative of a Florida mafia family (*International Herald Tribune*, 3 July 1993). With the repatriation of US ground troops in the early 1970s, the Golden Triangle heroin followed them and flooded US markets, shipped by Chiu Chau and ex-GI syndicates at a time when Turkey had prohibited poppy cultivation. As a result, from zero in the 1960s, South-east Asia became the source of 30 percent of US consumption by 1973, according to DEA estimates (quoted in McCoy, 1991: 392).

A similar pattern of covert operations and support for war-lords operating from remote mountainous regions, who in turn could act as patrons for local peasants growing poppy in these remote fastnesses, emerged in the 1980s following the Soviet intervention in 1979 to support a communist regime that had come to power in a coup in Afghanistan. Throughout the decade of US support for the various factions of 'Mojaheddin' (Islam-inspired) fighters, the latters' involvement in the production and trade in drugs was kept quiet. Yet production underwent a parallel boost in much of the country and laboratories operated in the Afghan–Pakistan border areas, and the South Asia region moved from being a self-contained area absorbing local production to being the second largest (to Burma) producer of opium in the world, and the Afghan–Pakistan border area became the largest source of supply of heroin to Europe. McCoy (1991: 445) reaches this assessment of the CIA's role: 'Although the CIA did not play the same paramount role that it had in the transformation of Burma's drug trade thirty years before, its covert warfare still served as a catalyst in the emergence of Afghanistan as a leading source of heroin for the world market.' This possibility had been anticipated in 1979 by an academic psychiatrist who was a member of President Carter's Strategy Council on Drug Abuse, Dr David Musto, who together with another member, J. Lowinson, wrote in the *New York Times* (22 May 1980) of their

> worry about the growing of opium poppies in Afghanistan and Pakistan by rebel tribesmen … [and about the US] going in to support the opium growers in their rebellion against the Soviets. … Shouldn't we try to avoid what we had done in Laos … in befriending these tribes as we did in Laos when Air America (chartered by the CIA) helped transport crude opium from certain tribal areas?

In the event the CIA, which was the main conduit for US $2 billion worth of covert aid in the 1980s to the *mojaheddin*, took the decision, on the advice of the Pakistan Inter-Service Intelligence (ISI), to use one among the many warlord groups as its main client – the Hezbi-i Islami guerrillas under Gulbuddin Hekmatyar. As the CIA ran training camps along the border and supplied arms, massively escalating its aid after the 1981 decision to support all-out war, this group received more than half of all supplies. Despite a questionable background of only limited popular support and a reputation for violence against defectors and rival groups, Hekmatyar not only transformed himself into the major rebel commander, but also into 'Afghanistan's leading drug lord'. Much of the US effort was subcontracted to the Pakistan military, itself the beneficiary of the policies of a military dictatorship and of US $3 billion in arms supplies, as well as its share of both aid to the Afghan rebels, which it controlled, and to the border drug traffic.

Evidence of this connection was in the public domain from the early 1980s; thus, a DEA Congressional affairs liaison officer was quoted in the press in these terms in 1983: 'the rebels keep their cause going through the sale of opium' (quoted by Scott and Marshall, 1991). But such issues only began to have widespread coverage in the US media *after* the end of the cold war and the Soviet withdrawal from Afghanistan in 1989 – e.g. in *Washington Post* articles in May 1990. It is also clear that this connection was known to policy-makers. Scott and Marshall (1991) quote a *New York Times* (10 April 1988) attribution to an 'Administration official' where he says, 'We're not going to let a little thing like drugs get in the way of the political situation. … And when the Soviets leave and there's no money in the country, it's not going to be a priority to disrupt the drugs trade'. This last sentence accurately presages the continuation of the Afghan–Pakistan trade after the cold war. Despite the fact that peace has not been assured over many parts of the country, Afghan production was estimated at 2800 tons in 1997 compared with 400 tons in 1980 (*Guardian*, 2 January 1998).

There were several parallels with events in Latin America in the 1980s when drug trafficking expanded rapidly. Coca, as opposed to opium, was the basic crop; grown in inaccessible highlands in various parts of the Andes. However, the intelligence-organised crime links took a different political form. In Nicaragua the CIA did support insurgents opposed to, or at least independent from, central governmental authorities as in Laos, Vietnam, Burma and Afghanistan, and these 'Contras' did, despite the denials, involve themselves in the drugs trade (see Scott and Marshall 1991). However, elsewhere in Central America and in the Andes the 'war against drugs' was inextricably enmeshed with, and often subordinated to, counterinsurgency measures against radical guerrilla movements operating against governments, some of whose agencies were involved in, or at least complicit in, the drugs trade.

Historically the first intermeshing of covert operations and drugs, and arguably still the most significant in setting future patterns, was in Nicaragua. US support to the 'contra' insurgents fighting the radical Sandinista regime has been well-documented; the illegal provision of military aid to the Contras, despite such support being prohibited by legislation, was brought out in the investigations of the 'Iran–Contra' affair. The chapter on that episode in this volume shows a triangular set of relations and infringements: Iran was covertly supplied with arms; payment was received for them under the counter; these funds were diverted to finance small arms, logistical support and training that could not be paid for under a Congressionally-approved budget. This activity was not in fact a direct CIA operation; it was further hidden by being under Oliver North's special task force under the White House-controlled National Security Council team. However, from the onset of the investigations there were suggestions of a fourth dimension to the connections: it was alleged that the Contras were involved in the drug trade and that the planes that covertly ferried them and their arms into the border areas of Nicaragua returned to the US with drugs.

Unlike the other three accusations, this fourth connection has not yet been fully admitted officially. Since the first media reports surfaced in late 1985, the CIA has either denied Contra involvement in drugs or made very limited admissions. In 1986 the State Department acknowledged 'limited (numbers)…of drug traffickers had *tried* to establish connections with the Nicaraguan resistance groups'. By 1987 a CIA official had gone on record as saying that 'not a couple of people ... but a lot' among the Contras were involved in drug trafficking. The FBI denied even that. The Congressional investigations into Iran–Contra did not record any direct findings on the issue; but did include in their report a memo purporting to refute the Contra–drug allegation. The Independent Counsel's probe did not have this issue within its terms of reference. The one official inquiry that did investigate the issue and confirm the connection was that of a Senate Subcommittee on Terrorism, Narcotics, and International Operations, under Senator John Kerry in 1989. Its Report (Kerry Report, 1989) concluded, *inter alia*:

> There was substantial evidence of drug smuggling through the war zones on the part of individual Contras, Contra suppliers, Contra pilots, mercenaries who worked with the Contras, and Contra supporters throughout the region ... [Moreover] US officials involved in Central America failed to address the drug issue for fear of jeopardizing the war efforts against Nicaragua.

The Subcommittee identified no fewer than four conduits of 'humanitarian' aid that were 'owned and operated by narcotics traffickers'. Its Report also came to some hard-hitting conclusions. It criticised refusals of intelligence agencies to cooperate in bringing individuals associated with the Contras to justice, and revealed 'ticket punching' whereby drugs traffickers buy immunity by allying themselves with US covert operations. And it warned that 'the credibility of government institutions ... [had been jeopardised by the Administration turning] a blind eye to domestic and foreign corruption associated with the international narcotics trade' (Kerry Report, 1989). The chief counsel to the Subcommittee felt that

> What we did was to make it very clear that the Administration's priority decision to defrock the Sandinista government was much more important than trying to deal with the drug problem. Ultimately money was so powerful that anyone in the region got involved in it (the drugs trade) up to their armpits. (Quoted in Scott and Marshall, 1991)

Despite these findings, denials continued: for instance, when the Arkansas entrepot was alleged in 1992, and again in 1996, when the accusation was made that two Contra exiles supplied what became a 'crack' epidemic in Los Angeles. The latter alleged that the CIA at least knew of these transactions, not that it orchestrated a money-for-dope operation. These latter stories appeared in the *San José Mercury*, and interestingly the documents were posted on a World Wide Web site and accessed by an estimated 100 000 surfers. Government inquiries were ordered into the accusations, but were largely internal and not made public.

Scott and Marshall (1991) argue that the Kerry Subcommittee findings were of great potential significance in a context where the denial of the drug connection to Iran–Contra and the cover-up around it generated a climate where drug traffickers and abusers of power like Oliver North and the other Iran–Contra indictees might feel invulnerable. It punctured a tendency, but only slightly, to invoke the anti-drugs cause to avoid media and Congressional scrutiny. They further argue, however, that the limited impact of the Kerry Report was not only because it received little media or public attention, it also derived from the absence in the Report of the longer term historical record of a CIA-drugs connection in Central America. In fact, that can be traced back to the CIA's support of Cuban exiles: 'at least 8% of the 1,500 (Bay of Pigs) invasion force has subsequently been investigated or arrested for drug-dealing' reported in *Newsday* 1973.

Scott and Marshall (1991) in fact posit the Cuban and Nicaraguan connections were symptomatic of a broader 'narco-terrorism' network between right-wing governments and political movements stretching from the 1980s Argentine military to governments headed by CIA clients in Honduras and Guatemala, as well as Bolivia and Colombia. Noriega himself was on the CIA payroll for 25 years before he was pilloried as a drug dealer, and the record shows the DEA informed the CIA of his involvement in drugs in 1972. Any action against him was vetoed because he was such a useful 'asset' as well as an anti-Sandinista ally – until his usefulness in that latter respect came to an end in 1986 (Hargreaves, 1992).

There is an even longer historical connection in the Golden Triangle– the same personnel, the same methods. For instance, among the old US 'China hands' that had to leave China in 1949 and who backed the Nationalist Chinese and other drug-lords in Burma and Thailand, and were involved in the setting-up what later became the CIA proprietary 'Air America', was Howard Hunt, who, with other China hands, was then transferred to oversee the 1954 CIA-backed coup in Guatemala, and in turn the Bay of Pigs invasion of Cuba – and who, of course, recruited some of his Cuban exile cronies to burgle the Democratic Party office in Watergate. It is also suggested that the latter was but a minor role related to a more general 'recruitment of a secret army of Cuban exiles, answerable only to the White House, and equipped to assassinate foreign leaders' (*Inquiry*, 5 March 1979, quoted in Scott, 1980). Even though the vast expansion of coca production and the export of cocaine to the US from and through Latin America was not so centred on CIA connections there as it was in South East Asia and Central America, the Agency's past role certainly has been a complicating factor in the context of drug enforcement in the Andean countries.

One example of this complicated context is Bolivia. Alongside Noriega in his Miami prison in the early 1990s was a Bolivian, Roberto Suarez, who had earned the title of 'cocaine king' by the end of the 1970s. He was a patron of the many coca growers in his own country and orchestrated the partial refinement and deliveries of semi-processed coca to the Colombian cartels, as well as providing a link with Bolivian military and government circles. Indeed, in 1980 he was one of the main plotters behind a military coup, with the Interior Minister Arce Gomez and General Garcia Meza who became President – plus the Nazi collaborator, later to be convicted in France as a war criminal, Klaus Barbie. The latter had been originally spirited away from France to Bolivia in 1951 with the help of the CIA to cover up his involvement in their operations in post-World War II. The coup was a pre-emptive strike against the threat to the drug lords of a projected shift to democracy, and heralded in a 'cocaine government' – the first instance of the traffickers 'buying themselves a government' (Hargeaves, 1992). Just before the coup the DEA had set up what one of its officials termed 'the biggest sting operation in law-enforcement history' against Suarez' network which lead to the arrest and indictment in Miami of his son and henchman, Alfredo Gutierrez. They jumped bail and were available to help in the coup. It has been suggested by the ex-DEA official involved, on whom Suarez put out a contract, that the CIA supported both the disappearance of Suarez' cronies and the coup (Levine, 1990).

Blaming the enemy

Of course the CIA's knowledge of, and at least peripheral role in, drugs in the various arenas was a subject in which the cover-up was a priority, especially with the growth of the drugs trade in the USA in recent years. Thus the CIA submitted testimony to the Church Committee looking into its activities in 1975, and even convinced the Committee, there was 'no substance' to 'allegations that the Agency's air proprietaries were involved in drug trafficking' in South-east Asia (Church Committee Report, 1975, quoted by McCoy, 1991: 386).

One cover-up device for doing this – to point the finger elsewhere, preferably at an enemy – was consistently used. Perhaps the first occasion was in South-east Asia: the drugs that began to come out of the Golden Triangle were at first attributed to the new Chinese Communist Government. That official Narcotics Bureau myth continued to be perpetrated until, and even despite, a scholarly study in 1960 exposed it and pointed instead to the fact that 'the narcotics business has been a factor in some activities and permutations of the China Lobby' (Koen, 1960: p. ix). In fact it was the Nationalist Chinese war-lords in northern Burma, and the Chiu Chau syndicates that had fled from Shanghai to Hong Kong and Bangkok, who were the opium traffickers. Similar intimations were made about the revolutionary government of Cuba, whereas it was the Bay of Pigs invaders and other Cuban exiles who were the traffickers. In what was termed in 1970, 'the largest roundup of drug traffickers' across the USA, it was found that over 100 of the 150 arrested suspects were people who had been part of the Bay of Pigs invasion force. In similar vein, 'with less than conclusive evidence, Washington was extremely vocal in accusing the Sandanista government of active participation in the drugs trade' (Hargreaves, 1992: 16) after it came to power having overthrown the Samoza dictatorship in Nicaragua. The left-wing guerrillas in Colombia, the M–19, were also targeted as having a drug connection. This kind of link was shaped into a conspiracy propounded by President Reagan in a 1986 address:

> The link between the governments of such Soviet allies as Cuba and Nicaragua and international narcotics trafficking and terrorism is becoming increasingly clear. These twin evils – narcotics trafficking and terrorism – represent the most insidious and dangerous threat to the hemisphere today. (Quoted in Scott and Marshall, 1991)

Under the Reagan and Bush Administrations this conspiracy was expounded as a new concept: '*narco-terrorism*'. This epithet had several useful attributes. It was, for instance, welcomed by two associates of Oliver North who were quoted in the Congressional Iran–Contra Report (1987: Appendix A, p. 686) as seeing a proposed propaganda campaign to link the Sandanistas and drugs in these terms: 'the chance to have a single issue which no one can publicly disagree with is irresistible'. The theory provided a rationale in the Andean Strategy for targeting 'old enemies' in the shape of insurgents in Peru and Colombia along with the 'new enemies', the cocaine cartels. It also served to give a new role to the US military – especially important, no doubt, after the end of the cold war. The WOLA Report (1991) quotes a former chairman of the Joint Chiefs of Staff: 'Certainly I think we'll put more emphasis on the drug war. And if there are resources tied to it, why, you'll see the services compete for those, and probably vigorously.'

There were indeed major expansions in the military budgets for Latin America in the early 1990s, but the terms required them to be related to the drugs war. WOLA (1991) quotes a member of the US military group in Colombia: 'Up until 1989 there were no restrictions. The aid was coming in under the old MAP (Military Assistance Program). When the MAP was turned into the FMF (Foreign Military Assistance) program, suddenly we had to tie all the aid into counter-narcotics.'

President Reagan had, meanwhile, made another contribution to declaring a 'war on drugs'. He signed a secret National Security Directive which defined drugs as a threat to national security; it undermined the health of America's youth, spawned a crime wave and attacked the social fabric. Narco-terrorism became more than just a word; it was thereby transformed into an operational formula. It pointed to a crusade, one that allowed the imagery of 'war', and also justified intervention abroad as 'self-defence' and, of course, defence of the hemisphere. Although, as Hargreaves (1992) points out, the rhetoric of war inevitably gets people to think in terms of 'victory', a future problem has been stored up as any objective analysis indicates that no victory is possible in this war and by these means: 'By calling it a war, the US is doomed to lose' (Hargreaves, 1992: 15).

The reality of the drugs trade and guerrilla activity in the Andes is different from the image of narco-guerrillas, although the situation does differ between the three main Andean countries. In Peru the Sendero Luminoso (Shining Path) guerrillas did have a powerful presence in the Upper Huallaga Valley, which was a major coca-growing area, but the extent to which the movement was involved in refining and transporting is doubtful. Moreover, it was suggested by a senior Peruvian official that 'militarizing the drug war will give the Sendero a growing army of 250,000 farmers' (quoted in WOLA, 1991), as the coca-growers would seek the movement's protection from the suppression programme, and thus the link that was formerly tenuous would be reinforced. In Colombia, the assertion that the M–19 and other left-wing guerrilla movement had an important hand in the drugs trade has been much publicised and politicised, according to Thoumi's study (1995) of drugs in that country. However, his findings are that

> while there have been connections between guerrillas and the illegal
> ... drugs industry (especially in the early 1980s when guerrillas
> offered a degree of protection and sought to 'tax' the farmers and
> traders), these relationships have been fundamentally unstable
> because the long-term goals of the two groups are diametrically
> opposed.

He suggests that they are no different from drug links with elected politicians or judges, yet no one speaks of 'narco-congress' or 'narco-judiciary'! In Bolivia, the links are even more tenuous as there has not been an active insurgent movement since the reintroduction of civilian rule in 1982. Yet elements in the US military still seek to spread the counterinsurgency gospel on the back of anti-narcotics programmes. Thus WOLA (1991) quotes a US Colonel, Robert Jacobelly, as talking about 'more of a latent insurgency in Bolivia at this point. Things will get worse, and that's related to the drugs trade' – his convoluted justification for using anti-narcotics and its resources to provide counterinsurgency training and other assistance!

Drug enforcement compromised

One basic consequence of the prioritisation of contra and other intelligence operations was to undermine the efforts at drug enforcement. This tendency is seen most obviously in the manner whereby the DEA takes a back seat in relation to the CIA. Organisationally, this is evidenced by the rule that 'no DEA country attaché overseas was allowed to initiate an investigation into a suspected drug trafficker or attempt to recruit an informant without clearance from the local CIA station chief ... their transmissions are made available to the CIA' (*International Herald Tribune*, 3 July 1993). McCoy (1991) compares the relative muscle of the two agencies and the 'internecine bureaucratic struggles for the opium hills of Asia': 'the US Bureau of Narcotics (precursor of DEA) opened its first office in Bangkok with just three agents in the late 1960s, more than a decade after a major CIA covert operation – backed by several hundred agents and a fleet of aircraft – had installed a 12,000-man opium army in the mountains of northern Burma.' This dearth of monitoring and operational drug enforcement presence in South-east Asia was itself not unconnected with CIA lobbying of the Eisenhower Administration to prevent the old Bureau of Narcotics and Dangerous Drugs (BNDD) setting up monitoring posts (*International Herald Tribune*, 3 July 1993).

The kind of consequences of this bureaucratic in-fighting is exemplified in this newspaper report: 'a pair of BN agents tried to seize an Air America DC-3 loaded with heroin packed into boxes of Tide soap powder. At the CIA's behest, they were ordered to release the plane and drop the inquiry.' The CIA has won out in countless struggles elsewhere. In Mexico the CIA required the drug agency in the 1970s to hand over a list of all its Mexican assets and co-ordinate operations (Scott and Marshall, 1991: 35). *The International Herald Tribune* (3 July, 1993) quotes a DEA investigation in Mexico as revealing that the country's director of federal security, a known CIA 'asset', was implicated in the kidnapping and murder of a DEA officer. Again Noriega's case is instructive: the CIA protecting him against the DEA until a different post-cold war agenda and a concern with the future of the Panama Canal led to the 1989 invasion.

In another notorious case, a highly visible joint US–Bolivian military operation sought to take out 50 cocaine laboratories. However, one 'vast drive-in lab', Huanchaca, near Santa Cruz had enough political protection to escape being on the list. A Bolivian investigator who announced he would make revelations was assassinated within hours. Bolivian sources, quoted by Hargreaves (1992: 155), maintained that the lab was CIA-run and servicing the Contras' supplies. In a 1993 case the US Justice Department investigated allegations that officers of a special Venezuelan anti-drug unit funded by the CIA smuggled more than 2000 pounds of cocaine into the USA, with the knowledge of CIA officials, and over the protests of the DEA.

McCoy (1991) generalises from such scraps of evidence that appear in the public record: 'Over the past forty years, CIA covert operations have often overwhelmed the interdiction efforts of the weaker U.S. drug enforcement agencies.' But the reality is not simply of a well-intentioned DEA being hampered by the CIA's hidden agenda and superior clout. 'The line between the two agencies has often been blurred' (Scott and Marshall, 1991: 35). This is seen at one level in the fact that the DEA, which had to find personnel used to clandestine activities in foreign countries when it took over from the ineffectual BNDD in the mid-1970s, recruited many of its personnel from the intelligence services, which were at the time under investigation by a Senate Committee (the Church Committee) and were drawing in their horns after the Vietnam war, and being warned off Angola by Congress. This interpenetration of staff sometimes meant that a DEA assignment was a cover for intelligence activity. Sometimes it meant that the DEA colluded with Contra-type activities – or that counterinsurgency activity has been accepted as part of the Andean strategy. In earlier periods the collaboration was more typically with corrupt police forces, such as the DEA-supported Thai Border Patrol, which became involved in the massacre of unarmed, demonstrating students in 1976 and thereby paved the way for a military coup (Herman and Chomsky, 1979: 227). A further complication is that the very nature of their investigations impels drug enforcement bodies to try to turn and use corrupt personnel who are part of the trade, and all too often they have a background of links with intelligence operations and with covert political operations.

Scott and Marshall (1991) argue that the widespread Contra–drug connection throughout Central America, and maybe beyond, gave rise to the most widespread examples of drug enforcement myopia and inaction. The DEA denied the very link which the Kerry Report (1990) confirmed. Such statements could hardly be ascribed to ignorance: the DEA itself employed and protected from prosecution a pilot supplying the Contras, who was mentioned by the Kerry Report as being suspected of 'continuing his own drugs business using his work for DEA as a cover'; the DEA's own Guatemala office 'compiled convincing evidence that the contra military supply operation was smuggling cocaine and marijuana' (*New York Times*, 20 January 1987); a former security aid to the Salvadorean death squads was on the DEA payroll. If not ignorance, then the DEA's statements constituted a cover-up – whether this was a result of corruption of some agents, an instinct to protect sources, or subservience of the DEA to the CIA or NSC.

Nor was the clash just one between two bureaucracies. One study (Youngers and Andreas, 1989, quoted in Hargreaves, 1992) estimates that there were some 58 federal agencies and 74 congressional committees that have some part in the drug war; and that 'turf wars, budget battles and bureaucratic infighting rage between them, resulting in fragmented and often conflicting policies'. But in the Andean strategy the US military and the Pentagon and State Department as well as other agencies responsible for military aid are also now involved directly. Problems arise because of a basic difference in approach. The war on drugs rests on the assumption that military operations are best suited to prosecute the campaign against producers and traffickers, and by implication, are also better qualified than civilians to maintain public order – a dangerous notion in countries where the military needed little excuse to sweep aside civilian political institutions. In contrast, DEA officials believe that US military and intelligence training in search-and-destroy methods, jungle survival as though they were engaged in a real war or 'low intensity conflict' situation, are inappropriate where there is no front line and no territorially-based enemy. Hargreaves (1992) quotes one DEA officer, Gene Castillo: 'The military's answer is to blow everyone up ... They call this a 'war' on drugs. It is a war of sorts, but it is still a law enforcement operation which has to be carried out according to the laws of the country we are in.'

In the Andes, strategy is not a matter for the DEA alone. As we have seen, the military forces of the US and of host governments are involved as well national police forces. In 1990 the US Southern Command with its headquarters in Panama declared drugs its number one priority, and its own budget for anti-drug activities in Latin America rose dramatically to US $100 million (WOLA, 1991). The US Military are involved directly in selecting targets, planning raids and co-ordinating operations with the DEA, and national police or military, but have developed the use of satellites, air reconnaissance and radar based in the US as part of a sophisticated regional intelligence network. There has also been massive growth in the military assistance budgets to the three Andean countries, which involves, of course, US personnel in advisory, training and logistics roles as well as actual weaponry. Likewise, the CIA has officially shifted its priorities to become more heavily involved in the war on drugs.

A more disturbing interpretation of the origins of the DEA itself has been raised by some analysts. Epstein (1991) argues that Nixon's war on heroin was part of 'a grand design' to set up a drug super-agency, under direct White House control, to become 'the strong investigative arm for domestic surveillance that President Nixon had long quested after'. It is certainly the case that his June 1971 declaration of the 'war' led to the assembling of the White House plumbers – many of them Cuban exiles – who were involved in the Watergate burglary, and much else besides. There were also suggestions (Scott, 1980; Kruger, 1980) that the plumbers were but the US version of an even more sinister 'narco-terrorist' link: the consolidation in the late 1960s and 1970s of an international network of extreme right-wing mercenaries involved in the drugs traffic, illicit arms and assassinations. It, purportedly, had links emanating from the Argentine intelligence personnel responsible for death squads with contacts throughout Latin and Central America, and related to a super-secret internal DEA intelligence group called 'Deacon 1', consisting of former CIA officers – all Cuban exiles – which developed greater loyalty to international fascist goals than those of the DEA. If these claims have any validity it puts a different light not only on what Nixon was trying to achieve with the plumbers and DEA – perhaps to infiltrate in order to control the right-wing narco-terrorist network – as Scott (1980) suggests, but also, of course, on Watergate itself.

Effects of compromising drug enforcement

At two points in time the use of drugs in the US and in Europe were in decline and the situations held out some prospect of reversing the growth of consumption. In the early 1940s, as a result of the League of Nations' efforts from 1934 and World War II, opium production fell, but the Sicilian and US Mafias' and the Corsican syndicates' special status with US military intelligence allowed them to control and expand the traffic. Then, in the mid-1970s, some temporary successes of the DEA's efforts in Turkey, Thailand and Mexico after a drought in the Golden Triangle cut the heroin flow to North America, resulted in a reduction in US addicts from about 500000 to 200000 (indicating, incidentally, how much addiction is driven by supply rather than demand). But in the subsequent 20 years, partly as a result of increased heroin from Afghanistan as well as Burma, world opium production increased fourfold. Seventy-three percent of the increased production in 1989 came from South-east Asia, where the CIA had worked with the drug lords for over twenty years. By the end of 1980, once the Afghan flow had begun and prices were lower, the number of US addicts had gone up to 450000 and continued to rise through the 1980s. Similar trends were occurring in cocaine from Central America and the Andes. Production there grew by an estimated eight percent per year from 1980 to 1988, and continued to escalate despite the Andean strategy. According to official sources quoted by WOLA (1991) coca production in South America grew by 28 percent in the first year of the war on drugs. These trends are supported by evidence of prices on the street, where falls are indicative of supply increases. DEA figures were $45000 per kilo of pure cocaine in 1984; $11000 by 1989 (Epstein, 1991: 11). During this period Presidents Reagan and Bush continued to trumpet that 'we've turned the corner in the war on drugs'. Attorney General Meese specifically claimed that Operation Snowcap in the Andes 'will cut the amount of cocaine being imported into the US by fifty percent' (quoted in Levine, 1991: 314). Demonstrably a false prediction.

Subsequently the war has had some successes. The Cali cartels in Colombia have been interdicted in their trade in drugs from Colombia, but the Medellin cartels have taken up the slack and refining has been moved by them to other countries. Indeed, even if the Andean strategy did achieve its goals for cutting coca production and refining, that would point up what some consider the fallacy in the logic of source-country strategies (WOLA, 1991). Apart from the many difficulties of implementation – host country resentment and conflicting agenda, corrupt officials, subordination to other foreign policy goals – reduced production in one place seems to lead to a 'balloon effect': squeeze in one place and it plops out elsewhere. But most fundamentally, the futility stems from the very limited linkage between cuts in production of coca or opium, particularly in any one country, and cocaine and heroin on the streets of Los Angeles or New York. The source country input has only an insignificant effect on price: as little as five percent in the case of cocaine.

The political effects of the phoney drug war

Source-country operations accounted for 70 percent of the total drugs war budget in the 1990s – although more than 80 percent of that was against cocaine in Latin America, with consequent neglect of the heroin traffic from South and South-east Asia. Compliance with this requirement is made easier by the US also requiring a 'certification' that such governments are co-operating with enforcement policies and programmes. There are several political implications. First, the prominent role of the military in these operations, plus military aid and the uncritical diplomatic support for the military in these countries, is said to increase the political muscle and centrality of generals who have a history of resisting rather than promoting democratisation. Second, the operations themselves drag governments, as Toro (1995: 69) said about Mexico, 'into a spiral of increasingly punitive programs that have rendered the manufacture and smuggling of narcotics more (rather than less) appealing and the organisation of this illegal market a threat to civilized and effective governance'. The other political consequence of the murky links between intelligence agencies and drugs and other international criminal networks is the institutional legacy. There may no longer be the same cold war and other foreign policy imperatives for the cosy relationship, but it must remain a matter of doubt how far a huge bureaucracy like the CIA can make a wholesale structural shift in its client networks, domestic alliances and practices.

These factors all render the war ineffective and counterproductive in terms of other goals such as democratisation. They also widen the gap enormously between rhetoric and reality.

Conclusions

> To an average American who witnesses the dismal spectacle of the narcotics traffic at the street level, it must seem inconceivable that the government could be implicated in the international narcotics trade. Unfortunately, American diplomats and CIA agents have been involved in the narcotics traffic at three levels: (1) coincidental complicity by allying with groups actively engaged in the traffic; (2) support of the traffic by covering up for known heroin traffickers and condoning their involvement; and (3) active engagement in the transport of opium and heroin. It is ironic, to say the least, that America's heroin plague is of its own making. (McCoy, 1991: 23)

The argument of this chapter has not been to crudely assert that the war on drugs is a total fabrication, nor that there has been a conspiracy consciously orchestrated by the CIA or other federal agencies to do the opposite and generate the spread of drugs. Rather, it has pointed to the crosscutting purposes underlying other forms of foreign intervention and domestic politics which have taken precedence over drug control. In the harsh resignation speech of William von Raab as Commissioner for Customs in 1989, he complained that there were too many in federal agencies with 'other interests more important than winning a war on drugs' (Levine, 1991: 315). Counterinsurgency and Contra-support efforts became entwined with local allies that found drugs trade convenient sources of funding, clientelist support and transportation. In this context the 'lying' consists at one level of turning a blind eye to these collateral activities and also of cover-ups about them. It has also involved, as we have seen, misinformation, in the sense of propaganda that pins the blame on 'enemies': the Chinese communists, the Cuban governments, the Sandinistas, 'narco-guerrillas' in the Andes, whereas the reality was that it was Chinese Nationalist war-lords, Cuban exiles, the Contras, and right-wing governments in Latin America that were the traffickers. There has also been a tendency to make false claims that the war is being won and the quantity of drugs on the street has been reduced, in the teeth of contrary evidence.

At another level, the role of some government agencies and personnel, and the inevitable knowledge by insiders of this role, plus their knowledge of the factors inhibiting the war, all raise the question of whether the 'wars' themselves do not have that element of *charade*. In part this might be seen as conscious: to show domestic voters a determination to tackle drugs by visible campaigns, but through pursuing one particular strategy among several options – repressive operations abroad, because other possible options, certainly the same degree of repression on the streets, have been ruled out for political or other reasons. In part it is also deliberately blurring interventions that on their own would be hard to justify, if only for isolationist or Vietnam-syndrome reasons. The 'war on drugs' serves the propaganda purpose of being a crusade, tackling what has been identified as a threat to national security. Moreover, it presents the cause of the problems of the inner cities, such as crime and violence, as essentially external, not a result of poverty and institutional racism. Whether deliberate or not, without postulating a grand conspiracy, the information fed to the public is of a holy war fought by brave federal officers and military personnel against vicious and powerful opponents. But this metaphor of the crusading war is, in the last analysis, counterproductive; if, as suggested here, that kind of war is unwinnable, then the continued supply will be seen eventually as a 'defeat' rather than a socio-economic problem. The reality has been a seemingly inexorable spread of drugs in US cities. This chapter has tried to show that this is a result of institutional forces; it is as much a by-product of the efforts of other federal officers and intelligence and military personnel.

Moreover, these depressing trends are world-wide: billions of dollars spent on a policy based on criminalisation and punishment, chiefly in the supply countries, while the supply grows and prices fall. Equally, scepticism about the campaign has grown. Representations were made to the UN General Assembly special session on drugs in June 1998 that the war on drugs has become more harmful than drug abuse itself. The signatories of this letter included several US mayors and three federal judges plus a former head of Scotland Yard's drug squad, as well as many writers, scientists and politicians. They represent an increasing constituency who, like the introductory quote, believe the war is a fraudulent deception.

8

The Scott Inquiry: Matrix Churchill and the Arms to Iraq Affair

Dave Bartlett

> The answers to Parliamentary Questions...failed to inform
> Parliament of the current state of Government policy on non-
> lethal arms sales to Iraq. This failure was deliberate.
>
> (Scott 1996: D4.42)

'On the floor of the House [of Commons] – save in rare moods of
resentment – the government controls the agenda' (Birkinshaw 1997:
168). One such occasion was 9 November 1992 when Prime Minister
Major was constrained, by the force of political opposition, and by the
strength of media and public disquiet, to announce an inquiry under
Justice Richard Scott into the export of defence equipment and dual use
goods to Iraq between December 1984 and August 1990, the prosecution
of three Matrix Churchill executives for contravening export licensing
regulations made under the Import, Export and Customs Powers
(Defence) Act 1939, and the use of Public Interest Immunity Certificates
(PIICs) in this and other similar prosecutions (Scott 1996: A.2: A.3; also
Birkinshaw 1997: 29; Doig 1997: 159; Norton-Taylor 1995: 31: 37; Leigh
1993: 255–6). Major thus gave way to widespread suspicion that ministers
and officials had conspired to break the Government's own export guidelines to supply the Iraqi war machine, that ministers had lied in
Parliament to avoid public and parliamentary criticism, had permitted the
prosecution of businessmen by Customs and Excise as a means of protecting themselves, and had sought to pervert justice by preventing the
disclosure of documents through Public Interest Immunity Certificates.

The Iran–Iraq war and Howe's 1984 guidelines

After the start of the Iran–Iraq war in September 1980, and with no
UN embargo on arms sales to the area, the British Government

professed neutrality and announced that lethal war materials would not be licensed for export to either combatant (e.g. Scott D1.4: D2.419). Political and commercial difficulties attended this position from the first. In 1979 Iran – which the US, Saudi Arabia and the Gulf States all actively opposed – held 74 outstanding contracts with International Military Services (wholly owned by the Ministry of Defence, MOD). By 1984 negotiations had resolved outstanding issues regarding 36 contracts and between 1981–4 Iran bought some £2000 million worth of goods from the UK. Similar difficulties attended consideration of restrictions on exports to Iraq which had increased from £201 million in 1979 to £874 million in 1982 and likewise totalled some £2000 million in the period to 1984. UK sales of defence-related material to Iraq totalled not less than £184 million in the first four years of the war as against similar sales to Iran of £13 million in the same period (D1.15). In the face of these considerations ministers agreed in 1981 that 'every opportunity should be taken to exploit Iraq's potentialities as a promising market for the sale of defence equipment' and that '"lethal items" should be interpreted in the narrowest possible sense, and the obligations of flexibility as flexibly as possible' (D1.10; also D1.3–16).

This approach led to the ambiguous and discretionary guidelines which became the hallmark of Government policy in the pursuit of its interest both that UK business be enabled to profit from the sale of defence related goods and establish access to potential future markets, and that Government retain control over the flow of material in accord with its perception at any time regarding the balance of foreign and economic policy interests. That such would be possible – without incurring the criticisms of friendly states and/or other potential customers, the parliamentary opposition, the press and the public – was the rationale for establishing Foreign Secretary Geoffrey Howe's Guidelines of December 1984 (D1.17–94: 146–7):

> (i) ... maintain our consistent refusal to supply any lethal equipment to either side; (ii) subject to ... fulfil[ing] existing contracts ...; (iii) ... should not in future sanction new orders for any defence equipment which in our view would significantly enhance the capacity of either side to prolong or exacerbate the conflict; (iv) ... continue to scrutinise rigorously all applications for export licences for the supply of defence equipment to Iran and Iraq. (D1.59)

Though agreed between officials and ministers in the Department of Trade and Industry (DTI), MOD, and the Foreign and Commonwealth Office (FCO) in November, and by Prime Minister Thatcher in December 1984, it was also decided that no statement of policy would be announced to Parliament (D1.87–90: 145: 148–150). Opportunities to make an announcement were ignored (D1.151–53) when ministers gave what Scott describes as 'inaccurate and potentially misleading' answers which did not comply with the principle that ministers have a duty 'not to deceive or mislead Parliament or the public' (D1.151: 160–1). Scott records that the announcement of the Guidelines when made in October 1985 (D1.154–5) was for 'political advantage' and that there was a 'consistent undervaluing by Government of the public interest that full information should be made available to Parliament'; the Government had consistently acted to its own 'political or administrative convenience' (D1.163: 165: D2.434).

Implementation of the 1984 guidelines

Despite the representation of the guidelines as superintending a policy of 'impartiality' and 'neutrality' which was 'strictly' applied to all defence related equipment (e.g. Scott D2.420–6), they continued to be applied with 'flexibility'. Howe described the Guidelines as no more than 'an aspect of the management of policy' (D1.81). Other ministers and officials regarded them similarly (D1.91–4: D2.9–18: 27–9) and Thatcher herself stretched policy beyond the Guidelines at a meeting with the Iraqi Prime Minister in December 1985 (D2.3–5). Moreover, the Export Credit Guarantee Department (ECGD) negotiated credits with Iraq beginning in 1983 and allocated £25 million of the second protocol for defence related purchases in 1985. The allocation was raised to £50 million (of which £5 million was allocated to support a contract for tank trackway) in the third protocol negotiated that year. The defence allocation increased again in 1987 and between 1984 and 1987 a minimum of £55.7 million of credit was advanced for military related exports to Iraq (D2.98–9: 115: also 65–120).

The Guidelines did nothing moreover to resolve difficulties regarding non-lethal, defence related equipment such as machine tools which DTI officials regarded as 'dual-use' – capable of civil or military production – and not covered by the Guidelines but coming under the 'industrial list' compiled to prevent high technology exports to the Soviet block. DTI's 'principal objectives [were] to maintain the best possible opportunities for trade with both countries, both in civil goods and services and "acceptable" defence exports' (DTI official, 1984, cited in D1.60: also D2.9–10: 60–4: 248: 280) and its officials were often in conflict with colleagues from FCO and MOD in the Interdepartmental Committee (IDC), an informal committee established in 1984 after the Guidelines were agreed to act as a clearing house for export licence applications (ELAs) for Iraq and Iran. IDC reviewed applications on the basis of recommendations from the MOD's Working Group (MODWG) on the defence enhancement capacity of an ELA. The failure of IDC to agree a recommendation resulted in its being passed to junior ministers, secretaries of state, and finally the Cabinet, for a decision.

In the period to November 1987 DTI issued export licences to Matrix Churchill, Wickman Bennett and BSA Tools for high specification, computerised numerically controlled (CNC) lathes described in ELAs as having such vague end uses as 'general mechanical engineering' (D2.269–82). Though some of these tools were known to have a defence capability and, while some ELAs experienced delay, all were approved. Anthony Steadman (Director of the Export Licensing Board (ELB) at DTI from May 1987) noted in November 1987 that 'no applications for CNC machines have been refused where a non-military use has been stated' and that in such cases it 'may be possible to get the FCO and MOD to accept, as a general principle, some by-passing of the IDC procedure' (D2.274–75).

Conflicting interpretations of the guidelines as between the DTI, MOD and FCO motivated attempts by DTI to seek an early revision of policy (cf. D2.9–26). Nevertheless, the guidelines provided a rhetorical support to Government policy and it was not until the circulation (to departments which included DTI's ELB) of a 30 November 1987 Intelligence Report that substantive difficulties arose. The Report named Matrix Churchill (recently purchased by an Iraqi front company and owned ultimately by the Iraqi Ministry of Defence), BSA Tools, Wickman Bennett, and Colchester Lathes as all involved in the supply of tools to manufacture a range of munitions at Hutteen and Nassr General Establishments, prominent military manufacturing facilities (D2.265–8: also 283–93: D5.2–24). The Report was based on information provided by Mark Gutteridge (a Matrix Churchill executive who later faced prosecution) to MI6 and was substantiated by a letter to Howe from a Matrix Churchill employee informing that the company was supplying 'machines [which] are going to be used to machine shell cases' in Iraq (D2.318), the March report of a businessman (D2.325), and a telex from the embassy in Baghdad concerning Hutteen and Nassr (D2.326).

In response to representations by the manufacturers of machine tools regarding delays which had attended ELAs and the possibility that licences might be revoked, Alan Clark (Minister for Trade at DTI) met representatives from the Machine Tool Trades Association (MTTA) who included Paul Henderson (Managing Director of Matrix Churchill who was also to face prosecuted) on 20 January 1988. The DTI minute of the meeting recorded that 'Choosing his words carefully and noting that the Iraqis would be using the current orders for general engineering purposes, Mr Clark stressed that it was important ... to agree a specification with the customer in advance which highlighted the peaceful (non-military) use to which the machine tools would be put' (G5.37). If this indicates that Clark gave a 'nod and a wink' to manufacturers, it was nothing to the understanding which the MTTA representatives believed they had received: the Minister had 'raised the discussion of applications for future export licences and their method of submission so that they had a good chance of being granted ... the intended use of the machines should be couched in such a manner as to emphasise the peaceful aspect to which they were to be put' (G5.37; also 2: 23: 33: 38: 43–4: G6.18–22: G8.1–5: G17.29–31].

Confirmation of official support for exports was provided in a memo from Ian Blackley of FCO: 'If it becomes public knowledge that the tools are to be used to make munitions, deliveries would have to stop at once. The companies should be warned of the falling guillotine, and urged to produce as fast as they can' (D2.35).

The 1988 revision of the guidelines

Formal discussions to review the guidelines were made possible by the August 1988 ceasefire which opened the prospect of potentially huge markets for civil reconstruction and military re-equipment to British industry. The Iraqi market was described as 'the big prize' and William Waldegrave, junior Minister at FCO, argued in October 1989 that 'I doubt if there is any future market of such a scale anywhere where the UK is potentially so well-placed .... We must not allow it to go to the French, Germans, Japanese, Koreans etc ... the priority of Iraq in our policy should be very high: in commercial terms comparable to South Africa' (cited in Norton-Taylor 1995: 59). Geoffrey Howe authored a paper in which he noted that 'the post-war reconstruction of Iran and Iraq will create major opportunities for British industry ... Opportunities for sales of defence equipment ... will be considerable' (Scott D3.12: also D3.1–12: 28; Norton-Taylor 1995: 60). Howe also noted the danger of alienating the Gulf states if arms supplies were resumed. The paper was forwarded to Thatcher with a note by Charles Powell (her Private Secretary, PS) emphasising the need to review defence sales policy to the two countries but raising the additional problem of public opinion regarding the Iranian controlled British hostages in Beirut and the recent gassing by Saddam Hussein of Kurdish civilians. Powell, in responding to Howe's paper, noted that 'the general strategy.. will.. require decisions over the next few weeks or months on a number of difficult and sensitive issues, such as the guidelines ... The Prime Minister will wish to be kept very closely in touch at every stage and consulted on all relevant decisions' (Scott D3.13–14).

On 21 December 1988 Clark, Lord Trefgarne (Minister for Defence Procurement at MOD) and Waldegrave agreed a new formulation of Guideline (iii) to deny only those exports 'which, in our view, would be of direct and significant assistance to either country in the conduct of offensive operations' (D3.30). The amendment was subsequently agreed when Waldegrave's PS wrote to Clark that the new formulation met 'our joint requirements, and should continue to be used on a trial basis for the time being ... Mr Waldegrave is content for us to implement a more liberal policy on defence sales, without any public announcement' (D3.42: also 16–47: 64–5: 107–14; Norton-Taylor *et al.* 1996: 56).

Evidence was not found by Scott which showed secretaries of state or the Prime Minister had given formal approval to the change (Scott D3.36: 40: 44: 65: 98–106: 110) and Thatcher's reading of a cabinet paper on the supply of Hawk jets to Iraq three months later (when she received two Notes which referred to the 'revised guidelines') might conceivably have been the first occasion when she (and John Major) may have become aware of the change in policy (D6.13–15: D4.14–16: also D6.1–28; Norton-Taylor *et al.* 1996: 57: 78–9).

While the sale of Hawks was rejected by the cabinet, other export orders for the Iraqi defence programme were authorised. In February 1989 MODWG was informed of the changed Guideline (iii) and reconsidered an ELA for the export of tactical radar to Iraq previously refused only in January, and now approved its export (D3.48–63; Norton-Taylor et al. 1996: 57). It was also in this period that ECGD had reviewed its relations with Iraq, and in November 1988 a further tranche credits totalling £340 million were agreed. By the end of 1988 ECGD's exposure totalled £1156 million and, despite the 'trigger' of overdue payments being repeatedly invoked, proposals for a further £350 million (and a more lenient 'trigger') were discussed in September 1989 (but against the opposition of the Treasury) as an inducement to encourage Iraqi repayments on previous credits. In the event £250 million was offered for 1990 (Scott D3.172–85).

The approval of a licence for the export of tactical radar to Iraq was balanced by an authorisation for the export of similar equipment to Iran but the February 1989 *Fatwa* on Salman Rushdie brought the new policy under renewed pressure and it was agreed in March that, while the new Guideline (iii) would continue to apply to Iraq, its predecessor would be reinstated when considering ELAs for Iran (D3.83–92: also 66–122). Waldegrave was later to argue that it was at this time that changes implemented on a temporary basis were rescinded and the original Guidelines reinstated, albeit with greater liberality and flexibility (D3.122: 113). While Waldegrave and other adherents of this '"interpretation" thesis' were found by Scott to have not had 'any duplicitous intention' this itself led him to comment that it 'underlines, to my mind, the duplicitous nature of the flexibility claimed for the guidelines' (D3.124).

Scott found that the reluctance of junior ministers to announce the changes resulted from the warnings of adverse reactions which embassies in the US and the Gulf feared would result from publicising any changes (D3.37–41: 110: D4.9). This fear predisposed ministers to refrain from formalising the position by putting the revision up to their respective secretaries of state and the Prime Minister. This omission was then invoked to claim that there was no need to make a public announcement of any change of policy since no such change had, or could have, occurred and provided justification for the early expressed position that no public announcement should attend the change (D3.36–44: 44: 98–104: 110–13: 125: *passim*: also D4.8–9: 42: 107–9).

This was an explanation which Scott describes as 'sophistry' (D3.125) but one which ministers used to justify statements regarding the Guidelines and policy on arms exports to Iraq. Thus in November 1988 Howe repeated his previous claims that the Guidelines '*prohibit* the export to either country of any equipment which would significantly enhance the capability of either side to prolong or exacerbate the conflict' (Italics added, cited in Norton-Taylor 1995: 41–2). Further written replies were signed by Waldegrave or Howe during 1989 and 1990 claiming that

> The Government have not changed their policy on defence sales to Iraq or Iran; British arms supplies to both Iran and Iraq continue to be governed by the strict application of guidelines which prevent the supply of lethal equipment which would significantly enhance the capability of either side to resume hostilities. (Scott D4.3: also D4.1–16: 22–4; Norton-Taylor *et al.* 1996: 66)

Similar assertions were made by Thatcher, John Major, Nicholas Ridley, Trefgarne, Clark, Lynda Chalker (FCO), Tim Sainsbury (MOD), John Redwood (DTI) and Lord Glenarthur (FCO).

Such replies to written or oral questions became a central issue of Scott's inquiry. He noted that Timothy Daunt (Deputy Under-Secretary of State at MOD) had argued (in a letter to Howe's PS) that while such statements were 'Arguably ... not misleading Parliament...[they] may be represented as culpably failing to inform Parliament of a significant change to the guidelines of October 1985' (cited Scott D3.115). Scott found of the claims that 'there had in practice been no change of substance in Government policy...that the guidelines had not been changed' (the interpretation thesis), that it 'does not seem to me to correspond with reality ... [it is] so plainly inapposite as to be incapable of being sustained by serious argument' (D3.118–19: 123). Such a representation was 'misleading', 'not accurate' or 'untrue' (D4.17–43; also Norton-Taylor *et al.* 1996: 66–8): Government had 'fail[ed] ... to be forthcoming in its public statements about its export policy to Iraq.... Parliament and the public were designedly led to believe that a stricter policy towards non-lethal defence exports and dual-use exports to Iraq was being applied than was in fact the case' [Scott D8.16: also D4.42: 62–3).

Matrix Churchill's machine tool export licences

The changing political environment and the accumulation of evidence following the November 1987 Intelligence Report regarding machine tool exports to Iraq were the context in which a series of ELAs from manufacturers were granted by DTI in the period following the January 1988 meeting of MTTA officers with Alan Clark, and despite the concerns expressed by FCO, MODWG, and the Defence Intelligence Staff (DIS).

In January 1988 an application by Matrix Churchill (ELA 0439) to export CNC lathes to Hutteen was permitted without licence despite a subsequent request for further information on end use by IDC and a recommendation by MODWG that no licence be granted (D2.332–5: D3.10: D6.55–6: 77). ELA 0440 was also submitted for a temporary export to the Baghdad trade fair and recommended for approval by IDC in March – after the goods had been sold and the ELA had been superseded by ELA 1029 (submitted in conjunction with ELA 1030 and unaccountably delayed with it until approval had been given regarding 0440); licensing proceeded 'on a wholly false basis'. So too did that for ELA 1030 which was passed by Steadman in April despite

FCO concerns as to destination and IDC not giving its approval until May. Most of these machines (which had received licences only for temporary export) were used on the missile programme at Nassr (D2.336–59: D5.66).

Further confusion and by-passing of the licensing procedures accompanied Matrix Churchill's ELA 2413 (an amalgam of the machines cited in ELAs 0440 and 1029) and ELA 52039 for temporary licences to export lathes for exhibition at the Baghdad Trade Fair in September. Steadman pre-empted any discussion of these applications (and of ELAs 62107 and 62108 filed by 600 Services Ltd and also for temporary export) by issuing immediate licences on the grounds that the items were required to be shipped urgently by the manufacturer and that 'in the policy paper to be circulated by FCO Ministers this week machine tools are one of the items for immediate relaxation under the guidelines' (D6.62–3: D2.355: D5: 66: D6.55: 57–72).

In October 1988 ELA 53234 (which was to be cited in the Matrix Churchill prosecution) was submitted for CNC lathes said to be for the 'production of metal components' at Nassr. A similar ELA – 54014 described by Lieut.-Colonel Glazebrook of MODWG as sufficient to equip a factory producing half a million 155mm shells a year (D6.106) – was lodged in November. No clarification of end-use or end-user was requested by DTI. MODWG recommended refusal of a licence and a briefing for Trefgarne argued that this was one of the Matrix Churchill applications which needed to be referred to the Prime Minister because MI6 sources indicated that the end use was munitions manufacture. Nevertheless, in December 1988 and January 1989 the Restricted Enforcement Unit (REU) advised that export be approved, citing as grounds the threatened closure of Matrix Churchill, that 'the security of our source ... [is] ... best guaranteed if reasonable exports of machine tools by Matrix Churchill were allowed to continue', and that continued exports would permit MI6 to continue to monitor the Iraqi procurement network. An export licence was granted in early 1989 (D6.73–106). (The REU was established in 1987 as a forum for exchanging intelligence on actual or suspected breaches of export controls between officials from DTI, MOD, FCO, Customs and Excise, MI5, MI6, and GCHQ. REU was usually chaired by Eric Beston, head of DTI's export control division and Steadman's superior at DTI [Scott C2.67–73]).

In January 1989 Matrix Churchill requested permission to export permanently the machines listed under ELAs 0440 and 52039 which had been granted temporary licences. The proposed destination was Nassr 'Project 1728'. These ELAs were supplemented in March by ELAs 22351 and 23006 (both cited in the Matrix Churchill prosecution) each with the original consignee stated as being Nassr and for the purpose of 'general metalworking' (D6.107–112).

By March 1989 DTI was aware that the order for the latter machines had been placed through Cardoen, a known Chilean arms dealing company, and a stream of intelligence had become available detailing the Iraqi procurement network for military material linking Matrix Churchill machine exports to military production at Hutteen and Nassr (D5.25–26: also 1–83: E9.10; Norton-Taylor *et al.* 1996: 70–1). Much of the information was provided by Gutteridge and Henderson of Matrix Churchill (e.g. Scott D5.26–61: G17.19–20; Leigh 1993: 102–8: 132–57: 162–7). By April MI6 was aware that 'Project 1728' was part of the Iraqi missile development 'Project 395'. The intelligence picture was reinforced in June by two further reports and by a paper from Glazebrook detailing Iraqi procurement which was, however, never completed by DIS nor presented to ministers (Scott D5.25: 64–79). The Working Group on Iraqi Procurement (WGIP, an adjunct to REU chaired by Beston and including Steadman and MOD and FCO officials) minutes recorded that 'the end user [of Matrix Churchill machine tool ELAs] was known to be the Iraqi missile programme' (D6.109). In July MODWG recommended refusal of export licences.

In September 1989 three further intelligence reports on Nassr and Project 1728 were issued and Matrix Churchill submitted ELAs 27098, 27099 and 18866 for temporary exportation. ELA 27099's originally specified destination of Nassr was later changed to a temporary licence without deleting the purchaser (an anomaly which was not noted by DTI). Trefgarne (who had exchanged posts with Clark in July) instructed that a licence for 27098 be issued despite FCO prevarication. In issuing 27098 Steadman also issued a licence for 18866 before details had been circulated to MOD or FCO. In evidence to Scott Steadman argued that 'I may have regarded 27098 as a test case' and that he had sought to facilitate 'the urgency of a decision from the company's point of view' and to avoid the 'cumbersome nature of the control procedures' damaging industry in general and Matrix Churchill in particular (D6.199). Six days later, after correspondence from and a phone call to Henderson, Steadman completed the non-authorised issue of an export licence for ELA 27099 despite the application being still under consideration by FCO, MOD and IDC. Scott concludes that there was collusion between Steadman and Matrix Churchill regarding the circumstances of the issue of this licence (D6.194–208: 216–20). (Similar events characterised the issue of temporary export licences to Bridgeport Machines Ltd in September 1989 and March 1990 (D6.209–17: 219: 225–45: 250).)

Matrix Churchill also submitted ELAs 27311 and 27315 in September for which 'metal turning of engineering components' was cited as the end-use (D6.115). These – with 52039, 0440, 23006 and 22351 – brought the total of Matrix Churchill's outstanding ELAs to six of which 23006 and 22351 were, with 53234 (above) to be the subject of the later prosecution). All were for high specification CNC machine tools destined for Nassr. These ELAs raised concerns in MODWG and the FCO and became the subject of dispute between Trefgarne and Clark, and Waldegrave who objected to the issue of four of the six ELAs but was rebuffed by the combined opposition of his two colleagues. At a meeting between the three ministers on 1 November 1989 Clark supported export in contradiction of the advice of MODWG and MOD briefing papers. Trefgarne's briefing papers (compiled by Steadman and uncorrected by Beston) contained a series of 'misrepresentations', while Waldegrave's opposition was diverted to conditional support by a briefing which included a series of inaccuracies. These briefing papers were each slanted in ways which downgraded the accumulating intelligence pointing to the intended military use of Matrix Churchill machine tools, and – in the face of DTI and MOD arguments that the Guidelines should be abandoned – Waldegrave agreed with Clark and Trefgarne to approve the issue of all outstanding Matrix Churchill ELAs (D6.108–11: 113–71: 193: also D8.4–15; Leigh 1993:183–94).

The decision was made despite the substantial and increasing evidence in further intelligence reports which linked Matrix Churchill ever more closely with Iraqi military programmes, and the 13 October 1989 GCHQ Intelligence Report which referred to a 'UK firm's' links with Cardoen in the construction of a munitions factory (Scott D5.25: D6.170–91: E9.10; Norton-Taylor *et al.* 1996: 70–4). In December Steadman was informed that the 'UK firm' was Matrix Churchill. Yet the company's licences for ELAs 23006 and 22351 (which were known to be related to contracts with Cardoen) remained unrevoked, and between December 1989 and June 1990 Matrix Churchill made four further licence applications (19890, 50380, 22269 and 22270) as well as applying to renew the licence on ELA 53234.

The 1990 policy review

MODWG recommended refusal of further Matrix Churchill ELAs in January 1990 but the dispute between ministers was resumed (Scott D6.221–224: 235–54) and in February DTI and MOD brought the matter before Cabinet where it was resolved to review policy on defence sales to Iraq and Iran. The process was interrupted by the March execution of journalist Farzad Bazoft in Baghdad, and by the publicity occasioned by the seizure of nuclear 'triggers' at Heathrow and the barrel sections of a 'super gun' at Teesside (D3.132–50: D6.250–4). In April, Iraq threatened to withhold payment on an estimated £1 billion of export credit guaranteed by ECGD and in June Ridley (then Secretary of State at DTI) minuted Thatcher on the need for a review of policy to take into account 'the policy and political arguments in favour of export controls, the commercial consequences for British industry and the financial risks for ECGD of continuing friction in our relations with Iraq' (D3.152–3). In July a policy review committee under Douglas Hurd (now Foreign Secretary) recommended revision of the existing Guidelines so as to implement 'limited and clearly-defined controls' which would ban only that material 'designed to kill', 'but not weapons platforms, equipment ancillary to weapons platforms, or any spares ... there should be no special constraints on the export of machine tools.' Implementation of the policy was to be deferred for 'several weeks' and its public announcement was intended to be 'by Written Answer during the Parliamentary spillover' (D3.164: also 152–65). Thatcher agreed the new policy which was, however, rendered irrelevant by Iraq's August 1990 invasion of Kuwait.

The Matrix Churchill prosecution

Customs and Excise had received a copy of the 13 October 1989 Intelligence Report and Peter Wiltshire (a Customs and Excise investigator) had attended the January 1990 REU meeting at which Matrix Churchill was named as the 'UK firm' involved in the Cardoen munitions factory contract. Nevertheless, no investigation into the company's exports was initiated until March 1990 after the seizure of machine exports by the German authorities (Leigh 1993: 2). A Customs Note recorded that investigators were 'warned off' the case (Scott G2.13) and the investigation caused panic in the DTI where Michael Coolican wrote Ridley asking if

> Ministers are willing to have the 1987 and subsequent decisions exposed and made the subject of court-room argument? .... The dirty washing liable to emerge from the action proposed by Customs and Excise will add to the problems posed by the [recently abandoned]

[super] gun [prosecution]. For DTI the timing is extraordinarily embarrassing given recent correspondence between ourselves, MOD and FCO. (G2.15–16)

Ministers and officials sought to bring the Customs investigation under political control (Norton-Taylor *et al.* 1996: 106; Scott G2.17–20: G3.7: 11–15: G5.94). Yet there were political advantages in the prosecution going ahead: In the face of increasing parliamentary criticism and media comment the matter could be hidden under the cloak of the *sub judice* rule and the obligation to answer inquiries avoided (Leigh 1993: 302; Scott A1.13; Phythian and Little 1993: 302). Moreover, officials had a range of tactics which could be implemented and the confidence that legal and public scrutiny could be avoided should the case come to trial.

Thus after Robin Butler (Cabinet Secretary) and Peter Gregson (Permanent Secretary at DTI) were made aware that officials 'had knowledge of intelligence in advance...that machine tools already licensed for export by Matrix Churchill were for the purpose of manufacturing munitions', Gregson expressed the intent of asking DTI lawyers 'whether it was in order for his officials...to make the factual statements which Customs has requested without volunteering the further information which they had about the intelligence information at the time' (Norton-Taylor *et al.* 1996: 108; also Scott G9.8).

The cover-up of government involvement in the export of defence related goods to Iraq was laid here (if not earlier) and in the subsequent period customs investigators and prosecution counsel were left in ignorance of a range of information available to authoritative actors. Central questions were those of the intended use of the Matrix Churchill machines and knowledge within government of their capability and purpose. DTI contended that Matrix Churchill lathes were 'dual-use', yet the Customs case was based on the contention that these same machines were 'specially designed'; that the 'package' of standard machine tools, software and accessories was designed for the production of military components and that Matrix Churchill had sought to deceive DTI (Scott D2.98–103: D6.267: G3.17–24: G5.13–73: G6.2–7: G17.2–8: G18.13–35: H1.7–15: K2.15; Norton-Taylor *et al.* 1996: 107–8; Norton-Taylor 1995:146–7). The defence, however, argued that government knew the purpose for which the machinery was intended, that this information had largely been supplied by Henderson and Gutteridge, and that manufacturers had been encouraged to export. Such a defence was dependent on the production of documents detailing the state of government knowledge, but the suppression of documents and evidence by the use of PIIC's acted to deny the defence the possibility of establishing the details of the government's knowledge.

The suppression of government information and the use of Public Interest Immunity Certificates

The suppression of evidence included false witness statements signed by officials on the advice or insistence of government lawyers and/or superiors. On the advise of Wiltshire that knowledge of the 30 November 1987 Intelligence Report could not be regarded as 'evidence', Steadman signed a statement prepared by Customs investigators which claimed that 'There was ... no evidence as far as I am aware to support these suspicions (that Matrix Churchill machine tools might be used for military production)'. Steadman's subsequent amendment of the statement to read 'hard evidence' was ignored by Customs officials who prepared a new draft excluding the entire sentence on the suggestion of Andrew Leithead (a lawyer in the Treasury Solicitor's Department). This final draft also included amendments suggested by Gerald Hosker (DTI Legal Department, later Treasury Solicitor). Leithead defended the amendments in part by arguing that Steadman's own version 'did not seem a sensible thing for the witness to say' (Scott G5.20: G6.24–38: 52–6; Norton-Taylor *et al.* 1996: 113–16; Norton-Taylor 1995: 149–52).

Beston also signed a statement which 'did not accord with and served to conceal the true position (Scott G6.4) and a supplementary statement seems to have been altered as a result of inter-departmental discussion. He gave evidence at the trial that he 'was not aware that there was conclusive evidence' that Matrix Churchill machines were to be used for military manufacture. Yet he had seen the 30 November 1987 Intelligence Report and had minuted Hosker that 'In the light of our knowledge in 1987/8 (and the decision to allow contracts to proceed for source protection among other things) I could not claim that HMG knew nothing ... I am not sure how this question could be answered honestly without causing some embarrassment at the very least' (G6.1; also G6.2–5: 47–52: 56; Leigh 1993: 168–81; Norton-Taylor *et al.* 1996: 111: 138; Norton-Taylor 1995: 152–3).

Documentary evidence was also concealed. Scott lists 22 documents which were either not brought to the attention of prosecution counsel or the significance of which seems not to have been recognised by them (Scott G9.2–4). During the trial itself defence Counsel demanded the disclosure of a further 27 documents (including Cabinet Office papers) which officials, investigators and the prosecution had failed to identify. The resultant search for this material revealed a further 16 documents for possible disclosure in Cabinet Office files alone. The claim by Alan Moses (Prosecution Counsel) that this material was 'not relevant' was dismissed by Scott in the case of five items which he described as 'relevant', 'of obvious relevance' or 'plainly relevant'. While Scott regarded the failure to disclose this material as part of a continuing attempt to mislead the judge and the defence (G15.1–21: 25–6: 29–30) he reported that he found no evidence suggesting a deliberate decision to withhold documents (G9.12–14). This conclusion seems problematic when viewed in the light of the third means by which officials sought to manage the disclosure of information – the use of PIICs.

In October 1991 treasury officials proposed sixteen DTI documents covering the formulation of government policy and departmental correspondence as a first tranche of material for suppression by PIICs at the forthcoming committal proceedings in the Matrix Churchill case. Peter Lilley (then Secretary of State at DTI) signed a certificate on the basis of advice that 'All the material falls within an established class for which public interest immunity has to be (not merely can be) claimed' (G11.1–3: 14: G13.1–4). At the request of MI6 the final Certificate did not append a list of the documents which it sought to suppress. Scott argues of these documents that they had an obvious importance to the defence case of the Government's knowledge and encouragement (G11.4) – especially those concerned with Clark's January 1988 meeting with MTTA. MI5 prepared PIICs for Kenneth Baker (Home Secretary) which were intended to preclude the possibility of the defence eliciting information related to security and intelligence issues through the questioning of witnesses. It precluded evidence on 'all sources of intelligence information' and talked of 'lives at risk' and 'matters [which] would be of value to a hostile power' (G11.5–13: G13.5–6). Paul Henderson was one such 'source' and the PIIC would prevent him from giving evidence as to his relationship with MI5 and the information which he had supplied to its agents.

PIICs were signed for the trial proper by Kenneth Clarke (Home Secretary), Michael Heseltine (President of the Board of Trade (DTI)), Malcolm Rifkind (Secretary of State for Defence) and Garel-Jones (junior FCO minister). Signature was demanded of ministers on the basis of inadequate and sometimes inaccurate briefings. Clarke's Certificate replicated that of Baker (above) save that cover was extended to documentary evidence and *released* the evidence of MI6 agent 'Mr.T'.

Heseltine was required to certify the 16 documents for which Lilley had previously signed together with a further five. He was instructed by officials that 'there is no discretion to waive PII: if documents fall into a category where it applies it must be claimed' (G13.52). He nevertheless refused to sign the certificate since, insofar as he had been given the time to examine the papers, it appeared that 'Departments had been well aware of the intended military use of the goods…. It would look as though he had been engaged in an attempted cover-up' (cited in Scott G13.58: also 59): 'no rational person who has looked at the files could have said that the documents should not have been disclosed' (G18.100: also G13.53–72). Heseltine was subsequently induced to sign this and a second PIIC after the intervention of Nicholas Lyell (Attorney General) (G13.7–62: 81–9) who is deeply criticised by Scott for his misrepresentations that ministers lacked discretion in signing PIICs in a criminal matter (G13: 125: 109–25). Leithead argued in defence of the suppression of information by PIIC that, 'if one was too generous with one's disclosure of documents…the whole system would get into disrepute', and that PII should be claimed for all documents which came under the categories of policy making or executive decision; 'when one is dealing with PII claims, one tends to take a rather sort of generous view…generous to the Government departments' (G13.93–4: also 63–75: 94–102: G16.1–8).

Scott lists 62 individual documents – some of which had been requested by the defence – which the PIICs were intended to jointly protect. Moreover, the bundles of PII documents, when handed to the judge, contained more than 15 MOD and FCO documents for which ministers had made no certification – they had simply been added by officials as an afterthought and on their own discretion (G11.2: G12.4: G13.39: 73: G14.9–10). Of a great swathe of these documents (the 'Category B' documents) Scott argues that their 'value…to the defendants…on the issue of Government knowledge and the Government's attitude to the export to Iraq of machine tools intended for the manufacture of munitions, seems to me to be so obvious as to be hardly worth stating…there was "nothing in reality to set against the balance in favour of" disclosure' (G14.5–6: also 11). It was only as a result of the judge ordering the disclosure' of the 'category B' documents that the defence was enabled to effectively cross-examine witnesses and establish Government knowledge of the purpose and destination of the machines in question and the case collapsed following the evidence given by Alan Clark.

Associated prosecutions and further evidence of a cover-up

The Matrix Churchill trial and the personal risk which prosecution had implied for the defendants was not an isolated case. The prosecution of BSA Tools executives for the export of lathes to Nassr under a licence issued in November 1987 and revalidated in January 1989, was withdrawn after the collapse of the Matrix Churchill trial (H1). Charges were also laid against Wickman Bennett executives in May 1991 for the export of machine tools to Nassr on licences issued in October 1987. As in the Matrix Churchill prosecution Customs employed the notion of 'special design' and the prosecution obtained PIICs to protect evidence of government knowledge and encouragement – that DTI had reconsidered the ELAs in the light of the 30 November 1987 Intelligence Report regarding the intended use of the machines, and decided that export should be permitted to continue (H1.21–2: H2.3: 34: 39–43: H3.1) The case was settled prior to trial with a privately agreed fine and the promise that the company would make no public statement. Similar arrangements aborted trails in the cases of charges brought against 600 Services Ltd (H3: J2) and Microwave Modules (J3). Euromac was prosecuted for attempting to export 'nuclear triggers' seized at Heathrow in March 1990 after US Customs mounted an operation involving *agent provocateurs*. Two of the three defendants were convicted and sentenced to imprisonment in 1991, but acquitted on appeal (Scott J4; Norton-Taylor *et al.* 1996: 147–8).

In the 'Dunk case' three defendants were charged with the export to Iraq of 200 machine guns on a false end-user certificate signed by a senior Jordanian army officer, convicted, and fined a total of £28000. Scott uncovered evidence which resulted in the overturning of the conviction on appeal on the grounds of an abuse of process (Scott J5; *Guardian*, 27 February 1997, Norton-Taylor *et al.* 1996: 147–50).

Paul Grecian (Managing Director) and four others associated with Ordnance Technologies (Ordtec) were prosecuted for the export of a fuse assembly line, fuse components and sub-assemblies between January 1988 and October 1990 said in the ELA to be destined for Jordan but delivered for transfer to Iraq. The defendants pleaded guilty in February 1992 after the use of PIICs to suppress documentary evidence which proved extensive government knowledge and precluding Grecian from giving evidence of the information which he had supplied to MI5. This material was discovered by Scott and the convictions were quashed on appeal because the prosecution's misleading of the judge 'amounted to a material irregularity' which had resulted in a conviction which was not 'safe and satisfactory' (Scott E10: J6; Norton-Taylor *et al.* 1996: 150–8).

Charges against Christopher Cowley (Space Research Corporation) and Peter Mitchell (Walter Somers) followed the impounding by Customs of parts of a 'supergun' barrel at Teesside docks in April 1990. Cowley and Mitchell were charged with exporting tubes which were to form the barrel(s) of an artillery piece with a range of up to 600 km. In November 1990 Customs abandoned prosecution after Counsel advised that the DTI and MOD had been involved in the affair from an early stage, had failed to investigate the companies warnings or assess the detailed drawings provided, and had advised that licences were not required (Scott J1: F1–F4; also Norton-Taylor *et al.* 1996: 91–103; Leigh 1993: 159–64; Cowley 1992). The affair was investigated by the Trade and Industry Committee (1992) which was denied evidence by DTI (Scott F1.2: F4.54–66) and Scott reported that he had also 'left some unanswered questions' (F1.4).

The aftermath of the trial and the continuing Government cover-up

After the collapse of the Matrix Churchill trial in November 1992 the question of the 1984 guidelines and their amendment in 1988 was recognised as a vital issue within government. In the Cabinet Office Nicolas Beven wrote, after an exploration of FCO files, that while ministers had wished to alter policy 'they decided [owing to the difficulties of a (public) announcement] to secure the same objective by a more flexible interpretation of existing policy' (D3.118–119). This 'interpretation thesis' (to which we have referred above and which Scott described as sophistry) permitted Robin Butler to argue that John Goulden (a senior FCO official) had 'misdirected himself' in January 1992 when he gave evidence to the Trade and Industry Committee that 'The guidelines announced by…Howe in 1985… applied until December 1988 when the third guideline was amended… It was updated to take account of the fact that there was a ceasefire' (Scott D3.116; also Norton-Taylor *et al.* 1996: 61–2; Norton-Taylor 1995: 2: 32–4). Beven's was one of a series of internal documents generated in the 'frenetic atmosphere' in the heart of government following the collapse of the trial (Norton-Taylor 1995: 29–31). Stephen Wall (PS in Major's office) recorded that 'It emerges…that the Howe guidelines of 1985 were amended by ministers in December 1988, but the amendment was never announced to Parliament' (Scott D4.51).

The substance of this account was reinforced by Timothy Daunt (MOD) who minuted that junior ministers 'took a conscious decision...not to make an announcement' about the 'agree[ment] to change the policy' (D3.115): papers disclosed at the trial seem to substantiate to some extent [the accusation that ministers] connived in bending the guidelines' (cited in Norton-Taylor 1995: 33).

Michael Heseltine warned of the dangers of maintaining the official line that what had occurred in 1988 was a flexible interpretation of policy not a policy change: 'To a sceptical audience that may seem a distinction without a difference' which would appear 'extremely disingenuous' and which 'underlines the unstable nature of the ground beneath ministers feet' (cited in ibid: 35). His advice was ignored and Beven's became the official position as presented by Butler to John Major in an official chronology of events which recorded that DTI, MOD and FCO ministers 'agree[d] unpublished relaxation of the Iran–Iraq guidelines' in December 1988 (cited in ibid: 29). In Parliament, Major, in reply to a question from John Smith (Leader of the Opposition) the day after the trial collapsed, declared that 'from 1985 until the Iraqi invasion of Kuwait the Government operated under guidelines first set out by the then Foreign Secretary' (cited in ibid: 31).

Thus the policy of disinformation and deceit continued. Establishing Scott's inquiry served not only to defuse the immediate political crisis generated by the evidence in the Matrix–Churchill trial and its collapse but, as with the trial itself, to bury the affair beneath the claim of *sub judice* and thus protect ministers by giving the excuse to refuse questions in the House, as well as avoid the possibility that the case would become an issue during the 1992 general election.

Moreover, in contradiction of Major's assurance that 'All papers that the inquiry calls will be made available [and] Lord Justice Scott will be entirely free to decide on the publication of his report and of the evidence he takes' (HC Debs., 16 November 1992, cited in Barker 1997: 10), civil servants and politicians sought to restrict the scope of Scott's investigation and his independent powers to call for evidence and interview witnesses. Scott's access to documents was obstructed and he faced a covert campaign to discredit him and the Report prior to its publication (Scott B1.2–15: Norton-Taylor 1995: 37–9: chapter 9; Norton-Taylor *et al.* 1996: 28: 31–35; Barker 1997). Scott talks of documents being 'discovered by chance', of 'The impact of a steady drip-feed of documents submitted in a piecemeal fashion [which] cannot be underestimated', and hints at attempts to intimidate Muttukumara, the inquiry's secretary (Scott B1.11–12; Norton-Taylor *et al.* 1996: 28).

The form of the Report and the timing of its publication were also not entirely under Scott's control (Barker 1997: 21–23; 1997(2): 46–7; Norton-Taylor *et al*. 1996: 28–30). Six ministers, two permanent secretaries and sixteen other officials received copies eight days before publication, while the opposition parties were offered a mere three hour preview in rigorously controlled isolation. The eight days permitted ministers and officials to select from the Report in preparing a disinformation campaign (Negrine 1997: 36; Norton-Taylor *et al*. 1996: 30) and a press pack prepared by DTI, Customs and Excise, the Office of Public Service, the Attorney General's Office and the Treasury (HMG 1996, see Norton-Taylor *et al*. 1996: 176–8; Thompson 1997: 3).

In the parliamentary debate which followed immediately on the distribution of the Report to MPs and the press, Ian Lang (then Secretary of State at DTI) proclaimed that it 'completely exonerates all ministers and civil servants from any sort of conspiracy or cover-up'. Waldegrave and Lyell were announced to have been pronounced innocent – the first of misleading Parliament, the second of misleading ministers as to their duty with regard to PII certificates – by the selective use of quotations which gave the words cited the opposite meaning from that bestowed by their original context (Norton-Taylor *et al*. 1996: 170–4; Guardian 15 February 1997; Negrine 1997: 36–7). Lang ignored Scott's central conclusions that

> The answers to Parliamentary Questions, in both Houses of Parliament, failed to inform Parliament of the current state of Government policy on non-lethal arms sales to Iraq. This failure was deliberate and was the inevitable result of the agreement between the three junior Ministers that no publicity would be given to the decision to adapt a more liberal, or relaxed policy, or interpretation of the Guidelines. (Scott D4.42)

Lang so distorted the findings of the Report as to use it as the basis for his own demand that Robin Cook resign from the *shadow* cabinet for his claims that the Government had connived in the supply of arms to Iraq in contradiction of its own Guidelines, misled Parliament as to the true position over a number of years, and had willingly permitted the possibility that innocent defendants would be imprisoned for want of access to documents which the Government had denied to their defence counsel. News management and the political control of a majority in Parliament effected by coercion of, and side deals with, individual Tory MPs and Northern Ireland Unionists ensured that the

Government won the division on an adjournment debate in the Commons on the strength of a single vote on 26 February 1996 (Norton-Taylor *et al.* 1996: 178–81: 183–6). Scott's Report subsequently fell into what commentators have described as a 'black hole of silence' (Norton-Taylor *et al.* 1996: chapter 15; *Guardian*, 14 August 1996, *Independent*, 15 February 1997).

Conclusion

Scott's Report provided a detailed examination of British policy making and the administration of government. Scott explored a range of issues which extended from failures of the state administration involving inaccurate briefings, the lack of coordination between departments, and the failure of intelligence to be available at the point of need, to the integrity of ministers and their preparedness to deceive Parliament, through constitutional issues regarding the obstruction of Parliament, ministerial responsibility and accountability, the use of Public Interest Immunity Certificates, and freedom of information, to the moral issues of permitting the supply of military equipment and arms to reprehensible regimes.

One of the principal themes which runs through Scott's account of events is the repeated ignoring by ministers and officials of intelligence evidence as to the purpose and destination of machine tools exported to Iraq. A second is the overriding concern of ministers to seize what was assumed to be the economic opportunity of increasing exports which Iraq's seemingly insatiable need to import offered UK industry. Combined with this is a general lack of concern as to what those goods were, or for what purpose they might be used. Finally is the scale and extent of ministerial deceit in seeking to hide involvement in supporting the export of arms producing machines from public scrutiny and parliamentary accountability. These issues are interlinked. The central concern of ministers was to promote exports and, to this end, ministers and civil servants may be fairly described as having conspired with machine exporters to ensure that their products surmounted the various licensing obstacles which had been established to enforce the publicly announced Guidelines and regulate the flow of defence related goods to Iraq.

To do other than ignore intelligence reports would have impeded the export imperative as it concerned the large market for dual-use, high technology machine tools (as well as other defence related goods) which ministers had accepted as acceptable exports under their own, private interpretation of the policy on promoting exports to Iraq. Similarly, public or parliamentary scrutiny would have risked impeding exports to Iraq by generating opposition sufficiently strong as to impose an external constraint on the policy as implemented by ministers. It was to avoid this possibility that the 1984 guidelines were formulated (and their announcement delayed) and later secretly altered without announcement. Ministerial deceit was a necessary adjunct. The deceit of ministers in concealing the practical meaning of the Guidelines as interpreted by themselves, and the implications of the export policy in relation to Iraq followed from the Government's drive to export all forms of goods, especially high technology defence related goods with a high value-added content and large foreign markets. Without the deceit, the policy as applied to Iraq was almost certainly untenable and would necessarily have had to be restricted to an approach more closely in line with the wording of the Guidelines.

With the Iraqi invasion of Kuwait the implications of the arms and machine exports was that British troops would suffer attack by what were in effect British-made munitions (and weapons platforms and ancillary defence equipment) in the hands of a leader who was portrayed by the ministers who had armed him as a latter-day 'Hitler'. It was at this point that an embargo on defence equipment was applied and enforced. Customs and Excise – as the responsible government agency acting with independent power – had initiated an investigation of Matrix Churchill some six months earlier and charged its executives (and those of other companies) with having previously exported defence related goods to Iraq. Prosecution and public trial threatened the Government with exposure of its previous approach to Iraqi defence exports, and ministers and officials engaged in a cover-up to maintain the secrecy of policy as implemented under the different versions of the Guidelines by seeking to ensure that evidence and documents were not available for public scrutiny via release to defence counsel for use in court. Ministerial endorsement of PIICs could in this case – as it had in earlier prosecution for similar offences – ensure the continued secrecy of policy implementation under the guidelines, and the deceit employed to protect it, at the cost of convicting the businessmen with who ministers had cooperated in the export of defence related material and who had cooperated with MI5 in supplying intelligence at personal risk.

That the endeavour failed was due to the perseverance of defence lawyers rather than the result of any institutional protection of which the defendants could avail themselves. It was the level and extent of the deceit in which ministers and officials engaged and its ramifications for the Matrix Churchill defendants, which moved Scott to the clear reply to the question of whether something constitutionally improper had happened asked him by the Public Service Select Committee, that, 'Yes, I think it did and I said so' (Norton-Taylor *et al.* 1996: 198–9).

9

The Pergau Dam Affair: Civil Aid and Arms Exports

Dave Bartlett

> The Government do not link arms sales and aid. Nor do we use the aid programme to finance arms sales.
>
> (FCO Minister, Lennox-Boyd, House of Commons Debate, 4 March 1994)

> Progress on the defence exports package negotiated in 1988 was certainly a factor in the final deliberations, in early 1991, on whether or not to commit funds to the Pergau project.
>
> (FAC 1994: para 87)

During the 1980s ministers were active in promoting the British arms industry world-wide. We saw in the study of arms to Iraq (chapter 8) that the Export Credit Guarantee Department (ECGD) was one agency used during the 1980s by the British Government to lubricate arms sales to Iraq in contradiction of the Government's own guidelines (Scott 1996 D2: D3). Asia and the Far East were increasingly important markets for British defence sales and exports of military material rose from £73 million in 1985 to £306 million in 1989. Total UK sales to the region amounted to almost £1.5 billion between 1987 and 1993 (FAC 1994(2): 118). Malaysia alone bought some £50 million worth of arms from the UK between 1988 and 1992 (ibid: 115–18).

It is therefore not surprising that Defence Secretary George Younger visited Kuala Lumpur in March 1988 and signed a protocol on arms sales with the Malaysian Government. It was to emerge, however, that the protocol had linked a proposed Malaysian order for Tornado fighter aircraft to the provision of civil aid. This linkage came to involve the Foreign and Commonwealth Office's (FCO) Overseas Development Administration (ODA) in funding the Pergau Hydro-electric Dam under the Aid and Trade Provision (ATP). The project involved the largest single cash sum ever provided for a single ATP-supported scheme and was ruled illegal by the High Court in 1994.

Civil aid for development

ATP is jointly managed by the ODA and the Department of Trade and Industry (DTI) as one way of assisting British companies to gain commercial contracts in aid recipient countries while observing the ODA's normal social, economic and environmental criteria that projects must represent sound investments, promote economic and social development, and provide value for money (FAC 1994(2): 170). Aid should, 'promote sustainable economic and social development and good government in order to reduce poverty, suffering and deprivation and to improve the quality of life for poor people' (FCO 1993, cited in ibid: 112). This policy followed from the terms of the Overseas Development and Cooperation Acts 1980 and 1990. Section 1(1) of the 1990 Act empowers the Secretary of State 'to furnish any person or body with assistance, whether financial, technical or of any other nature [for the purpose of] promoting the development or maintaining the economy of a country or territories outside the United Kingdom, or the welfare of its people' (cited in FAC 1994(2): Appendix 11: 279).

Douglas Hurd, when Foreign Secretary, described to the Foreign Affairs Committee (FAC) how it has always been British policy that development aid should not be provided for arms purchases, nor that there should be any 'conditional linkage' between the provision of such aid and arms sales (FAC 1994(2): 34–5). Any possibility of a link between the sale of arms and the provision of aid was always denied by ministers. In July 1989 Tim Sainsbury (then Defence Minister) argued that 'It would not be acceptable to Her Majesty's Government to link overseas aid to the [Malaysian] arms package' (cited in *Guardian*, 19 February 1994), and in March 1994 Lennox-Boyd (junior FCO Minister) claimed that 'the Government do not link arms sales and aid. Nor do we use the aid programme to finance arms sales' (cited in WDM 1995: 1). Similar statements have been made by Lynda Chalker (Minister for ODA) (e.g. HC Debs., 20 December 1991, col 331W; also *Guardian* 19 February 1994; *Independent*, 4 February 1994) and Douglas Hurd (FAC 1994(2): evidence, para 9: 16–7, pp 34–5; HC Debs., 18 February 1994, col 124W).

The March protocol and the arms–aid linkage

On 23 March 1988 Younger made a two day visit to Malaysia to pro-mote arms sales during which he signed a Defence Export Protocol (a Memorandum of Understanding, MOU) with the Malaysian Govern-ment in which he pledged that the UK Government

> undertook to bring to bear the resources of its Ministry of Defence in order to grant certain facilities, including: – aid in support of non-military aspects under the programme, with the details to be agreed by both Governments. HMG took note of the Malaysian Government's desire that this grant should amount to no less than a specific value of the equipment, and agreed to discuss this in the context of the MOU. (cited in FAC 1994: para 25)

Younger permitted the Malaysians to understand that they would receive civil grant aid as a percentage of the value of arms sales: 20 per-cent – £200 million – of the value of arms sales then envisaged as amounting to £1 billion. (A summary of the March protocol is repro-duced in FAC 1994(2): Annex A, 15: also Appendix 10: 278.)

The background to Younger's signing of the protocol remains the subject of contradictory accounts. Arms sales had been under discussion since the beginning of the year and the possibility of arms–aid linkage had been raised in a meeting in London between Younger and the Malaysian Finance Minister earlier in March 1988 (FAC 1994: para 19; FAC 1994(2): 192). Spreckley (High Commissioner in Kuala Lumpur) admitted that he 'knew there was a deal brewing on the arms side' (FAC 1994: para 20: 22: 390–430; FAC 1994(2): 101), yet Hurd (who suc-ceeded Geoffrey Howe as Foreign Secretary) was later to claim that the FCO was unaware of any discussions linking civil aid to arms purchases until mid-April (FAC 1994(2): 278). Howe (the then Foreign Secretary) visited Malaysia a fortnight after Younger's March visit but claimed to have not discussed the details of the agreement at that time (FAC 1994(2): 193–4).

Hurd also claimed that FCO officials were not involved in briefing Younger prior to his departure. Younger himself argued the contrary and *seems* to be supported in this by Howe (ibid: 36–7: 87–8: 192–4). Both are clear, however, that Younger understood prior to his March visit that there could be no linkage between arms sales and aid (ibid: 88; *Independent*, 17 January 1994). Nevertheless, Younger permit-ted the insertion of the linkage clause drafted by the Malaysians

(FAC 1994 (2): 88–9: 106) without consulting colleagues in London on the wording of the protocol which he signed without authority (ibid: 36–7: 38: 88–93: 104–7). What was to become clear was that 'This was a Ministry of Defence-driven initiative, negotiation and agreement' (Hurd): the Ministry of Defence (MOD) 'was taking the lead', 'they had responsibility' (Spreckley), and that 'the Foreign Office and Foreign Secretary were not consulted before the protocol was signed' (Howe) (ibid: 37: 103: 4: 105: 194).

While Younger admitted to recognising that linkage was implicit in the protocol, he and Spreckley each denied that the protocol was a contract which bound either of the parties in any way (FAC 1994: para 24–9: 30–2; FAC 1994(2): 89–92: 94–5: 98: 105). This was not an interpretation which FCO or ODA shared. Hurd later admitting to have recognised the protocol as an 'entanglement' of two distinct policies (aid and arms sales) and as presaging a potentially huge demand on the aid budget: 'There was a temporary and incorrect entanglement – incorrect in the sense that it ran against British policy' (FAC 1994(2): 33: also 39–42; Howe evidence, FAC 1994(2): 196–201; *Independent* 3 March 1994, *Times,* 3 March 1994). These fears were accentuated in May when the Malaysian Government indicated its desire for £300 million in civil aid on the basis of a revised estimate for arms sales of £1.5 billion. Ministerial discussions resulted in agreement that the policies must be disentangled by means of two 'separate but parallel letters'. Thus on 28 June 1988 Younger wrote the Malaysian Finance Minister informing him that the 'linking of aid to projects was governed by international rules which would preclude the sort of arrangement which the Malaysian Minister for Finance had seemed to envisage' in March (FAC 1994: para 34; FAC 1994(2): 14–5). Meanwhile the British High Commissioner wrote offering up to £200 million of ATP assistance (a similar figure to that agreed in the March protocol) for future development projects yet to be identified and agreed – an offer which was of itself unusual (FAC 1994: para 36; FAC 1994(2): 15). The two letters were delivered simultaneously and it is inconceivable that they were not co-ordinated in a move described as meeting the requirement that if the Malaysian addition to the March protocol (i.e. the contentious linkage clause) 'was going to be withdrawn something had to be put in its stead and something that would bear comparison' (FAC 1994(2): 108). Moreover, not only did the Malaysians receive prior notice of the letters, but 28 June was also the day on which Younger met his Malaysian counterpart at the British Army Equipment Exhibition, and the Minister for Trade announced in the Commons that ECGD would make an additional arrangement to cover the £1 billion of expected arms purchases (FAC 1994(2): 108–9: 239).

Hurd claimed in evidence to the FAC that 'the two subjects having been delinked.... The two policies were thenceforth pursued in parallel, but neither was conditional on the other' (cited in ibid: 3: also 39–42: 201–6). Yet, on the day following the delivery of the 28 June letters, Prime Minister Thatcher wrote to Mahathir Mohamad, Malaysian Prime Minister, requesting that she visit Malaysia. And, in August (two days after that visit), wrote again confirming – in a single paragraph – both the details of the arms package and that £70 million in grant aid and £130 million in ECGD support would be available for civil projects (FAC 1994: para 30: 33–8). The FAC concluded that the 'aim and effect of the three letters [in June and August] was to assure the Malaysian Government that the arms deal and an aid package would nevertheless both proceed in parallel' (FAC 1994: para 41; also FAC 1994(2): 39–42: 43). Moreover, in September Thatcher and Mahathir signed an MOU which covered arms sales involving GEC and British Aerospace products (Tornado fighters, submarines, artillery and missiles) totalling £1 billion after the two Prime Ministers had excluded officials and negotiated the final details in private (*Financial Times*, 4 February 1994). (The September MOU is never given more than incidental mention in FAC 1994, CPA 1994 or NAO 1993. A summary of the MOU is reproduced in FAC 1994(2): Annex A: 116–17.)

Younger admitted that the British commitment made in this MOU to arrange concessionary finance for any funding shortfall that the Malaysians encountered, was 'all a bit abnormal' (FAC 1994(2): 99–100). He was also reported as claiming – in reference to the March Protocol – that 'A verbal undertaking was given by somebody – not myself – to link aid to the defence project' (*Economist*, 5 February 1994, cited in FAC 1994(2): 118; also *Independent*, 17 January 1994). The assumption has always been that the 'somebody' was Prime Minister Thatcher. Yet Younger denied Thatcher's involvement in the affair (FAC 1994(2): 88: 96: 97) while also admitting that she 'took a very keen interest in our relationship with Malaysia' and that she had 'leant' on Lord King (chair of British Airways) in 1985 to ensure that BA would relinquish landing rights at Heathrow in favour of the Malaysian national airline following an agreement with Mahathir (*Guardian*, 19 February 1994; *Economist*, 12 February 1994: 26; also FAC 1994(2): 53; *Independent*, 17 January 1994). Thus Thatcher's refusal to appear before the FAC to give evidence (FAC 1994(2): 332) has left a series of questions unanswered.

The original March protocol was thus superseded without its ever having being really withdrawn; it was the 'father' of the June letters and the subsequent September MOU (FAC 1994(2): 108). We have noted Hurd's claim that the 'potential link' had been removed. It was this glib claim which underpinned the Government's defence of its funding of the Pergau project on the grounds that although a 'moral commitment of some kind' remained, 'there was no linkage, that had disappeared' (Howe, FAC 1994: para 39–40). If these formulations seem unconvincing, scepticism was only increased when Hurd admitted that 'it is unrealistic to think that a British Government...would not be ready to pursue in parallel defence sales on the one hand, and civil contracts for British companies, sometimes with ATP support, on the other (ibid: 3).' Moreover, the Malaysian Foreign Minister has claimed continuing linkage (FAC 1994(2): 130; *Guardian*, 9 February 1994) while one British businessman is recording as having argued that 'You and I know that there is a connection between winning arms sales in Malaysia and offers of aid...the question is whether anyone was stupid enough to leave explicit evidence (cited in *Financial Times*, 5 February 1994).

The funding of the Pergau dam

If the doubts regarding linkage remain, questions also arise regarding the project for which the civil aid was destined. Pergau had been examined as the possible site for a hydroelectric station by the World Bank in 1987 when it was concluded that Malaysia should concentrate on generating electricity from gas-fired power stations until the turn of the century (FAC 1994: para 64–5; NAO 1993: para 8–10). It was only after the signing of the September 1988 MOU that the Pergau dam project became an issue in London. In October a consortium of Balfour Beatty and Cementation Ltd informed DTI of their intention to apply for ATP funds for the project. The consortium followed this approach in November with a formal application citing a preliminary price of £315 million, and ODA (at the request of DTI) agreed to inform the Malaysian Ministry of Energy that the project was a possible candidate for ATP funding. In January the consortium prepared a 'firm contract proposal' with a revised costing of £316 million. Despite ODA concern in December 1988 that the project was uneconomic and of the need for a full economic appraisal, the consortium, DTI and the British High Commission in Kuala Lumpur were resistant and argued that such an investigation would 'disturb the commercial negotiations' (CPA 1994: 6; FAC 1994: para 66–7). Not until 12 March 1989 was a two-person appraisal team sent to Malaysia to conduct a two-day study – a delay which ODA regretted and a study period which it considered was 'wholly unsatisfactory'. The initial conclusions were phoned to London by the High Commission on the 14th (some 24 hours after the team arrived in the country) (CPA 1994: 16–7: 19; FAC 1994: para 60–71). It was on this basis that Thatcher made an oral offer (on the 15th) to Mahathir then visiting London. Thatcher's offer was for £68.25 million ATP assistance conditional on a full economic appraisal.

The appraisal when delivered on 29 March concluded that the economic viability of the project at the consortium's price was marginal (NAO 1993: para 15; CPA 1994: para 11). This conclusion was however made obsolete by the consortium's 25 percent price increase to £397 million – a price hike made despite the consortium having lobbied the Prime Minister's Office for the March offer to be made on the estimated price of £300–£320 million (NAO 1993: para 15; CPA 1994: 16–7: 23: 24; FAC 1994: para 73–4: 84). ODA's doubts as to the economic viability of the project at the new price – 'this project would be thoroughly uneconomic' – were drawn to the attention of ministers in the expectation that, with such unfavourable terms and assessments, the Malaysians would negotiate the price down or cancel the project (CPA 1994: 7–8: 18–9; FAC 1994: para 75: 77–8).

Ministers viewed withdrawal from the commitments as politically impossible and in April 1989 the British Government made a formal offer of ATP assistance on the Pergau project of £68.25 million on the original £316 million price together with an expressed willingness to consider additional finance (FAC 1994: para 77–8: 81). In May ODA completed a price investigation which recommended a £29 million reduction from the original £316 million price estimate and, after a further economic appraisal, concluded in February 1990 that the project would be '"a very bad buy" and a burden on Malaysian consumers' (NAO 1993: para 20; CPA 1994: para 16–7: 19). Yet the original offer was renewed in October 1989 and again in April 1990: 'The fundamental point is that we [ODA] felt a ministerial decision had been taken to give an indication of support' which ODA could not retract (CPA 1994: 8). Not until the offer lapsed again in October 1990 did ODA decide against extension until the completion of a review of the Malaysian power sector. This decision followed the reorganisation of the Malaysian electricity authority and the announcement that the generating company – Tenaga National Berhad (TNB) – was to be privatised. The new study concluded that the project would not be economic before 2005 and that if proceeded with sooner would, over its 35 year life, cost Malaysian electricity consumers £100 million more than the alternative gas generation (NAO 1993: para 22: 31).

Nevertheless, in December 1990 and following the Malaysian's November decision to buy Hawks instead of the original Tornados, Mahathir confirmed during a London visit that the Pergau dam project was to go ahead. Further consultations followed with the Malaysian Government in January 1991 when a second price investigation – this time of the £417 million costing – recommended that the new, higher price was reasonable and acceptable after minor adjustments which reduced the total by £4 million (ibid: para 28). The price investigation was followed by a further economic review which concluded that at a price of £417 million (with a UK element of £308 million and thus an ATP component of £108 million) the project remained uneconomic (ibid: para 38).

The hardening of the ODA position against the Pergau project resulted in two memoranda of dissent from Tim Lankester (Permanent Secretary at ODA) which outlined the economic case against proceeding with the project and informing Lynda Chalker (the Minister) that the project was an 'abuse of the aid programme' which should 'not be implemented for the foreseeable future.... This was not a marginal project such that the economics could be readily set aside in favour of commercial or political considerations.... With such a large amount [of money] at stake it was important not to finance a knowingly bad investment' (CPA 1994: 9–10: 16). Lankester argued that the project did not contribute to the development of Malaysia and the FAC noted that he viewed it as inconsistent with policy statements made by ministers to Parliament regarding the basic objectives of the aid programme (FAC 1994: para 50–1). In his 5 and 7 February 1991 memoranda Lankester informed the Minister that he would require a Ministerial Direction to meet the expenditure if a decision to proceed with the project was finalised (CPA 1994: para 39–40: 5–6).

While Lynda Chalker, Tim Sainsbury (Minister for Trade at DTI) and Chris Patten (Chalker's predecessor at ODA) each opposed the project (FAC 1994: para 81; FAC 1994(2): 237: 247–8; *Independent on Sunday*, 13 February 1994), Alan Clark (Minister for Procurement at MOD) argued that withdrawal 'would have an adverse impact on UK relations with Malaysia in general and on the defence sales relationship in particular' (cited in WDM 1995: 3–4). This was not dissimilar from the argument made by Charles Powell in a letter to the FCO in February 1991 on behalf of Prime Minister Major, and it was this position which informed the decision by Douglas Hurd (now Foreign Secretary), in consultation with John Major, to go ahead with the project at the contract price of £417 million that same month (FAC 1994: para 53).

The political defence of the aid–arms linkage

On 4 July 1991, four days prior to the signing of the financial agreement committing funds and less than one month before work began on site, Hurd issued a Ministerial Direction ordering expenditure for the Pergau project from the ODA budget. Under the order ODA was committed to an expenditure of £108 million over five years which included support of £70.5 million in the third year of the project – a sum which constituted 70 percent of the total ODA budget in that year and enforced financing by a 14 year loan involving a total cost to ODA of £234 million over the period. ECGD provided a further £45.8 million in interest rate subsidy (NAO 1993: para 35–9: 56: Appendix 2; CPA 1994: para 55: 7).

ODA's funding of Pergau came under increasing scrutiny. The suspicions of the media and opposition politicians that the provision of ATP assistance for the project contravened the prohibition on linkage between civil aid disbursement and arms sales followed an *Observer* article in May 1990 which claimed a link between arms sales and the Pergau project aid package (*Economist*, 15 January 1994: 30–1). Accusations were made in Parliament that the Pergau contracts had involved the payment of bribes totalling £35 million (*Guardian*, 5 February 1994; *Independent*, 3 February 1994).

From 1989 ministers issued a series of misleading or inaccurate replies in answer to verbal or written questions which focused on the funding of the Pergau project and its linkage to arms sales. In May 1989 Thatcher claimed (in contradiction of Spreckley's 28 June 1988 letter) that 'There is no memorandum of understanding between the British Government on aid; offers of support [under ATP] are made for specific projects on a case-by-case basis' (cited in FAC 1994: para 43). In June she denied any linkage between the two deals in a written reply which ingenuously stated that the 'provision of overseas aid as an *integral* part of a negotiated agreement on the defence package was not possible' (italics added, cited in CPA 1994: 10), and in November that civil aid 'is not used in connection with sales of military equipment' (HC Debs., 14 November 1989, col 121W). In May, June and July Tim Sainsbury gave three singularly uninformative replies to questions to the Defence Secretary from Joan Lestor MP (HC Debs., 17 May 1989, col 191W: 13 June 1989, col 397–8W: 7 July 1989, col 302W). The subterfuge was accomplished in part by the refusal to reveal the fact or content of Spreckley's 28 June 1988 letter to the Malaysian Minister of Finance which had balanced that admitted to have been sent by Younger (HC Debs., 25 January 1994 col 145–6; 8 February 1994, col 124W; FAC 1994: para 43).

The continuing suspicions and political controversy in the wake of a report on the affair by the National Audit Office (NAO 1993) led to parliamentary investigations by the Committee of Public Accounts (CPA 1994) and the Foreign Affairs Committee (FAC 1994) into the details of the case and the possibility that linkage had been established between aid assistance and arms exports, and the role of individual ministers and departments in the affair. In its conclusions the FAC found that 'Ministerial replies to certain questions [in Parliament] were literally true, though less open and less informative than the House has a right to expect' (FAC 1994: para 44: also 42–5). In the face of mounting press criticism and political pressure Hurd admitted in January 1994 that there had indeed been a 'brief entanglement' between aid provision and arms sales to Malaysia when he gave an incomplete account of Younger's March 1988 protocol. He admitted that the Protocol had made reference to 'aid in support of non-military aspects' but omitted to disclose that it had outlined a formula which linked the level of aid to the level of arms orders (HC Debs., 25 January 1994, cols 145–6; FAC 1994: para 42). Not till February was it admitted in a written reply that the protocol had linked arms sales and civil aid at a level calculated as a percentage of the former (*Economist*, 12 February 1994: 26; *Financial Times*, 4 February 1994).

Hurd later admitted that he took the decision to order funding of the project in the context of 'a wider perspective ... What swayed me was that there had been a clear undertaking *at the highest level* ... If we had broken our word the consortium would have lost the business' (italics added, FAC 1994(2): 32–3). This, he argued, could have had serious adverse consequences for Anglo-Malaysian relations and UK exports (CPA 1994: para 41–4: 8–9, 10–11). Moreover, Lynda Chalker admitted in evidence that the 'wider' factors which Hurd brought to bear on his consideration of the ATP funding for Pergau included the sale of arms (FAC 1994: para 87).

Misleading or inaccurate replies to Parliament were supplemented by restricted access to documentary material. Professor John Toye noted in his submission to the FAC in 1994 that the NAO Report (1993) was completed without the benefit of documents which government departments had marked 'not for NAO eyes' (FAC 1994(2): 290). While ODA denied the allegation (ibid: 326), Lennox-Boyd later admitted that the FCO had retained six files. The withheld FCO documents are reported to have included a memorandum from Chris Patten detailing his opposition to the Pergau project when Minister at ODA, and objections put forward by Howe and Chalker (*Independent* 3 February 1994, 6 February 1994).

Legal endgame

In 1994 the FAC concluded that 'Progress on the defence exports package negotiated in 1988 was certainly a factor in the final deliberations, in early 1991, on whether or not to commit funds to the Pergau project' (FAC 1994: para 87). The provision of aid which resulted from this link was subsequently found to have been illegal. In June 1994 leave was granted to the World Development Movement (WDM) to seek a judicial review of Hurd's decision to proceed with ATP assistance for the Pergau project. In November the High Court found the funding of Pergau to have been unlawful under Section 1 of the Overseas Development and Cooperation Act. The project had been made for political and economic reasons: it had been 'economically unsound' and had failed to promote the development of the Malaysian economy or the interests of its people. Hurd was found to have exceeded his powers in allowing funding of the project to be a charge on ODA funds and the Government was ordered to cease future payments in support of the project from ODA funds (the next payment of £11 million was due in December) and to 'make good the deficiency in the overseas aid budget'. Leave to appeal the decision was denied and WDM was awarded costs (*Guardian*, 11 November 1994; *Times*, 11 November 1994; WDM 1995: 1). Hurd's initial response was to announce that the Government would continue to meet its contractual obligations to fund the dam. He followed this with the announcement that the Government would not reimburse the aid budget for the £24.37 million ruled to have been illegally spent between July 1991 and March 1994 and that Pergau project assistance due in 1994/4 and 1995/6 (£65.5 million) would be funded from the Treasury Reserve. ECGD considered that the judgement did not preclude its continued support for Pergau (NAO 1995: para 6–32; HC Debs., 13 December 1994, cols 773–4; WDM 1995: 1–2).

Conclusion

The story of the Pergau project is a tale of British ministers lying in Parliament and to the electorate to prevent public knowledge of agreements which they knew to contravene their own stated policy and to be politically controversial in the extreme and possibly illegal. The details of the deals which those activities sought to conceal were of considerable economic significance to large companies in the construction and arms manufacturing sectors of British industry with important links to the party which formed the government of the day and individual ministers.

The sums of money involved were huge – £417 million (increased to £457 million by March 1995) for the construction of the Pergau dam and associated generating equipment, and £1 to £1.5 billion of prospective orders for defence equipment. With deals of this size in prospect by non-competitive tendering procedures it would be surprising if companies such as BICC and Trafalgar House, or their respective subsidiaries – Balfour Beatty and Cementation – which formed the consortium which was the sole bidder for the Pergau dam contract, and British Aerospace and GEC-Marconi had not engaged in lobbying ministers to support deals which guaranteed large profits. Indeed the FAC concluded that the consortium had 'put pressure on the Prime Minister to make a firm offer [of aid assistance for the Pergau dam project] at her meeting with the Malaysian Prime Minister on 15 March 1989' (FAC 1994: para 84).

Toye has argued that the ATP programme was initiated in response to the political influence of powerful interest groups and that it continued because of the appetite of industrial interests for state subsidies. Such subsidies are said to reinforce the means to exercise further 'political leverage' through donations to political parties and the recruitment of retired politicians and civil servants (FAC 1994(2): 292). Geoffrey Howe has been a non-executive director of BICC since 1991 or while Lord Carrington was succeeded as Chairman of GEC by Lord Prior (both one-time senior Conservative ministers) in 1984. The company has also recruited senior civil servants (SCMI 1990:para 1136: 1146: 1181–3), and three of the largest donors to the Conservative Party are also three of the largest UK construction firms operating in Malaysia and have benefited on a grand scale from the ATP programme: Trafalgar House, BICC and Biwater (*Economist*, 5 March 1994: 30; *Independent on Sunday*, 13 February 1994; Toye evidence, FAC 1994(2): 290). Moreover, such companies have an almost institutionalised access to the ministers and officials responsible for the allocation of ATP funds and advancing the interests of British industry in the world market. Such access includes the rotation of personnel between industry and ministerial or civil service positions (Scott 1996 D6.29–54: D2.363–396: 391–6; *Guardian*, 19 February 1994; WDM 1995(2): 35–6; Nolan 1995: 5: 53–6). Industry representatives also sit with ministers and officials on DTI boards. The British Overseas Trade Board (headed by the Secretary of State at DTI) and the Overseas Projects Board include officials from ODA and ECGD as well as representatives from companies which are the principal recipients of ATP funds (*Guardian*, 19 February 1994; *Independent on Sunday*, 13 February 1994).

If Toye's assessment is correct, the situation which he describes is one which ministers would seek to protect from the attention of political opponents and from investigation by the media. In the case of the Pergau dam project the linkage between civil aid and arms sales is clear. The decisions of ministers to advance the two schemes were variously defended in terms of economic benefits and jobs, and the 'national interest'. The 'national interest' was, with 'commercial privilege', deployed to defend the decision of ministers that the arrangements should be conducted privately and that the details should remain secret and free from challenge in Parliament or by the media and public. The denial of information to Parliament of the details of the various MOUs and other agreements with Malaysia concerning arms sales and the Pergau dam project necessarily followed from the recognition in 1988 that linkage between the two deals had occurred and was contrary to stated policy and of questionable legality under the provisions of the Overseas Development and Cooperation Acts, and thus likely to raise potentially serious political difficulties.

The fear of scrutiny necessitated that ministers dissemble or lie by omission since to reveal details of the private arrangements which had been made would invite public debate and the probability of a political challenge to, and repudiation of, both the general policy of linking civil aid to arms sales and its implementation in the particular case of funding for the dam project. Any such challenge would have possibly serious political implications for the Government and individual ministers and for the economic interests which had benefited from the arrangement and stood to benefit from similar arrangements in the future.

If scrutiny was to be avoided, dissembling was inevitable since the truth invited the outcome which ministers sought to avoid. This intent was undermined by the probing of journalists whose reports (in part at least) moved individual parliamentarians to challenge the executive. This ultimately forced ministers to admit the existence of documents which they had previously denied. Ultimately the courts became involved when WDM mounted a private legal challenge to the government's implementation of policy and the ruling that ministers had acted illegally confirmed the Government's original fears as to the possible outcome of public scrutiny of the policy.

10
Shoot to Kill

Maureen Ramsay

> There is no shoot to kill policy, there never has been, and as
> far as I am concerned there never will be.
>
> (James Prior, Secretary of State for Northern Ireland,
> *Guardian*, 12 January, 1984)

The nationalist community has repeatedly made allegations that at
various times during the current 'troubles', the British Government, via
the British Army and local police forces, has authorised or at least
endorsed a 'shoot to kill' policy in Northern Ireland. The term 'shoot
to kill' refers to the unlawful killing of known or suspected Republican
activists through their deliberate engagement by security forces in
armed confrontation. The existence of a 'shoot to kill' policy has
always been vigorously denied. This chapter will first outline the context in which alleged 'shoot to kill' incidents have occurred. It will
then examine in more detail some notorious shoot to kill cases to
assess whether official denials are attempted cover-ups to conceal the
truth and if so, whether they are justified.

The context of the alleged 'shoot to kill' incidents

Northern Ireland was artificially created in 1921 when Britain decided
to partition Ireland into two separate political entities – the Irish
Republic, a sovereign state, and Northern Ireland, with a degree of
internal self-government and a federal relationship with Great Britain.
This was seen as a pragmatic solution to the conflicting demands of the
Unionist and Catholic populations. Partition confirmed the conflict
within the six north-east countries between the largely Protestant,
unionist and loyalist majority (approximately one million) who wanted

to remain part of Great Britain, and the largely Catholic minority (half a million) who hoped that eventually Northern Ireland would become part of the Irish Republic.

The territorial definition of Northern Ireland guaranteed an inbuilt Protestant/Unionist majority in the Northern Ireland Executive, and allowed Unionists to rule in the interests of that majority. The current disorder in Northern Ireland began in 1968 when civil rights marchers campaigning on behalf of the Catholic minority took part in a series of demonstrations to protest against their systematic discrimination in jobs and housing and their exclusion from power.

The civil rights marches of 1968 and 1969 provoked the fear amongst Unionists that civil rights organisations were a front for republican and nationalist politics and that acknowledging their demands would be an unwelcome move towards an united Ireland. The Unionist-dominated Northern Ireland Government responded by banning marches. The mainly Protestant Royal Ulster Constabulary (RUC) and their auxiliary force, the B Specials, became involved in violent clashes with demonstrators which were followed by rioting, further demonstrations, counter-demonstrations and sectarian violence. The RUC and B Specials made unprovoked attacks on Catholic areas, killing six people (confirmed in the Cameron Report 1969). The B Specials were accused of indiscipline, brutality and the indiscriminate use of firearms during the riots in August 1969 (Scarman Report 1972). The local security forces were not only discredited, but their heavy-handed sectarian approach escalated the problem of disorder.

In August 1969 the British Army were brought in to share control of security with the RUC and to act as an impartial peace-keeping force. The British government disbanded the B Specials and replaced them with the Ulster Defence Regiment (UDR) in the hope that these would be seen as fairer than the hated B Specials. At first the Catholic community welcomed the intervention, but hopes of fairness and impartiality soon dimmed and a stream of complaints about indiscriminate searches and harassment of Catholics increased tensions.

The attempt by the Army and the RUC to jointly control the situation culminated in the disastrous internment without trial policy introduced in August 1971. The RUC provided lists of people to be interned and the Army carried out the arrests. There soon followed widespread accusations of the selective use of internment against republicans and numerous complaints about human rights violations, systematic brutality and the torture and ill-treatment of detainees (reviewed in the Report of the European Commission on Human

Rights 1976). These abuses unified most Catholics and led to growing support for the Irish Republican Army (IRA). Violence increased dramatically, culminating in paratroopers shooting dead 13 civilians on an illegal march against internment in Derry on 31 January 1972. This event, later to be called 'Bloody Sunday', irretrievably poisoned the relationship between the Army and the nationalist community. The state's failure to prosecute soldiers confirmed the view that the security forces were above the law. The discrepancies between official and eyewitness accounts of the event and the still controversial Widgery tribunal findings which effectively exonerated the soldiers are believed by many to be evidence of a cover-up to prevent the truth emerging: the truth as to whether the paratroopers had implemented a prearranged plan, a 'shoot to kill' policy when they opened fire.

In the aftermath of Bloody Sunday, Stormont was suspended and direct rule imposed from London (March 1972). The army in effect remained in control of security. Internment without trial as a way of dealing with disorder continued until 1975. Mass screening and regular house searches further alienated the Catholic community and led to an increase in the number of terrorist incidents and sectarian murders. During this period, a policy of combating terrorism through obtaining convictions escalated. To this end, in 1973, the notorious 'Diplock courts' were introduced where those suspected of terrorist activities could be tried without jury and convicted on the basis of uncorroborated confessions. In 1974 the Prevention of Terrorism Act (PTA) allowed suspects to be held for seven days before being charged or released. After internment was phased out, and overall responsibility for security and law enforcement was restored to the police in 1976, there was increasing emphasis on trial in non-jury courts and convictions obtained through confessions. In order to secure confessions two new interrogation centres were opened, Castlereagh in Belfast and Gough Barracks in Armagh. By 1979 there were more than 1600 formal complaints of beating and ill-treatment at these interrogation centres and although the Bennett Committee Report in that year recommended a new code of interrogation, not a single RUC officer was charged (Boyle *et al.* 1980: 39).

An alternative to combating terrorism through convictions was to prevent offences occurring in the first place. In the late 1970s the army appears to have concentrated on preventative action, recruiting informers, gathering intelligence and engaging in undercover operations. The Special Air Service (SAS) and other specially trained units were then deployed to lay ambushes for suspected IRA members on active service. Between 1977 and 1978 the SAS killed ten people, seven IRA members and three civilians in undercover operations (Boyle 1980: 25, Jennings 1990: 113, Urban 1992: 81). The number and type of incidents together with the release of inaccurate information from the Lisburn press office suggested that the army were deliberately covering up the truth about the nature and circumstances of the killings (Curtis 1984: 77; Murray 1990: 232; Urban 1992: 60–1). The use of misleading cover stories led to accusations that the army was following a 'shoot to kill' policy, that the SAS were effectively executing suspected republican terrorists in pre-planned ambushes. After adverse publicity and widespread protests, the role of the SAS seems to have come under critical review, particularly from the RUC (Urban 1992: 81) and SAS involvement in covert operations of this sort ceased.

However, the early 1980s saw a continuance of this pattern of dealing with terrorism, both through securing convictions and though eliminating suspected terrorists in undercover operations. The Bennett Report (1979) with its new controls on police conduct had made obtaining confessions through interrogation more difficult. Uncorroborated confessions were replaced by a new method of securing convictions. The RUC initiated a 'supergrass' system in which 'reformed' terrorists in exchange for money and a new identity, implicated a large number of their former colleagues. Between November 1981 and November 1983, more than 600 people were arrested and charged with offences related to paramilitary activities. Mass trials began in 1983, many of those charged were eventually released because evidence was withdrawn or rejected by the trial judge or on appeal (see Greer 1990: 73–103).

Combating terrorism through undercover operations had been transferred from the Army to the RUC. There had been a build up of specialist police forces since the introduction in 1976 of the general policy of army withdrawal and police primacy. By 1982, there were again allegations that a 'shoot to kill' policy was being pursued. The apparent return to this strategy using the RUC rather than Army special forces was seen by nationalists both as a response to the increase in violence and to the political success of Sinn Fein during and following the Hunger Strikes in 1981. A 'criminalisation' policy in 1976 had withdrawn 'special category' status for prisoners convicted of terrorist offences and deemed them ordinary criminals. Prisoners refused to accept criminal status and their protests culminated in the Hunger Strike of 1981 in which 8 IRA and 3 INLA (Irish National Liberation Army) men starved to death amidst a glare of world publicity. The intransigence of the British Government in conceding to political status or recognising political motivation for terrorist crimes, and its steadfast refusal to intervene as ten men, one after another, died, caused renewed anger, bitterness, and a major upsurge in street protests and violence. In the period of the hunger strikes from March– October 1981, there were 1205 demonstrations as well as a dramatic increase in IRA violence against the security forces and in the use of plastic bullets by the RUC and the army in an attempt to control the situation. In 1981, 30000 plastic bullets were fired by the security forces, 17000 in March when Bobby Sands, the first hunger striker, died (Guelke 1992: 102). The upsurge in IRA violence against the security forces was coupled with the emergence of Sinn Fein as a political force. Bobby Sands was elected to Parliament in April 1981, two other hunger strikers were elected to Parliament in June 1981, Provisional Sinn Fein gained five seats in the October 1982 Assembly elections.

Against the backdrop of IRA attacks on security forces and the threat posed by their political success, three infamous 'shoot to kill' incidents occurred in 1982. They were all the result of undercover operations by the RUC. In the early 1980s responsibility for acting on military and political intelligence seems to have been given to specially trained mobile undercover surveillance units, the basis of whose training was 'firepower, speed and aggression'. It was these units who were involved in the shooting dead of a number of active, but unarmed, IRA and INLA members in 1982. The circumstances of the killings, the use of cover stories and the failure to prosecute the police officers involved, fuelled the belief that the killings were the result of a deliberate police conspiracy to shoot to kill suspects.

After these incidents and the hostile publicity generated by them, there was pressure on the RUC to abandon their aggressive force operations, and responsibility for specialist operations and for intercepting terrorists appears to have been restored to the SAS (see Urban 1992: 217). Urban points out that after five years of not killing anyone, between 1983–3 the SAS killed nine IRA members in ambushes based on informer intelligence (Urban 1992: 61, 246). The killing of active IRA members remained relatively high. Miller writes that between 1982 and June 1991 there were at least 67 killings by security forces in disputed circumstances (Miller 1994: 100). The most notorious of these were the ambush and lethal shooting by the SAS of eight IRA men engaged in an attack on an unmanned police barracks at Loughgall on 8 March 1987, and the killings by the SAS of three unarmed IRA members in Gibraltar in 1988. These incidents once again conjured the spectre of a 'shoot to kill' policy and the inquiries which followed were surrounded by claims of cover up and whitewash.

This brief survey suggests that since 1968, the security forces have used two alternative tactics for dealing with public disorder and terrorism. These can be broadly and crudely categorised as either attempts to secure convictions through repressive legislation and the criminal justice system, or through brute force. To assess whether or not 'brute force' has included a deliberate 'shoot to kill' policy, initiated by the security forces or as a political directive, some of the most notorious cases will be examined in more detail.

Sunday, 30 January 1972: Bloody Sunday

On Sunday, 30 January 1972, later to be called Bloody Sunday, thirteen civilians were killed by British soldiers and fourteen others were injured during an illegal civil rights demonstration against internment in Derry. The disinformation and whitewash used to justify these acknowledged facts, together with the still unresolved questions concerning the events, continue to fuel the suspicion that a pre-arranged plan, a deliberate 'shoot to kill' policy was in operation on that day.

Background

The violence on Bloody Sunday took place in the vicinity of Bogside on the edge of an area known as Free Derry. The predominantly Catholic district of Bogside had been under effective control of the IRA and was an established no-go area for the RUC and British troops. Free Derry and its unpoliced population was a challenge to the security forces, an embarrassment to Stormont and a source of outrage to Loyalist leaders. Democratic Unionists attacked the Unionist Government for its weakness in tolerating the no-go areas and campaigned for a tougher security policy. Political pressure was growing for the government to act decisively and return the no-go areas to a state of law and order.

The demonstration was organised by the Northern Ireland Civil Rights Association (NICRA) in protest against internment without trial which had been introduced the previous August, and was in defiance of a six-month ban on public demonstrations imposed under emergency legislation. The week before there had been a similar demonstration outside the internment camp at Magilligan which had been broken up with CS gas, rubber bullets and an excessive use of force by the British Army, in particular by soldiers of the Second Battalion of Green Jackets and the First Battalion of the Parachute Regiment (1 Para). A repeat of the violence at Magilligan was forecast the day before Bloody Sunday when the Army and the RUC issued a joint statement:

> Experience this year has already shown that attempted marches often end in violence and must have been foreseen by the organisers. Clearly the responsibility for this violence and the consequences of it must rest fairly and squarely on the shoulders of those who encourage people to break the law. The security forces have a duty to take action against those who break the law. (Quoted in McCann, 1992: 72)

The same day, the Democratic Unionists, outraged at the violation of the ban, announced 'We were approached by the Government and given assurances that the Civil Rights march would be halted by force if necessary' (*Sunday Post*, 30.1.72). The political and military stage was set for the prevention or the break-up of the march by similar methods to those used at Magilligan.

The demonstration

According to the Widgery Tribunal held in the wake of Bloody Sunday, General Ford, Commander of Land Forces in Northern Ireland, put Brigadier MacLellan in charge of the overall plan to police the march (Widgery Report 1972: para 16–23). He gave the order to erect barriers cordoning off Creggan and Bogside. Lt. Col. Wilford, Commander of the Paras, drew up the plan for a scoop-up arrest operation in the event of rioting breaking out. A support company, 1 Para under the command of Major Loden, were deployed behind the barricades to carry out the arrest operation.

The march set off peacefully, but rioting broke out when a small group of demonstrators, their path blocked by the Army and the RUC, began throwing stones and bottles at soldiers behind the barricades. Soldiers responded with rubber bullets and water cannons. The rioting petered out and most of the marchers had been peacefully dispersed. Then apparently without warning, the support company began firing. Within thirty minutes thirteen demonstrators were dead.

That night, in order to justify the soldiers' actions, senior Army officers at Lisburn HQ issued an official statement claiming that the paratroopers were sent in after

> they came under nail bomb attack and a fusillade of 50–80 rounds from the area of Rossville Flats and Glenfada Flats. Fire was returned

at seen gunmen and nailbombers. Subsequently, as troops deployed to get at the gunmen, the latter continued to fire. In all, a total of well over 200 rounds was fired indiscriminately in the general direction of the soldiers. Fire continued to be returned only at identified targets. (*The Times*, 31 January 1972)

The next day the Ministry of Defence (MOD) gave a press briefing relayed through the British Information Services, the Government News Agency, designed to substantiate the Army's version of events. It was claimed that soldiers fired only at identified targets and that at all times the soldiers obeyed their standing instructions to fire only in self-defence or in defence of others threatened. The statement listed a series of incidents to demonstrate that soldiers had returned fire at nailbombers, petrol bombers, snipers and gunmen with rifles or pistols. (see *The Times* and other papers, 1 February 1972).

The official version of events was from the beginning hotly contested and contradicted by virtually all eyewitnesses who claimed that the soldiers had opened fire without warning or justification, and that none of the dead or injured had been armed, firing weapons or throwing bombs. In response to the outcry following the killings, the British Government set up a Tribunal of Inquiry chaired by Lord Widgery, the Lord Chief Justice of England. From the outset, the Widgery Tribunal and its findings were suspected as a cover up of the truth and a poorly disguised attempt to exonerate the soldiers.

Widgery's report failed to resolve the conflict of evidence between the soldiers and other witnesses and came to conclusions that were inconsistent with his own findings. All the soldiers testified that they fired in response to a perceived threat from identified people who were firing at them or threatening them with nail or petrol bombs. Despite the counterclaims by eyewitnesses, evidence given by priests, journalists, wounded marchers and uncommitted observers, including British ex-servicemen, Widgery found in favour of the soldiers' version of events. He believed that 'in general the accounts given by the soldiers of the circumstances in which they had fired and the reasons why they did so were, in my opinion, truthful' (para 104). He professed himself to be entirely satisfied that the Paras had opened fire in response to an armed attack on them and concluded that he could find 'no reason to suppose that the soldiers would have opened fire if they had not been fired upon first' (Conclusion 10). Yet Widgery did not find any independent evidence to back up this supposition. Rather, his own findings directly challenged the assumption that the soldiers had come under heavy and sustained attack. He found that:

> Although a number of soldiers spoke of actually seeing firearms or bombs in the hands of civilians none was recovered by the Army. None of the many photographs show a civilian holding objects that could be identified as a firearm or bomb. No casualties were suffered by the soldiers from firearms or gelignite bombs. In relation to everyone of the deceased there were eyewitnesses who said that they saw no bombs or firearms in their hands. (para 65)

Moreover, his own conclusions were self-contradictory. If soldiers had fired at identified gunmen or bombers, this did not square with his conclusion that 'none of the deceased or wounded is proved to have been shot whilst handling a firearm or bomb' (Conclusion 10), nor with his view that 44 shots fired in Glenfada Park where four were killed were 'fired without justification', nor with his conclusion that when these four men were shot, the groups of civilians were 'not acting aggressively', nor that the soldiers' behaviour in the Park was 'bordering on the reckless' (para 85) and that the twelve shots fired by soldiers in Rossville Flats were 'unjustifiably dangerous for people round about' (para 101).

The only evidence that backed Widgery's conclusion that although 'none of the deceased was shot while handling firearms or bombs ... there is a strong suspicion that some others had been firing weapons or handling bombs in the course of the afternoon' (Conclusion 10) was the police photograph of nailbombs in the pockets of Gerald Donaghy, one of the four shot in Glenfada Park, and traces of firearms residue on three of the deceased.

In Donaghy's case, Widgery rejected the obvious explanation that nail bombs had been planted on him while he was in police and military custody after his death (para 88). The car taking Donaghy, who was still alive, to hospital was stopped at a military checkpoint and driven by a soldier to an Army First Aid post. Here Donaghy was examined by a medical officer, who pronounced him dead. Soldier 127 was called to the First Aid post to examine the car, saw Donaghy's body on the back seat with nail bombs protruding from his pocket. Widgery decided that on balance of probability Donaghy had been carrying the nailbombs, despite the fact that Young, who had carried the wounded Donaghy to Raymond Rogan's house and had searched his body for identification, Raymond Rogan himself, a doctor who examined him there, a reporter who was sheltering there and the Army Officer who had made a detailed examination of Donaghy at the First Aid checkpoint, testified that they had seen no nail bombs, and they could not have failed to notice them had they been there.

Widgery's suspicion that three of the deceased had been handling guns was based on uncritical acceptance of forensic reports of lead deposits on their hands. The unreliability of such evidence is now well-established. On 5 December 1991, a Special History programme broadcast on Channel 4 showed that the traces of firearms residue on the men was likely to have come from contact with the soldiers, who themselves had been firing and who manhandled their bodies after their death (see Dash 1972: 81–5; McCann 1992: 233; Mullan 1997: 62).

Widgery's conclusions were not credible at the time, and though the whole truth has not yet emerged, recent discoveries further confirm Widgery's unwillingness to acknowledge contradictory evidence and give it due weight.

Recent findings

A confidential minute dated 1 February 1972 from a Downing Street meeting between Edward Heath (the then Prime Minister), the Lord Chancellor, Lord Hailsham and Lord Widgery has recently been discovered in the Public Record Office in London. The minute reveals that Heath reminded Widgery that when conducting the inquiry 'It had to be remembered that we were in Northern Ireland fighting not only a military war but a propaganda war' (HO219/50 item 13, Public Records Office, London). This memo reinforced the suspicion that there had been government and judicial collusion to prevent the truth emerging and that Widgery's report was nothing more than a propaganda document in this war, designed to conceal politically embarrassing facts and to protect the military personnel involved in the killings.

A memo dated 10 March 1972 written by the Tribunal secretary and recently released from the Public Record Office reveals that Widgery, on the advice of civil servants, only read a small number of the 500 eyewitness statements collected by NICRA and the National Council for Civil Liberties (NCCL), (HO219/64, Public Record Office, London, reproduced in Mullan 1997: 274). The statements were rediscovered by Don Mullan, himself an eyewitness on Bloody Sunday, in a plastic bag in a community centre in Derry. Mullan compiled and edited these accounts (Mullan 1997). He argues that evidence in these previously unpublished documents, together with statements made by Paras and other regiments now released from the Public Record Office, contradict the findings at the Widgery Tribunal that soldiers on the ground opened fire after coming under attack themselves. He substantiates this claim by showing that eyewitness statements, army statements made by Paras and other regiments in the aftermath of Bloody Sunday, police and army radio transcripts on the day do not contain any reference to soldiers coming under attack from nail or petrol bombs. There are no reports of anyone armed on the barricades or of positions coming under fire. However, there is evidence to suggest that not only did Paras on the ground open fire first, but that in addition snipers were firing from the city walls which overlook the Bogside and Creggan estates. Eyewitness testimony insists that gunfire came from the walls and that soldiers were shooting to kill or wound. Post-mortem reports confirm that three of the dead were hit by bullets travelling downwards and backwards. The victims were shot as they faced away or were running away from the Paras and the bullets must have come from another source, from in front and above them. In the opinion of a ballistic expert, the three were killed by a single marksman using a telescopic lens, firing from the city walls. Analysis of police and army transcripts, the Brigade Log Book and recently released statements by soldiers on the walls confirm that at least two 'hits' were registered on demonstrators from the walls (Mullan 1997: 53–6).

These new findings are significant because they raise the possibility that the Paras were not the only military involved in the killings in Bloody Sunday. They add weight to the suspicion that the gunfire was deliberately aimed at targeted and verifiably unarmed people. This suspicion had already been aroused by the fact that the deceased were men of military age and they were all killed by a single shot aimed at the head or trunk. This had suggested controlled and discriminate shooting with the soldiers targeting particular people.

This new evidence also further discredited the findings of the Widgery Tribunal. It supports the view that Widgery was politically dishonest when he ignored the overwhelming evidence that the killings were unjustified, when he failed to concur with the coroners verdict at the inquest of those who died that the soldiers action was 'sheer unadulterated murder' (*Irish Times*, 22 August 1972). Fresh evidence to support this verdict is still emerging. In June 1997, the Irish Government presented the British Government with an assessment of the new material and called for a new independent inquiry into the events of Bloody Sunday (Irish Government 1997). The new material includes all the evidence presented by Mullan, plus analysis of other eyewitness accounts given to the Government in 1972, analysis of statements by soldiers released from the Public Record Office in 1996 and investigative reports by the press and other media.

According to the Irish Government's assessment, the 500 statements recorded by NICRA and the NCCL which were submitted to, but not substantially considered by, the Widgery Tribunal, together with the 101 statements given to the Government, confirm the view that on Bloody Sunday the British Army deliberately shot and killed unarmed citizens without justification and that British Army snipers fired shots from the vicinity of the city walls (Irish Government 1997: 6,16). These eyewitness statements are clear, internally consistent and mutually collaborative, unlike the statements given by soldiers to the Military Police and later to the Treasury Solicitor for the Inquiry on or after the 30 January 1972. These were released from the Public Record Office in 1996 and analysed by Walsh (1997).

Walsh shows that the statements made to the Military Police and the statements subsequently made to the Treasury Solicitor contain 'serious and relevant discrepancies, inconsistencies and alterations' (Walsh 1997: 27). The changes reduced some of the conflicts in different soldiers' accounts in earlier versions and had the effect of making the attack seem more justifiable. Both sets of statements were available to the Counsel for the Tribunal for the Army, but earlier statements were not made available to the Counsel for the next of kin. The Tribunal both ignored evidence which challenged the reliability of the statements made by the soldiers at the Tribunal and concealed the existing evidence damaging to their accounts (Walsh 1997: 65–6).

Portions of transcripts of statements by a paratrooper, referred to as Para AA, were given to the Irish Government, by a journalist, Tom McGurk, and were published in a Dublin newspaper, the *Sunday Business Post* on 16 March 1997. In these transcripts, Para AA alleges that soldiers lied to the Tribunal and Tribunal staff altered aspects of the soldiers' statements in an attempt to justify the killings (Irish Government 1997: para 254, Para AA transcript: 22–3). Para AA's account supports the eyewitness claim that the Paras deliberately shot at unarmed and fleeing citizens. He also claimed that the use of lethal force was sanctioned in advance by the army. Para AA alleges that the anti-tank platoon of the Support Company had on the previous day been encouraged by its Lieutenant to get some 'kills' (Irish Government 1997: para 32, Para AA: 22).

Channel 4 News broadcast a number of programmes relating to the events of Bloody Sunday. On 17 January 1997, during a major investigative report on Bloody Sunday, it was asserted that the British

Army fired from the walls. On 29 January 1997, Channel 4 News reported that a former soldier confirmed this. On 18 March 1997, a former paratrooper, possibly Para AA, claimed that officers working for the Widgery Tribunal changed the version of events initially presented by him.

According to the Irish Government, the assessment of the new material provides 'fresh grounds for the belief that members of 1 Para wilfully shot and killed unarmed citizens' (p. 176). It also

> reinforces original doubts that the Widgery Tribunal was inherently and wilfully flawed, selective and unbalanced in its handling of the evidence at the time. It effectively rejected the many hundreds of civilian testimonies submitted to it and opted instead for the unreliable accounts proffered by the implicated soldiers. Contrary to the weight of evidence and even its own findings, it exculpated the individual soldiers who used lethal force and thereby exonerated those who were responsible for their deployment and actions. (Irish Government 1997: 177)

There has always been the belief in the nationalist community that the killings on Bloody Sunday were the result of a political and military decision made in advance. Whether the British Cabinet, Faulkner's government or the military commanders approved the killings in advance, whether the soldiers were acting under orders or without authorisation, remains unknown. What is known is that the soldiers who killed thirteen people on Bloody Sunday were not acting in self-defence nor responding to a concerted attack on them; that those who died were unarmed; that those who killed them lied about the circumstances of the shootings; that the British judiciary covered up these lies and justified the killings; that the British Government, by its failure to prosecute any of the soldiers involved, sanctioned the killings in retrospect.

Just lies?

It is clear that lies were told about Bloody Sunday and that the judiciary and the government sanctioned these lies and thereby justified the killings. But if the justice of the lie depends in the first instance on the justice of the end for which it is told, then it is difficult to see what just end, what national or public interest could be served by lies to cover up the circumstances of the killings of thirteen unarmed civilians or by the killings themselves. Lies to cover up the fact that the killings were unlawful could be *explained*, but not justified by political expediency. That is, by the need to conceal political and military decisions for which there could be no democratic consensus or general approval; by the ideological imperative to misrepresent nationalist/republican opposition and so to justify nationalist deaths; by the state's need to present its forces use of violence as legitimate and by the practical need to clear the soldiers directly involved and to protect them from prosecution. If shooting dead thirteen civilians had been a legitimate use of force in response to attack, there would have been no need for deception.

If the security forces, the military, the judiciary and the government had acknowledged the circumstances of the shootings, could these killings be justified as a means to a just end? Shooting to kill the demonstrators could be *explained*, but not justified in terms of the interests the British state had in placating the Loyalists and shoring up Stormont, by the political necessity of demoralising Free Derry, curbing the civil rights movement and denting nationalist/republican opposition to British rule. There could be no consensus on the justice of these ends. The ends in question were precisely the injustices the civil rights association and the nationalist community were trying to redress. Killing unarmed people as a means only added to this catalogue of injustices.

Disinformation or the killing of innocent people could not be considered to be just means. Endorsement of disinformation about the circumstance of the shootings had counterproductive consequences. The legal system and the government's attempt to justify and legitimate the killings undermined any residual faith the nationalist community had in these legal and political institutions; any faith they may have had in justice and the rule of law; in democratic accountability and control. The disinformation and the killings proved to be incompatible with any ends which might have been thought to be achieved by them. The immediate effect was a wave of protests against the killings and the British presence in Northern Ireland, riots, strikes, demonstrations, the torching of the British Embassy in Dublin, and the withdrawal of consent for the Ulster regime. A few months later Stormont fell. The government's collusion in violence effectively killed the civil rights movement, but intensified rather than curbed nationalist opposition and dramatically increased support for the IRA.

It is generally acknowledged that the events of Bloody Sunday marked a watershed in the nationalist community's attitude towards the security forces and increased violent opposition to British rule. It is also acknowledged that the judicial and government endorsement of the deception and of the killings effectively granted the security forces an unlimited licence to kill. If soldiers could get away with lies, if they were not brought to justice for the killings of unarmed citizens, they would not be brought to justice for shooting suspected republican terrorists. The events of Bloody Sunday paved the way for legitimating the unjustified use of lethal force in the shoot to kill incidents that happened intermittently, but in clusters, throughout the years.

The 'Stalker' shoot to kill cases 1982

The best known examples of alleged shoot to kill operations are three incidents which occurred within five weeks of each other in 1982 shortly after control of security had been transferred to the RUC. They took place against the background of the political success of Sinn Fein and renewed attacks on the security forces following the Hunger Strikes of 1981. The most recent attack had been on 27 October 1982 in the Kinnego landmine explosion in which three police officers were killed. The first incident happened two weeks later.

On 11 November three men, Eugene Toman, Sean Burns and Gervais McKerr were shot dead after a car chase outside Lurgan, Co. Armagh. The RUC officers involved in the event were interviewed by detectives from the RUC's CID. On 15 November Sgt. Montgomery gave his first version of the events. He claimed that Mr Kerr, the owner of the car, had stopped briefly after being waved down at a Vehicle Check Point (VCP). As one of the constables approached the car, the car accelerated and he jumped or fell out of the way. Montgomery assumed the constable had been hit and said that as the car drove off, he heard shots and saw flashes coming from the back of the car. The crew, assuming they were under attack, gave chase and opened fire. The car crashed into the verge. Montgomery said he heard a metallic sound like a weapon, so he ordered the men to open fire again. He also claimed that a number of warnings were shouted as they approached the car (*The Irish Times*, 13 November 1982; *The Guardian*, 5 June 1984).

The original statement from the RUC press office gave the impression that the police officers involved were part of an ordinary police patrol and that the shootings happened after a routine police roadblock. But the police officers were members of the RUC's Anti-Terrorist Squad engaged in a top secret operation to apprehend Toman and Burns who had been implicated in the Kinnego landmine explosions by an informant. The incident was no chance encounter. The three men had been under surveillance for some time. After the CID had conducted the initial investigation into the car shooting the evidence was passed to the DPP. The officers were re-interviewed and charged with murder. After the lifting of the Official Secrets Act (OSA), in the trial, Montgomery admitted the true nature of the operation, but stood by his original account of the shootings. This account was contradicted by the facts that all three men shot dead were unarmed, that a total of 109 bullets were fired into the car from the front or side rather than the back, which would have been the case if the officers account was correct, and that Toman had been shot through the heart (Curtis 1984: 77–8; Urban 1992: 151). Despite this, the police officers were acquitted of murder. Lord Justice Gibson held that the three policemen had no case to answer. They had acted in self-defence and had used reasonable force in attempting to arrest the men. He commended the RUC men for their courage and determination in bringing the deceased to this 'final court of justice'.

The second incident occurred three weeks later. A seventeen-year-old civilian, Michael Tighe, and his friend Martin McAuley, were shot at a hayshed near Lurgan. The original official police story was that police officers had been carrying out routine anti-terrorist patrols when they saw a gunman moving towards a hayshed at the rear of an unoccupied farm in a remote country lane. The police officers approached the hayshed, heard muffled voices and the sound of rifles being cocked. Two warnings were shouted and McAuley appeared pointing a rifle. The officers opened fire, wounding McAuley. One of the police officers then saw Tighe on some haybales pointing a rifle and he opened fire, killing Tighe.

At the trial of McAuley for the possession of firearms, and after the lifting of the OSA, the police officers changed their story and admitted that they were part of an undercover team. They had not arrived at the hayshed by chance but were acting on information supplied by an informer. It was later discovered that the hayshed was bugged, had been under surveillance for weeks and was thought to be the store for weapons used in the Kinnego landmine explosion. The officers claimed that the original version of events had been given on orders from Special Branch who had concocted the story to protect intelligence sources. Despite this and the facts that there was no ammunition found in the shed, that the guns recovered from the shed were 50-year-old unloaded rifles, that McAuley insisted Tighe was unarmed and that there was no initial warning or chance to surrender, no officers were charged (Stalker 1988).

The third incident happened on 11 December outside Armagh city when two unarmed, high ranking members of the INLA, Seamus Grew and Roddy Carroll, were shot and killed by police officers. This incident took place less than a week after the Ballykelly pub bombings which had killed off-duty members of the security forces. Responsibility for the bombings had been claimed by the INLA.

The official RUC version of events upheld by Constable John Robinson, who was later charged with the murder of Grew, was that Grew and Carroll broke through a random road-block (*The Irish Times*, 2 September 1983). The car was intercepted by Robinson who said he heard a bang, thought he was being shot at, returned fire, emptying a magazine into the passenger side of the car, and killed Carroll. He then reloaded and fired four shots into the closed driver's door, killing Grew. He claimed he was acting in self-defence as he suspected the men were armed.

Again, after the OSA had been lifted, Robinson testified that he was a member of the RUC Special Support Unit, the same undercover unit that had been responsible for the two previous incidents, and that he was taking part in a secret operation. This was to capture the INLA leader, Dominic McGlinchley, who was thought to be travelling in Grew's car. The car had been under surveillance and had been followed across the border into the Irish Republic without the permission of the Irish authorities. The car was waved down by a police car just after it had crossed the border back into Northern Ireland.

On oath, in his defence Robinson admitted that the original road-block story was fabricated by senior RUC officers to conceal the extent of the operation and to protect information sources. At the trial forensic tests could produce no sound equivalent to the shots Robinson allegedly heard before he opened fire. Forensic evidence also showed that Grew could not have been shot through the closed door as Robinson had claimed. The door must have been open and Grew must have been shot while he sat in the car or while attempting to leave the car. Both the deceased were unarmed and no weapons were found in the car (Urban 1992: 132). Despite this, Robinson was acquitted by Judge McDermott who said that the prosecution had not satisfied him that Robinson was not acting in self-defence. He suggested that Robinson's actions were 'reasonable in the circumstances' (*The Daily Telegraph*, 21 March 1984; *The Guardian* 29 March 1984, 6 April 1984).

The Stalker inquiry

The differences between official police accounts and evidence given in court, together with what had been revealed about the involvement of military intelligence, prompted the police authorities to hold an inquiry. John Stalker, Deputy Chief Constable of Greater Manchester, was appointed on 24 May 1984 to lead the inquiry into what became known as a 'shoot to kill' policy. His brief was to investigate the circumstances of the shootings and to determine whether there had been an attempt by RUC officers to pervert the course of justice. Stalker claimed that his attempts to discover the facts were obstructed from the start. He believed that Special Branch officers had organised a cover-up of the circumstances of the shootings and that they were trying to prevent him discovering the truth. His request to interview an informer crucial to establishing the pre-planned nature of the operations was blocked by senior RUC officers. Sir John Hermon, the Head of the RUC, initially refused to release the tape of the bugging device that had been in the hayshed. Stalker had maintained that this MI5 tape would be all the evidence he needed to prove or disprove allegations of a shoot to kill policy. The tape might reveal whether or not the officers had opened fire without warning and could therefore conclude his investigation (Stalker 1988: 66).

In May 1986 , 18 months later, his request for the tape was agreed, but just before Stalker was about to fly to Belfast to inspect it, he was removed from the case. He was officially suspended and charged with ten disciplinary offences relating to his conduct as a police officer in Manchester. In 1987 the Police Authorities rejected all ten charges and reinstated Stalker to his former post. Stalker was convinced that the trumped-up allegations against him were part of a 'dirty tricks' campaign to remove him from the inquiry. He resigned from the police force and subsequently published a book about the affair (Stalker 1988). Colin Sampson, the Chief Constable for West Yorkshire, completed the inquiry. The Stalker/Sampson report eventually concluded that there were reasons to charge some RUC officers with offences, that MI5 as well as police officers should be charged with conspiracy to pervert the course of justice, and that the six men had been shot in unlawful circumstances.

The report, which has never been published, was passed to the DPP in January 1988. The DPP discussed it with the Attorney General, Sir Patrick Mayhew, who announced in the House of Commons that for reasons of 'national security' it would be unwise to proceed with charges (HC Debs, vol 126, cols 21–35, *The Times* and *The Guardian*, 26 January 1988). He also indicated that there was no evidence of a 'shoot to kill' policy or of any offences being committed. The decision not to prosecute was followed by general outrage. The Irish Government expressed 'dismay', the European Parliament called for the report to be reconsidered, Ken Livingstone, MP denounced Sir Patrick Mayhew as an 'accomplice to murder', the press responded cynically. The government had seemingly covered up a 'shoot to kill' policy.

Stalker's investigations had highlighted evidence that pointed to the existence of such a policy. The three incidents occurred in a short space of time directly after the setting up of specialist undercover anti-terrorist mobile support units. Officers from the same units had been involved in all the incidents indicating a pre-planned attack. Their training in 'firepower, speed and aggression', the accuracy and efficiency of their weapons suggest their purpose. The fact that each incident followed long surveillance operations, that a police informer had implicated Toman, Burns, McKerr and McAuley in the Kinnego landmine explosion, that the hayshed was thought to be the store for the explosives and that it was bugged, that the killings of Grew and Carroll were linked to a covert operation to detain McGlinchley, that all the victims were suspected IRA or INLA members believed to have been involved in attacks on security forces, suggest a carefully planned and targeted operation – a policy of creating ambushes in order to shoot to kill suspected terrorists. The facts that forensic evidence contradicted evidence in the Montgomery and Robinson cases; that the policemen had given incorrect information to the CID after being debriefed by Special Branch and that the RUC investigation after the incident was unprofessional, inept and lacking in crucial information indicates a deliberate concealment of the truth. This together with the obstruction of the Stalker inquiry, the removal of Stalker from the case on trumped-up charges, the acquittals and the government's decision not to prosecute, indicate knowledge, support and sanction for these operations at the highest level.

Stalker's own verdict was that 'The circumstances of these shootings pointed to a police inclination if not a policy, to shoot suspects dead without warning rather than arrest them. Coming as these incidents did, so close together the suspicion of deliberate assassination was not unreasonable (Stalker 1988: 253). He told *The Times* 'I never did find evidence of a shoot to kill policy as such. There was no written instruction, nothing pinned on a notice board. But there was a clear understanding on the part of the men involved whose job it was to pull the trigger that that was what was expected of them' (9 February 1988).

Just lies?

It cannot be proved that there was a shoot to kill policy in the sense of an order from the Government or the RUC to eliminate IRA terrorists whenever the opportunity arose. But the deliberate concealment of the truth in court, the use of disinformation to protect the security forces from due process and the legitimating of their actions suggest sanction for something approximating a shoot to kill policy. At least it suggests a policy of counter-terrorism which allows security forces to kill unarmed suspects who have been under surveillance and who pose no immediate threat and to go unpunished when they did so.

According to the RUC, the deception about the circumstances of the killings was justified, it was honourable disinformation for what might loosely be termed national security reasons. Disinformation about the circumstances of the shootings was for the just end of protecting informers and to retain the ability to exploit information in covert operations. When the deception was exposed in the Stalker/Sampson Report, the government justified the decision not to prosecute in the interests of 'national security'.

Deception might be justified for a just end – to protect intelligence sources and military operations. It is, however, difficult to see how the false stories from official sources could be justified in this way. Disinformation about chance encounters, suspects breaking through road-blocks and opening fire can hardly be necessary or the only way to protect informants, nor could shooting to kill be necessary or the only way to apprehend suspects who have been under surveillance for some time. It is even harder to see how national security interests demand that the security forces involved in the killings went unpunished. National security would have to be stretched to implausibly include the automatic exemption from due process of law and from conviction of state personnel involved in covert operations.

Neither the disinformation nor the killing of unarmed suspects could be justified by reference to a just end. The release of inaccurate statements by the Army Press Office, disinformation in the media and the courts, the failure to prosecute could be *explained*, but not justified, by the need to make the officers' actions seem more defensible by attempting to present the killings as lawful, to preserve the myth of a 'clean kill'. This is why the killings were followed by false statements that the incidents were chance encounters, that the suspects drove through a checkpoint, that they were armed, pointed a gun, opened fire or were believed to have opened fire. It was necessary to deflect allegations of deliberate ambush and extra-judicial executions. The government's attempt to silence the inquiry and to bring no prosecutions could be *explained*, but not justified, by the need to conceal the covert role of British Army intelligence and the philosophy, strategy and tactics of the units which carried out the specialist operations in order to avoid political embarrassment, and by the need to boost the morale of the RUC.

Even if the deception could be justified for a just cause, even if a shoot to kill policy could be justified as a means to defeating terrorism, the costs of lying and the costs of killing unarmed suspects outweigh any benefit that the security forces, the judiciary and the government sought to bring about. The lies and the failure to prosecute had counterproductive consequences. Rather than legitimising the killings, they confirmed the nationalist view that the security forces were above the law, that they were not subject to the normal legal constraints on the use of minimum force, that they were unlikely to be convicted or even charged and that even when the lies were exposed and it was confirmed that they had killed people who posed no immediate threat, they would be protected in the interests of national security. Rather than justifying the deception or legitimising the killings, the judiciary and the government's action and inaction eroded respect for the administration of justice in Northern Ireland. It called into question the political legitimacy of a government which sanctions state violence exercised by its agents who are neither responsible to Parliament nor to the electorate. The state sanctioning of lies and violence not only corrodes democratic ideals, but is incompatible with the state's aim of defeating political violence. The continued opposition in Northern Ireland has shown that as long as justice and the law are opposed, political violence will be sustained.

Conclusion

The case-studies discussed in this chapter are only two examples of deaths in disputed circumstances which support the allegation that at various times the RUC and the British Army have operated a shoot to kill policy in Northern Ireland. This has always been vigorously denied. But the circumstances of the killings of unarmed citizens in 1972, the alleged shoot to kill incidents in 1977–8, 1982, 1982–5 and 1988 suggest the possibility that shooting to kill is one of the tactics for dealing with the problem of public disorder and politically motivated violence, which was resorted to at various times by different sections of the security forces. The number of incidents, the situations in which they occurred, the fact that those directly responsible for the killings were either highly trained soldiers with a reputation for aggressive action or members of specially trained mobile undercover surveillance units, all indicate the deliberate and planned use of lethal force.

Whether or not shoot to kill was a response to an explicit political or military order, it was always condoned and sanctioned by the higher authorities. The official cover stories, the acquittals and the failure to prosecute those responsible show that the security forces have effectively been granted a licence to shoot to kill. Despite the protests when one of these incidents occur and despite the obvious disinformation and whitewash which inevitably follows them, the authorities and those directly responsible for the killings have been able to get away with both their lies and their unjustified use of lethal force.

11
BSE: Mad Cows and Deregulation

Dave Bartlett

We can say with confidence that beef can be eaten safely by everyone, both adults and children.

(John Gummer, Minister of Agriculture, May 1990)

There is no evidence whatsoever that BSE causes CJD and, similarly not the slightest evidence that eating beef or hamburgers causes CJD.

(Gillian Shephard, Minister of Agriculture, June 1994)

In the early 1980s the UK rendering industry underwent important changes in both production process and organisational structure. The period saw the introduction of the new energy-saving, Carver– Grenfield, 'continuous batch', rendering process which reduced operative temperatures to a range of only 80–90 degrees (as against the previous 130 degrees) without the sterilization processes required in other countries. A new Conservative government, ideologically committed to deregulation, removed many of the state's previously established regulatory procedures in the areas of public health, planning and the environment (Gifford n.d.) and, in April 1981, legislation established self-regulation in a rendering industry which was becoming increasingly concentrated in large-scale plants and subject to strong pressures towards monopoly ownership (Shaoul 1996; *Observer*, 22 December 1996).

The change in the process of rendering sheep remains and cattle carcase waste was made despite MAFF (Ministry of Agriculture, Food and Fisheries) research showing the need for high temperature processes to kill the scrapie agent in waste sheep meat (Dealler 1996: 4: 7: 18). The new rendering process and the transformation of a part of the product into inputs for high protein compound feeds for cattle (and other farm stock) are generally regarded as the route by which cattle became exposed to scrapie – a transmissible spongiform encephalopathy (TSE) infectivity which has been endemic to the British sheep flock for over two hundred years – which was said to have broken the species barrier and appeared in cattle as a Bovine variant TSE – BSE. Subsequently the new disease infected not only individuals in a range of domestic, farm and zoo animals, but also appeared in the human population as a variant form of Creutzfeldt-Jakob Disease (CJD).

The British Government – and particularly MAFF – sought to defend the meat industry from adverse consumer reaction to the information that beef potentially contained an infectious agent with lethal effects for the human population by denying, until March 1996 – and in the face of increasing evidence to the contrary – both the seriousness of the BSE epidemic in cattle and the possibility of a species jump from infected cattle to the human population. Ministers and officials insisted that beef was safe to eat and underpinned this stance by providing misleading or inaccurate information to Parliament and the public. The failure to fully research the problem or initiate effective veterinary and public health measures was subordinate to these larger deceits.

The early cover-up

The official explanation (above) of the origins of BSE has not been proved and one alternative hypothesis suggests the possibility that BSE has been endemic, if rare, in cattle for decades (Dealler and Kent 1995: 11). In this account the changes in rendering practice and the increased level of forced cannibalism which occurred as the bovine derived content of ruminant feed rose to 55 per cent, occasioned the spread of BSE through the national herd (possibly in combination with the development of a more resistant variant of the disease). Moreover, the official assumption that BSE occurred only among animals that had ingested contaminated feed and that vertical transmission between dam and calf was not possible has been contradicted by the evidence. Horizontal transmission between cattle is also probable, and TSEs may also be spread through contact with exposed soil and though ground water (Lacey 1994; Cliffe 1996; *Financial Times* 18 May 1996; *Times Higher Education Supplement*, 20 March 1997; Dealler 1996: 72–5: also 79–80: 12–14; Dealler and Kent 1995: 5–7: 11).

Though the first case of BSE is generally thought to have occurred in a Hampshire herd in 1985, with the first confirmed case recorded from a farm in Kent in November 1986 (Lacey 1994: 2: 23), it is now known that 'bovine scrapie' was diagnosed in a cow from Pitsdown Farm, West Sussex, in September 1985 following the death of ten cattle from a 'mysterious disease' since December 1984 (*Guardian*, 10 February 1998; Elliot 1998; Channel 4 News, 9 March 1998), and it remains possible that MAFF vets were aware of the condition as early as 1982 (*Sunday Times*, 1 July 1990; Dealler and Kent 1995: 11). In 1988 and 1989 MAFF reported six cases as having occurred in 1986, but in 1993 increased the figure to over 60 (Lacey 1994: 23). Since the incubation period of BSE is 4–6 years, sub-clinical infection of cattle found to be infected in 1986 must have occurred between 1980 and 1982, and all confirmed cases of BSE recorded prior to 1990 must have been infected pre-1986 (ibid: 25–5: 65).

Government vets are known to have been prevented from publishing or discussing details of the newly recorded disease. In June 1986 MAFF embargoed the publication of an article which described an infected antelope as having contracted 'scrapie' (Elliot 1998) and in July 1987 Colin Whitaker (a vet) was instructed to remove the words 'scrapie-like' from the title of a slide to be shown as part of a paper to be presented to the Cattle Veterinary Association (*Guardian*, 11 March 1998). By the end of 1987, 420 cases of BSE had been confirmed in Britain, yet the first report of BSE appeared in the specialist press only in October 1987 and after MAFF had insisted that its original title be changed from 'Scrapie in cattle' (Wells *et al.* 1987), and in two short notes a year later in the *Veterinary Record* (*Veterinary Record* 122(18), October 1988; also Shaoul 1996: 6; Lacey 1994: 2: 24–5; Elliot 1998). In 1989 the *British Veterinary Journal* recorded the case of a large farm with a high incidence of BSE infection whose private vet had been warned against talking to the press about the case, and from where Edinburgh Neuropathogenesis Unit (ENU) personnel were ejected by a MAFF official (Dealler 1996: 51).

This lack of public acknowledgment of BSE was the first stage of a long-running attempt by MAFF to control the agenda and prevent public awareness of the issue and its implications for human health. MAFF's reticence on the subject mirrors its performance in a number of other food safety scares; the sharp rise in disease due to listeria during the 1970s and 1980s, the 1988 salmonella outbreak (Gifford n.d.: 26) and the 1996–7 Scottish outbreak of E.coli 157, are the more serious from a range of examples. In each case MAFF's initial approach was denial followed by a reluctant admission of minimal risk until forced to acknowledge a degree of serious risk in the face of overwhelming evidence and public disbelief in its stance. In the case of listeria MAFF initially announced that the bacteria did not cause disease and was not associated with food, and the Central Public Health Laboratory (CPHL) was embargoed from giving information about food and food poisoning (Dealler 1996: 31–3: 165–6). A similar blackout on information was employed in the case of BSE and the CPHL was instructed against preparing reports on BSE and CJD for public dissemination in 1988 (ibid: 34–5: 39).

The Southwood and Tyrrell Reports

Despite MAFF vets diagnosing BSE in 1985, the Department of Health was not informed until March 1988, when officials recorded that action to counter a 'potential plague' was urgent (Elliot 1998). In May MAFF established the Southwood Committee to examine the implications of BSE for animal health and the human population. In June 1988 confirmed cases of BSE had reached 867 (Lacey 1994: 62), yet none of what are regarded as the normal preventative or eradicative measures in such epidemics (e.g. foot and mouth, fowl pest) were initiated: there was no quarantine or slaughter policy, no restrictions on the movement of cattle, no withdrawal of possibly infected land from associated production, or even sample slaughtering to evaluate the scale of the problem.

BSE was made a notifiable disease on the recommendation of the newly established Committee which also recommended that infected cattle should be compulsorily slaughtered and the carcases destroyed with 100 percent compensation. The acceptance of this second recommendation in July was intended to remove meat confirmed as infected by BSE from the human food chain (but not for a further month – almost two years after the disease was diagnosed). Compensation was, however, offered at only 50 percent – a rate which it is widely suggested resulted in the under-reporting of BSE incidence. In July the addition of ruminant derivatives to ruminant feed (cannibalism) was banned on the advice of the Committee which recommended an indefinite extension of the ban in November when they also advised that milk from 'suspect' BSE infected cattle be destroyed, and that a register of the offspring of infected cattle be established. While the ban on suspect milk was implemented, again, with some delay, the last recommendation was not introduced until October 1990 (Lacey 1994: 61).

One month after the Southwood Commission was established the *British Medical Journal* published evidence that BSE posed a potential public health threat (Holt and Phillips 1988: also Morgan 1988; Dealler 1996: 4: 7: 18). Yet the Southwood Report assessed such a threat as 'remote': it is 'most unlikely that BSE will have any implications for human health'. Thus, despite 'the possibility that BSE could be transmitted orally cannot be entirely ruled out, [and] known affected cattle should not enter the human food chain', the Report *declined* to recommend that foods containing the spleen, brain and lymphatic tissue (offals with a known high rate of infectivity) of cattle be labelled as such – the 'risks as at present perceived would not justify this measure'. Manufacturers of baby foods 'should, however, avoid the use of ruminant offal and thymus' (ibid: 67–9).

The moderate nature of Southwood's recommendations and the delay in their implementation contrasts with the pro-active policy of some competitor countries where measures included the slaughter of the entire herd when a diseased cow was discovered. The Report mirrored MAFF's argument that BSE constituted a transitory problem and that there was no evidence of maternal or horizontal transmission. It extrapolated from the statistics and these assumptions to argue that cattle were a 'dead-end-host' and that the epidemic would peak in 1993 with a cumulative toll of 17–20 000 animals, before rapidly declining and disappearing in 1996 (ibid: 61–2: 66–7).

The Southwood Report recorded 2160 confirmed cases of BSE from 1667 farms between November 1986 and December 1988. Despite the Report's reassuring prediction that BSE cases would stabilize at the rate of 350–400 per month (one per thousand), reported cases had risen to 500 per month in January and increased to 900 in December 1989: confirmed cases for 1989 totalled 7136 as against the predicted 4800 (Lacey 1994: 73). In June 1989 the report of the Tyrrell Consultative Committee (established in 1988 on Southwood's recommendation) implicitly questioned some of the earlier Committees' findings. It reported the need for reassurance that BSE would not spread to 'new species', and re-opened the questions of vertical transmission from dam to calf and horizontal transmission within herds by recommending that these questions should be researched. The Committee also called for spot-checks on the brains of apparently healthy cattle and noted the 'urgency' of investigating the relation of BSE to CJD – an 'urgency' which it felt could be satisfied by monitoring the incidence of CJD over the following decades (Tyrrell 1990; also Lacey 1994: 74–82).

MAFF prevaricated on these recommendations: the Report was not published until January 1990 and, while the current £1.3 million research budget was to be raised by £2.2 million, this was delayed until the new financial year (ibid: 82–3). Delay and part measures also attended the June 1989 specified bovine offals (SBO) ban: not until November were the brain, spinal cord, spleen, thymus, intestines and tonsils – all organs of only marginal commercial value – of cattle over six months to be removed from the human food chain. High value cattle parts – liver, kidney, blood, muscle and bone marrow (each with a higher known rate of infectivity than tonsils) – were not included in the ban (Lacey 1994: 83–5: 87; Dealler 1996: 274; also Dealler and Kent 1995: 8–9).

The suppression and manipulation of the scientific evidence

In addition to the suppression of information discussed above, MAFF also has a record of suppressing research into BSE. Examples of research being suppressed in the UK include Harash Narang's research at the Newcastle Public Health Laboratory Service (PHLS) into diagnosing the pre-clinical occurrence of BSE infection (Dealler 1996: 108–11: 119–20; *Guardian*, 13 July 1998; *Observer*, 24 March 1996), Stephen Dealler's statistical work on the scale of the epidemic and its risks for public health (below), and Robert Perry's evidence of the transmission of BSE to the human population (Dealler 1996: 108–11: 119–20; *Observer*, 24 March 1996).

Narang has documented details from his own case in a submission to the 1998 inquiry. He had been actively involved in research on scrapie, CJD and BSE since 1969 and had a record of published research in the field from which he developed the hypothesises of a virus as the infective BSE agent rather than the transmissible Prion which the ENU identified as the cause of the disease in 1987. Narang published details of a negative staining technic for the diagnosis of BSE in 1987 (which he successfully demonstrated to ENU and the Central Veterinary Laboratory, CVL, in 1988 and 1989) and, from 1988, recorded a quantitative and qualitative change in the incidence and form of CJD disease in the North East region which he recognised at autopsy as 'atypical'. This research on the transmission of BSE to humans and further research to develop urine and blood diagnostic tests for BSE and CJD, was halted or disrupted in 1990 by lack of funding, the destruction of his experimental materials on the orders of the head of PHLS, the advice of Ray Bradley (head of CVL) that the private collection of experimental material from abattoirs would be illegal, and his dismissal in 1994 on the grounds of redundancy after two disciplinary inquiries. (Narang 1998: para 1.5–1.10: 2.1–2.21: 2.38–2.73). In this period PHLS attempted to imposed an embargo on the scientific and public dissemination of the results of Narang's work (ibid: 2.18: 2.24–6: 2.33: 2.37–2.38).

Restraints on research were also reported in 1988 by the University of California's San Francisco Department of Biology (recognised as being at the frontline of BSE research): MAFF simply refused access to BSE infected material – apparently because the Department disagreed with the official thesis that BSE would not infect the human population because it was a variant of scrapie (Dealler 1996: 61–2: 63). Similarly Dr Joe Gibbs of the US National Institute of Health reported that he was refused BSE material by MAFF to conduct research (*Despatches*, 11 December 1997).

MAFF's dominance of the arena enabled it to control the scientific agenda and manage outcomes. In the case of the Southwood Committee, four members from the scientific community selected by MAFF sat with three civil servants. Specialists in TSEs were excluded and, of the seven, only John Wilesmith (head of epidemiology at CVL) had expertise in the field while the scientific members had no expertise in public health or published research in TSEs (*Times Higher Education Supplement*, 29 March 1996. Lacey 1994: 58–9; Dealler 1996: chapter 3: 3–31: 108–9; Dealler and Kent 1995: 7). The Committee's members had no detailed knowledge of contemporary or foreign research into either TSEs or BSE (Southwood himself was a professor of Zoology) and were largely dependant on Wilesmith and MAFF officials for guidance and even basic information – the experimental work of Dr Gibbs conducted in 1980 in the US which established that monkeys could contract a TSE by ingesting BSE infected material was not provided to the committee despite Southwood being aware of its existence (*Despatches*, 11 December 1997).

The dependence on MAFF officials which Southwood experienced was one of the control techniques which Richard Lacey (Professor of clinical microbiology at the University of Leeds) has described from his own experience of participating in government advisory bodies (Lacey 1994: 56–7). Second is the intimidation implicit in the existence and threat of the official secrets legislation (in 1997 a *Newsweek* reporter recorded researchers refusing him information for fear of prosecution under the Act (*Newsweek*, 24 March 1997). Third is the state's control over a variety of patronage resources and the power to apply sanctions to dissenting voices. This last includes research grants and the funds which support organisations such as Narang's PHLS. His evidence suggests that PHLS was embarrassed by the involvement of a senior researcher – especially one who dissented from the 'official' position – in a field which had been placed off-limits by a higher authority and risked cuts to its budget if his work was not restrained (Narang 1998: para 2.32: 2.57–2.60: 2.67: 2.71).

Censorship was a another strategy used by MAFF to control the agenda. This was how Ian McGill described events surrounding the proposed publication of a scientific paper on the death in May 1990 of a Siamese cat (Max) from feline TSE. A MAFF press release concerning Max had claimed that there was 'no evidence' that the disease 'is transmissible nor is there any known connection with other animal encephalopathies' (Lacey 1994: 93–4). In 1991 McGill and Gerald Wells were instructed by their superior at CVL – acting on the orders of Keith Meldrum (MAFF's Chief Veterinary Officer from June 1988) – to remove references suggesting a causal linkage of the death with BSE: 'we are not willing for the paper to be published unless these references are removed' (cited in *Despatches*, 11 December 1997).

Thus 'politics drove the science' (McGill, cited in ibid). Southwood has indicated two of the political considerations which directly influenced his committee's recommendations. First, if the Committee regarded the human risk of BSE to the human population as 'remote', there were the more immediate financial consequences of possibly undermining consumer confidence in the UK meat industry to be considered (Southwood, BBC2 *Horizon*, 17 and 18 November 1996). Second, was the existing political consensus: the Committee examined the need for a ban on the use of offal in human food products (a ban which was introduced in 1989, above) and decided that, since many of their recommendations were already regarded as 'pretty revolutionary' by MAFF, such a proposal was simply a 'no-goer' on tactical political grounds (*Times Higher Education Supplement*, 12 April 1996). Dealler has suggested that changes were made to the Southwood Report prior to publication (Dealler 1996: 40) and this perhaps explains the appearance of a congratulatory statement in the Report welcoming MAFF's speed in introducing regulations and the positive response of the food and farming industries (Lacey 1994: 70–1). If this was so, then MAFF had avoided Southwood's own precautions when – following the preparation of the first draft by MAFF officials – he had insisted that the Report be written by Dr Pickles from the Department of Health who had delivered the document to him in person to avoid its interception by MAFF (Elliot 1998).

The Southwood Committee's failure to recommend an SBO ban was utilised by MAFF officials to argue that, since it had not been recommended, there were no scientific grounds for its introduction. This reasoning permitted ministers and officials to reformulate Southwood's conclusions and to argue that there was 'no risk, or indeed any proof of such a risk' to public health from BSE (Meldrum statement to the EU's

Standing Veterinary Committee, cited in EP 1997(1): 9): 'independent experts have concluded that BSE is most unlikely to have any implications for human health' (cited in CEG 1996: 4). It was a rhetoric which was to form the basis of government policy through to 1996: 'we can say with confidence that beef can be eaten safely by everyone, both adults and children' (John Gummer, Minister of Agriculture 1989–93, House of Commons Debate, 21 May 1990).

The assertion that 'there is no scientific evidence' of any public health threat from BSE infected cattle led to the refusal to publicly address or admit to the existence of evidence which suggested that (at the least) the 'balance of probability' would provide a more cautious and safety conscious underpinning to public policy. Not until September 1996 did Ian Pattison (Chief Medical Officer, Ministry of Health) explain that 'safe' means 'negligible risk... it should *not* imply no, or zero, risk'. Such arguments are best viewed as acrobatics in language skills and excuses for misinformation after the event: he had previously advised that 'There is absolutely no evidence whatsoever of a risk to human health' (cited in *Financial Times*, 10 January 1990) and Gillian Shephard (Minister for Agriculture, 1994–5) had cited this official in 1994 when arguing that 'the Chief Medical Officer continues to advise that there is no evidence whatsoever that BSE causes CJD and, similarly, not the slightest evidence that eating beef or hamburgers causes CJD' (cited in CEG 1996: 1).

It was by means of ministerial statements such as these that scientific advisors were described by Tyrrell as having been 'edged into a position of apparent responsibility for public policy-making' as a means of removing responsibility from those who control political decisions (paraphrased in *Times Higher Education Supplement*, 5 April 1996: 12 April 1996). Tyrrell was later to compare MAFF's response to his own report as like 'a plot from *Yes Minister*' and as having left a 'bad taste' (*Times Higher Education Supplement*, 8 July 1998).

The accelerating public health crisis and MAFF's response

In 1989 the incidence of confirmed cases of BSE increased to 7136 per annum and to 1500 per month by December 1990 with the year's total standing at 14 000 – an exponential rise far in excess of Southwood's projections. The Government faced increasing public awareness of, and press interest in, the epidemic and its human implications, to which MAFF reacted by releasing reassuring press statements (Lacey 1994: chapter 6). In February 1990 the impending publication of experimental results which confirmed the species transmissibility of BSE to mice was dismissed by MAFF as 'unnatural' but as confirming MAFF's historic position by providing 'further evidence that BSE behaves like scrapie' (MAFF release, reproduced in ibid: 91). The events associated with the death of a Siamese cat (Max) in May have been referred to above. On 13 May 1990 the *Sunday Times* headlined 'Leading food scientist calls for slaughter of 6m cows'. MAFF responded with three releases repeating the official position that since BSE derived from scrapie and there was no evidence for the vertical or horizontal transmission of the disease, then cattle were a 'dead end host' and there was no threat to human health (Lacey 1994: 94–7). In September new evidence emerged of the susceptibility of pigs to TSEs. A reassuring MAFF press release argued that the Tyrrell Committee saw 'no new implications for human health as a result of this experiment' (ibid: 121–3).

Nevertheless, in February 1990 the compensation to farmers for BSE diseased animals was raised to 100 percent and in September the SBO ban was extended to cover its use in all animal feeds including pig and poultry feeds and pet food. MAFF now announced the introduction of the requirement that farmers keep birth and movement records for all cattle. This followed an EU Commission requirement that computer records be kept for individual cattle and that only cattle from herds shown to be free of BSE for the previous two years be permitted for export. We will see below that this requirement was sabotaged by MAFF.

Infection continued to rise during 1991 with 25 000 confirmed cases, of which 17 percent were cattle under three years old and born at around the time of the feed ban (Lacey 1994: 135–8: 140–1: also 130–1). In March MAFF admitted to the first case of a calf born to a BSE mother since the feed ban but nevertheless itself infected. MAFF now had publicly to admit the 'possibility' of maternal transmission while claiming that this had 'no significance for public health' (ibid: 126–7). 35 000 confirmed cases of BSE (in a 3 per cent smaller herd and in wild contradiction of all the official estimates) were recorded during 1992 and, by December 1993, 6246 confirmed cases of BSE infection had occurred in cattle born after the introduction of the feed ban (ibid: 156). In June 1992 Nicholas Soames, junior Agriculture Minister, had admitted in Parliament that BSE had been experimentally transmitted to five species in addition to cattle (ibid: 143–4). By 1993 BSE had been confirmed as having crossed 23 species barriers to animals which included domestic cats and pigs, and a range of zoo animals including monkeys and apes (Dealler 1996: 147: tables 1–4, pp 264–70; also Lacey 1994: 147). Moreover, medically unexpected deaths were now occurring in the human population – in 1993 two medically unusual deaths from CJD of farmers with BSE infected herds were reported, and in May a fifteen-year-old girl (Vicky Rimmer) was diagnosed CJD positive – a disease which is normally restricted to the old and middle-aged (Lacey 1994: 157–8: 163–4; Dealler 1996: 230). In May 1995 Stephen Churchill became the first victim to succumb to what was to be labelled later as 'new variant'–CJD.

Pressure on the Government increased with the rise in public disquiet following a *Sunday Times* article on 13 March 1994 revealing that of 316 calves born of BSE infected dams and reared in MAFF experimental facilities to guarantee against infection from contaminated feed, 19 had contracted BSE. The evidence for vertical (if not horizontal) transmission was now clear (Lacey 1994: 174–5) yet it was not until June that the SBO ban was extended to include the guts and thymus of cattle under six months (ibid: 178–9). MAFF shifted its explanation of the epidemic by arguing that its continuing force resulted from farmers (and feed processors) having continued to administer contaminated feed despite the 1988 ban (ibid: 138–9: 155–6; Narang 1998: para 2.64; Dealler 1986: 185–8). This explanation was not disinterested. In 1990 the Institute of Environmental Health had warned MAFF of widespread contraventions of the SBO ban (ITV, *World in Action*, 17 June 1996). Enforcement procedures were not, however, tightened until July 1995. In the meantime the February 1992 changes in the inspection and reporting procedure and the April 1994 reduction in compensation to the market value of older cattle – both on the advertised expectation that the numbers of infected cattle was expected to fall (Lacey 1994: 139–40; Dealler and Kent 1995: 5) – resulted in accusations from individual farmers and environmentalists that BSE infected cattle were being mis-diagnosed by MAFF vets. They argued that this effectively prevented their subsequent slaughter by private vets from counting in the BSE statistics and contributing to the growing evidence of vertical transmission (Lacey 1994: 164–9; Dealler 1996: 203–5: 234–5; Dealler and Kent 1995: 5).

Thus the statistics on the incidence of BSE and the scale of the epidemic were becoming a matter of increasing controversy. In November 1993 Dealler published preliminary calculations revealing significant under-reporting of BSE in 1989, 1992 and 1993 (Dealler 1993; 1996: 138–71: 177–9: 186–93). MAFF's published statistics for the latter years concealed an under-reporting of infection among cattle born after the feed ban and the likelihood of vertical transmission (Dealler 1996: 208–11: tables 20–1). Dealler's calculations also suggested that a large number of the population had already consumed the small quantities of infected meat necessary to develop the human form of BSE. Publication was preceded by an editorial in *Nature* pointing to the long-standing knowledge of the possibility of inter-species cross infection by TSEs and raising the question of possible jail terms for individuals shown to have failed to take action to prevent the transfer of BSE to the human population if such was to be shown to have occurred (*Nature*, September 1993, reproduced in Lacey 1994: 160–2).

In July 1994 the EU extended its existing ban on the export from Britain of cattle without a certificate of origin which recorded the home herd as BSE-free, to cover the previous six years, and expanded it to veal calves (ibid: 179; Dealler and Kent 1995: 9–10). By September 1994 the total number of cattle confirmed as having been infected with BSE stood at almost 140 000 including some 12 400 born after the feed ban (Lacey 1994: 2: 25: 179). Although the numbers of confirmed BSE cases continued to run at about 800 per week, the year's recorded total fell to 25 570 (Dealler 1996: 225; Lacey 1994: 161). By the end of 1995 BSE had been confirmed in 159 000 cattle on 32 000 farms in the UK and the May 1996 total of 165 000 confirmed cases of BSE were calculated to include some 27 000 animals born since the introduction of the 1988 feed ban (ITV, *World in Action*, 17 June 1996). These statistics reveal that either mass criminal activity (feeding contaminated feed to cattle long after the ban, either from old stocks or from feeds contaminated in the plants) by farmers had gone entirely undetected by MAFF inspectors, or that the assertion of the non-transmissibility of BSE between cattle had been false.

The continuing deficiencies in inspection procedures are given a note of conspiracy by the revelation, in 1996, that MAFF documents showed officials to have been instructed that the EU's 1990/1994 requirements regarding the certification of exported animals were to be deliberately ignored. Civil servants had been instructed that checks should be made on only 10 percent of exported stock and in March a MAFF junior minister admitted that in 1995 alone 1800 consignments of animals to the continent had been exported with documents which ministers were now told were illegal (Dealler and Kent 1995: 9–10; *Guardian*, 14 December 1994, 12 April and 20 August 1996). Moreover, in the wake of the widespread accusations since 1990 that the SBO ban was being widely contravened, and the accusations of under-reporting of BSE infection which followed the 1992 changes in the inspection procedures, it was not until September 1995 that procedures were tightened, and not until November that the mechanical removal of meat from the backbone (the site of the spinal cord) was banned (a failure which had helped conserve costs for slaughterhouses). Yet in April 1996 deficient procedures were still being recorded in slaughter houses and Douglas Hogg (Minister of Agriculture) admitted four instances of serious failure to extract infectious spinal cord from carcasses between January and March alone (CEG 1996: 9).

The human health risk and political crisis

In November 1995 Dealler and Kent published revised estimates of cattle succumbing to BSE and of the scale of the threat to the human population (Dealler and Kent 1995). Dealler calculated that seven percent – 230 000 animals – of cattle born since the 1988 feed ban were BSE infected. He calculated that by 2001 (and assuming that no cattle born after 1991 became infected) the UK population would have consumed an estimated 1.8 million cattle which would otherwise have died of BSE if they had lived to ten years old, and a further 8 million cattle which might not show the signs of BSE even at that age because infected later in their life cycle than the younger group (Dealler 1996: 212–13: tables 22: 27). Millions of the human population could thus be calculated to have already eaten infected meat and many of these to have consumed a potentially fatal dose (ibid: 212–13: 169–70: tables 14–15: 29–30; Dealler and Kent 1996).

November also saw the public broadcasting of estimates that some three-quarters of a million infected cattle had been eaten by the human population – 250 000 of them since the feed ban was introduced. Narang conducted tests for the programme which resulted in his diagnosing 29 percent of a sample of cattle described as free of BSE as being infected with the disease. Meldrum confirmed this result when, after refusing to answer whether the numbers of BSE infected cattle consumed by the public was known, he admitted that for every cow with BSE symptoms two others incubating the disease would have entered the human food chain (ITV, *World in Action*, November 1995; also Dealler 1996: 224–8: 234: 236: 237). The programme aroused renewed and extensive press and radio interest. MAFF officials, however, continued to parrot the claims that 'There is no evidence that there is any threat to humans from BSE', and that inspectors removed all infected cattle at markets and prevented infectious material entering the food chain. Prime Minister Major repeated the claim that 'there is currently no scientific evidence that BSE can be transmitted to humans or that eating beef caused CJD … beef is a safe and wholesome product' (Dealler 1996: 242).

However, in March 1966 the ENU identified a degeneration of the brain in young victims of CJD similar to that seen in BSE-infected cattle, and informed SEAC who advised the Government that the ten CJD deaths in victims aged between 25 and 41 possibly resulted from ingesting BSE-infected meat (*Times Higher Education Supplement*, 8 May 1998; Elliot 1998). The situation was judged so serious that Deputy Prime Minister Heseltine suggested that almost 12 million cattle would have to be slaughtered and Hogg that the entire national herd might have to be sacrificed (*Guardian*, 1 August 1998). On the 20th the Government, fearing that this information would be exposed in the media and that its own credibility and ability to manage opinion and determine the agenda would be undermined, made an announcement in the Commons. Stephen Dorrell (Minister for Health) admitted that BSE might be related to a new – 'variant' – strain of Creutzfeldt-Jakob Disease (nv-CJD). Ian Pattison and Ministry of Health officials admitted that projections of the new disease indicated that it could become a major public health problem; 'at one extreme there is a risk of an epidemic' (ibid: 246; Gifford n.d.: 22). Only now was MAFF constrained to issue new regulations banning the use of all mammalian meat and bonemeal in all animal feed (in June all such feeds were recalled and in August it was made a criminal offence for it to be retained on farms or in mills) and expand the list of SBOs to include headmeat and lymph glands.

Nevertheless, the Government continued in its claims regarding the safety of British beef. Hogg declared that the bans imposed by France and Belgium on the import of British beef were illegal and sought a directive to that effect in the European Council. One week later, however, that body itself banned the import of British beef into the entire Union. In the ensuing negotiations the Government was forced to concede the slaughter of all cattle over 30 months old – a cull which claimed 1.65 million animals in the following year but a 'concession' which, with others, failed to remove the ban.

The Ortega Report and the aftermath

The inadequacies of the British Government's response to the BSE epidemic contradicted the emergent consensus based on the existing evidence of the seriousness of the BSE epidemic, and may be measured by the position of the Consumers in Europe Group (CEG 1996), or by the resolution of the European Regional Conference of the OIE in 1990 that measures against the disease 'must include *at least* the identification of all cattle and the slaughter and destruction of *suspect* animals' and that the *'suspicion* and occurrence of BSE should be made compulsorily notifiable' (italic added, OIE 1990: resolution 1; 3).

The UK Government's failure to take these precautionary measures was examined by an EU Committee of Inquiry. The Ortega Report indicted the British Government for having contravened Article 5 of the European Treaty by failing to honour undertakings made to the Council in 1990 regarding surveillance of herds and the inspection of slaughterhouses and carcasses, by failing to implement the EU requirement of the computerised identification of cattle and their movements, and by failing to prevent exports of cattle from BSE-infected herds or to ensure that exported animal products complied with health standards (EP 1997(1): Part I, section 2: 11–12: 13).

On 17 February 1997 the European Parliament voted by 422 to 49 (with 48 abstentions) in support of the Report (*Strasbourg Notebook* 1997(2); 1997(1); EP 1997(3)) which also recorded the British Government's 'blocking tactics', its refusal to release documents and the refusal of Hogg to give evidence to the inquiry. The Report recorded that the EU's Standing Veterinary Committee had endorsed the British Government's position that there was 'no risk' to public health from BSE, and that this resulted in part from its BSE subgroup being chaired by Ray Bradley (head of CVL 1969–91, subsequently a MAFF advisor) who had also acted as rapporteur to the full Veterinary Committee. The Report also notes that the committee minutes have been seen by some as suggesting that Bradley (who was assisted by a temporary Commission official who was also formerly employed by MAFF) may have withheld evidence from the full committee (EP 1997(1): 25: 32).

The Report also records that dissident experts had 'admitted that they were subject to massive British pressure' (EP 1997(2): 5). The Commission itself had also come under political pressure to cease BSE-related checks in British slaughterhouses (EP 1997(1): 28: 29; 1997(2): 13) and Jacques Santer, Commission President, claimed to have 'received threats and pressure on a major scale from the British government' (*News Report,* Strasbourg, 15 January 1997; also EP 1997(2): 13). The Report argued that in using such tactics, 'the UK Government has...exerted pressure on the Commission's veterinary services... thus avoiding inspections and preventing publicization of the extent of the epidemic' (EP 1997(1): 14–15: also 28).

The Government committed £3.5 billion to the slaughter of 3.65 million cattle initiated in 1996. Yet the EU's lack of confidence in the capacity of the British state to enforce regulations, or in its determination to do so, was evidenced in March 1997 when a fresh scandal erupted over a 1995 report which the Meat Hygiene Service (which had taken responsibility for abattoir hygiene from local authorities) had forwarded to MAFF. It detailed failures of dirty plant and contaminated carcasses in abattoirs as well as the failure to properly remove spinal cord material. Bill Swan (its author) accused MAFF of suppressing the report by rewriting it to reflect what MAFF claimed was a 'considered view' and by failing to publish it. Despite MAFF claims that the document had been circulated to interested parties who included the Scottish Office and Ian Pennington (then heading the inquiry into the recent outbreak of E.coli infection in Scotland) all denied knowledge of its existence (Channel 4 News, 6 and 7 March 1997; *Guardian*, 6 March 1997; 7 March 1997; 8 March 1997).

The 1998 BSE inquiry

In January 1997 projections for the scale of a possible human epidemic of nv-CJD made on the basis of the existing data and a variety of limiting factors gave an estimate of possible outcomes which ranged between 213 and 80000 human deaths per annum by the year 2040 (Channel 4, News, 15 January 1997). At the end of September two independent studies each concluded that their data 'provide compelling evidence' of a link between BSE and nv-CJD (*Guardian*, 30 September 1997). By the end of the year official nv-CJD victims totalled 23 (an increase of nine over the year) rising to 27 by July 1998. In December SEAC was reported as describing BSE and nv-CJD as virtually the same disease (*Guardian*, 23 December 1997) and the new Labour Government announced an independent inquiry under Lord Justice Philips to investigate the BSE affair. MAFF was reported as supporting the new inquiry as a means by which to avoid litigation by the families of nv-CJD victims (Channel 4 News, October 1997). Such an inquiry had been rejected by the Conservative Government in March 1996 with the arguments that it would undermine public confidence in beef and offer an excuse to continue the European ban, but that a judicial inquiry might become necessary at a later date to deflect further investigation of the affair by Parliament (*Guardian*, 1 August 1998).

At the time of writing, the Inquiry had not published its report. However, evidence presented to it elaborates on many of the details reported above. The Inquiry took evidence suggesting that a BSE-like disease had occurred sporadically in the US since at least the 1960s, which suggested that BSE was endemic to cattle, if rare (*Guardian*, 10 March 1998). It heard Roy Anderson, an Oxford professor of epidemiology, describe CVL as secretive and recount how he had been repeatedly refused access to the MAFF database on the spread of BSE to conduct a new statistical analysis of the incidence of BSE infection (*Times Higher Education Supplement*, 8 July 1998). The Inquiry was also shown video evidence that cattle were being buried in secret pits on a massive scale at least until 1997, and heard Lacey's estimate that as many as one million BSE-infected cattle were being disposed of in this way every year as a means of hiding evidence of the continuing epidemic by farmers seeking to have their farms declared free of the disease. MAFF had rejected the video evidence (Guardian, 18 March 1998; Channel 4 News, 17 and 19 March 1999).

Narang gave evidence that the official figures for the human death toll were inaccurate. He presented evidence that a victim of what was probably nv-CJD had succumbed in 1984 and that at least 16 deaths to the disease were not officially attributed to it in the period to the end of 1997. This suggests that, as with BSE, deaths are being attributed to an inappropriate cause and that the scale of the human epidemic is already being underestimated (Narang 1998: para 3.1–3.3: 4.1).

Richard Southwood also gave evidence. He reported Derek Andrews, Permanent Secretary at MAFF, as having expressed the hope in 1988 that, in the face of the possible conclusion that meat from BSE-infected cattle should not be consumed, the recommendations of the committee 'would not lead to an increase in public expenditure'. Southwood also gave evidence that the Committee's estimate in 1988 was that BSE would infect a total of some 70 000 to 90 000 cattle but that the Report limited the figure to 25 000 after Wilesmith had criticised the larger figure as being 'much too high' (*Observer*, 23 March 1998, *Guardian*, 12 March 1998, 6 March 1998).

Conclusion

The Government's failure in attending to the BSE epidemic has been explained in terms of MAFF's institutional commitment to the achievement of having rebuilt agriculture and provisioning the population with cheap food in the period since 1945, and to sheer incompetence or the desire to protect past decisions by actions which compounded the original error. MAFF officials may well have performed their duties in the context of the Ministry's established institutional interests, nevertheless they operated in the political climate established by the government of the day, at the direction of ministers and within the parameters established by their decisions. The incoming Thatcher government was ideologically committed to deregulation. In 1979 it ignored the recommendation of a Royal Commission on Environmental Pollution that the feeding of rendered animal remains to ruminants be banned and abandoned existing draft regulations on animal feed. In 1981 legislation established self-regulation in the rendering industry (Gifford n.d.; Shaoul 1996; *Observer*, 22 December 1996). The UK food safety regime was further loosened when a Food Safety Act introduced the defence of 'due diligence' by which food manufacturers could claim to have undertaken reasonable precautions to avoid infringement of regulations, and an Environmental Protection Act introduced the concept of 'Best available technique not entailing excessive cost' (Shaoul 1996: 22: 52).

In its discussion of the UK Government's responsibility for the BSE crisis the Ortega Report found that the problem lay in 'the attitude of the government, which has failed to ensure the proper application of [legislative] measures…doubtless under pressure from the meat industry' (EP 1997(1): 14–15). Shaoul explored these themes in an examination of the relationship between the British state and the meat industry. He shows MAFF to have supported large-scale restructuring in the slaughter and rendering industries where monopolist and oligopolist enterprises became dominant during the 1980s. In this period horizontal mergers and vertical integration resulted in the emergence of Prosper de Mulder (PDM) with a share of 64 percent of the red meat waste market (Shaoul 1996: 40: 41–60: 58). MAFF submissions to the Monopolies and Mergers Commission (MMC) in 1991 and 1993 are recorded as indistinguishable from those of the rendering industry and as supportive of PDM's performance. MAFF granted derogations to abattoirs from full compliance with EC health regulations in 1977 and 1992 (ibid: 31–2) and complained of the additional costs and inconvenience which BSE-related regulations threatened to impose on the industry (ibid: 48–49: 54–5). The Department of the Environment was also supportive of the existing regime in evidence to MMC (ibid: 49) and in 1993 granted derogations to renderers in respect of EC environmental regulations (ibid: 49–50: 52–6). Shaoul argues that the MMC has also consistently placed the financial interests of PDM above considerations of public health in three reports (1985, 1991 and 1993) which supported concentration in the rendering industry and the easing of environmental regulation (ibid: 44: 58: 41–60).

It was the Government's ideological commitment to a policy of deregulation and the support which ministers, civil servants and state agencies thereby gave to creating the conditions for reducing costs (and thus increasing profits) in the food industry which led to the abandonment of established public health protections in the 1980s and, between 1992 and 1996, to the rejection of recommendations that an Animal Feeding Stuffs Advisory Committee be established. The latter was rejected on the grounds that 'it is almost bound to recommend tightening regulations' (Soames, cited in *Guardian*, 23 March 1998; also Channel 4 News, 20 March 1998). We have noted the hope expressed by the PS at MAFF in 1988 that Southwood's recommendations 'would not lead to an increase in public expenditure'.

Deregulation policies were politically controversial in themselves and the rising incidence of a range of food-related threats to human health held the risk that informed debate of the issues involved would undermine the Government's strategy to re-orientate the economy on strengthened free-market principles. As the crisis developed the scale of the BSE epidemic undermined the official position that BSE was not transmissible between cattle or across the species barrier and therefore represented no threat to the human population. The government's early inaction conditioned later choices. New measures to protect veterinary and public health would have involved a vastly higher level of public expenditure than would have been necessary at an early stage of the crisis and contained the risk of alerting the opposition, the media and the public to the existence of the potential dangers which policy implemented to deregulate food production – and thus the Government itself – had been largely responsible for creating.

Informed public debate was avoided by the expedient of continuing to deny the existence of any veterinary or public health problem and by the suppression of evidence and information. Government enrolled individual members of the scientific community to obtain what could be presented as scientific support for the contention of 'no threat to the public from eating beef'. Investigations were 'managed' by civil servants and findings and advice were manipulated and/or presented to imply scientific support for the Government's position. 'Dissidents' in the scientific community were rubbished or ignored.

Inaccurate or false statements by ministers and officials which constituted lying by omission and commission were necessary if the official 'line' were to be credible and deregulation policy continue to be politically viable. They were the inevitable corollary of the desire to protect both the industry and the Government from effective scrutiny and from public and political accountability.

Conclusions

Maureen Ramsay and Lionel Cliffe

Examination of the political contexts in which lying takes place in these case studies has revealed that political explanations for deception are not the claims of realpolitik, nor are they requirements of successful policy, still less the desire to serve the national or the public interests. The cases discussed in this book reveal that these political deceptions were not driven or justified by needs of this sort.

The Watergate lies were defended by federal officials under the guise of national security. National security justifications in this case functioned to cover up illegal acts by Republican party officials seeking to ensure the re-election of Nixon. Lies told to the American public about Vietnam were not motivated by the need to promote the national interest, but by the need to avoid democratic accountability for actions and policies which were incompatible with the beliefs and values of many American citizens. Debate about the escalation of the war under President Johnson was suppressed because he could not rely on popular support for such policies. Nixon's clandestine bombing of Laos and Cambodia and his attempt to mislead the public over the 1970 invasion of Cambodia were motivated by concern about public and congressional resistance to widening the war in Indochina. The 'war on drugs' had a different logic. A particular strategy of exporting a war on drugs was adopted with a great fanfare to give the illusion this widespread problem was being tackled and to avoid confronting the powerful interests behind the drug trade. The Reagan administration's attempt to conceal trading arms for hostages with Iran and its illegal supply of arms to Nicaragua cannot be explained by the need to protect national interests. Secrecy was necessary to avoid the effects of popular disapproval about dealing with a regime linked to terrorism and US military support for the Contras in Nicaragua.

There was a similar motivation behind the British government's attempt to cover up arms sales to Iraq after the Iran–Iraq war in contradiction to the government's own stated policy. The Scott Report (1996) showed that the cloak of national security and appeal to the national interest was used to defend the decision not to announce the policy on arms sales. But a more plausible explanation for the decision was to minimise public hostility to arms trading with oppressive regimes and the fear that public concern over Iraq's human rights record could jeopardise post-war deals with Iraq (Phythian and Little, 1993:305).

When British ministers lied to Parliament and the electorate about the link between the provision of overseas aid and arms sales in the Pergau Dam affair, the decision was defended in the national interest by the need to increase trade and to protect jobs. But the deception itself cannot be adequately explained or justified with reference only to these broad aims. The policy originally was concealed in order to prevent Parliament and the public from recognising the significant role private political and economic interests of politicians and industrialists played in the affair.

The British government's attempts to minimise public knowledge of the risks of BSE being transmitted to humans can only be justified or explained by the need to protect the public interest if the interests of the beef industry are identical to the public interest. If the public interest includes public health, then the decision which effectively subordinated public health to the vested economic interests of the rendering, food processing and farming sections of industry may partially explain the need for misinformation, disinformation and the managing of public opinion during the BSE crisis, but cannot justify it.

Lies endorsed by the legal system and government about the killings on Bloody Sunday have yet to be officially admitted. Inaccurate statements, disinformation given to the media and in the courts, and the state's failure to prosecute in the 'shoot to kill' incidents were defended in the interests of national security. But, the massive efforts at deliberate concealment of the truth in all these incidents, even to the extent of fabrications against Stalker, cannot be justified or explained with reference to this end. Deception was rather the result of political expediency, and can be explained by the need to present the unjustified uses of lethal force as legitimate and by the need to conceal political and military decisions from the judgements of the public.

In all these cases, political deception is not explained by any national or public interest, but variously by personal ambition, by the desire to stay in or consolidate power and to protect the interests of the policy makers, by the need to conceal the influence of corporate, commercial or unelected sectional interests on policy making, by the need to minimise public hostility and to avoid political exposure and democratic accountability for actions and policies which are at odds with public beliefs and convictions.

These deceptions are not justified on consequentialist grounds for two reasons. One, because they cannot be defended as necessary to achieve a 'just end', and two, because even if their perpetrators believed they were acting in the national or the public interest, the justice of the means is questionable given that harms caused by the deceptions outweighed the good intended. In all these cases lies and secrecy had negative or counterproductive effects. The costs of the deceptions as we have seen were variously political, personal, financial, economic and social. Moreover, any justification for these deceptions is further undercut because they violate democratic principles. If citizens are misled or not told the truth, if through secrecy and deception they lack the information to participate in and consent to decisions, if the government does not represent their views and is not held to account for its policies, then this undermines the democratic ideal and shows that real existing democracies are undemocratic in that they do not permit genuine participation and real accountability.

The political deceptions discussed in this book are not justified on consequentialist grounds nor are they justified in a democracy. But what is wrong and unjustified here is not simply the deception, but that deception itself is possible, because of the various ways political power is insufficiently checked and controlled in so-called democratic societies. This is a formal procedural problem, an institutional or structural wrong about the absence or violation of processes which legitimate a democratic state. But there is a more substantive wrong in that the circumstances that cause lies to be necessary involve not just a violation of democratic procedures, but a violation of democratic values and norms. This happens when the circumstances that require lies to be told are themselves the result of the power of economic and private interests to achieve their own selective ends at the expense of democratic governments' obligation to act in the general interests to further the common good.

In the Pergau Dam affair, it is not just the lies told about civil aid and arms that is wrong, nor just that Parliamentary action was unable to mount an effective challenge to obtain any redress. What is wrong is a situation where powerful industrial interests can predispose a state to act in support of private economic interests.

In deceptions about food safety in the BSE case what is wrong is not just the lack of information about public health. What is wrong is the myopic policy of de-regulation that in part caused the problem to arise by removing protections in order to increase profits in the food industry . What we need to morally evaluate is policies which put producers before consumers, policies that protect the 'free market' at the expense of public health. What needs to be criticised is the inappropriate political and industrial interests that determine decisions on food safety, the lack of executive authority about what happens on farms, and the state's lack of independence from the interests of the food retailing, processing and rendering sections of industry. More broadly, we need to call into question the post-war commitment to intensive agriculture and modern farming practices and methods of animal rearing.

In the 'shoot to kill' incidents, it is not just the lies sanctioned by the judiciary and the government that is wrong, but the actions and policies that the lies were intended to cover up – the unjustified use of lethal force by the security forces and the state's failure to address the causes of the initially unjust situation in Northern Ireland. In the many cases of US covert interventions, and specifically in the Iran–Contra affair, it is not just the lies, cover-ups and the fact that decisions were made by a foreign policy making machinery located outside government not subject to democratic accountability that is wrong, and in this case of dubious legality. The policy of supplying arms to foreign governments and leaders of repressive regimes, and to overthrow governments, has to be questioned. Similarly, what was wrong in the arms to Iraq affair was not just the fact that ministers deceived Parliament and the public about export licensing of arms at the end of the Iran–Iraq war, nor just that the structures and accepted practices of the British parliamentary system made it possible for politicians to hide the policy. What is wrong is the underlying economic strategy which seeks to remove every obstacle to capitalist profitability. That is, the whole policy of arms-related sales and the arms economy which in order to boost civilian and military trade and to get return on investment must export and continue to export arms to odious regimes.

In this book we have argued against political realists who believe that secrecy and lies in politics are necessary, inevitable and justified on consequentialist grounds. We have argued that justifying secrecy and lies is particularly problematic in politics because of the difficulty in agreeing on a just end and because secrecy and lies often cause more harm than good, not least because they are incompatible with democratic principles. We have further argued that trying to defend secrecy and lies in politics diverts attention from the fact that many cases of deception in politics are not defensible on consequentialist grounds. What we should be concerned with in politics is not whether lies are necessary, inevitable or justified, but the conditions that make lying possible and the situations that create the need for lies. It is these which require moral scrutiny and improvement.

We have attempted to bring theoretical and analytic perspectives to bear on individual cases of government deception in order to offer some explanation of how liberal democracies accommodate lies as well as why political lying is such a pervasive phenomena within them. Although we do not offer a new or general theory that explains all and every government deception, our exploration and arguments in individual cases about how governments lie, why they lie and what they lie about, can be synthesised and drawn together. Our analysis suggests that these cases are only examples which illustrate, and are symptomatic of, patterns of deceit which inevitably arise and will continue to arise as a result of the structures, institutions and power relations in real existing democracies.

It would seem that political deceptions are possible because of the private, secretive and exclusive nature of state power that characterises liberal democracy (c.f. Markovits and Silverstein 1988). This is compatible with Robertson's (1982) view that deception is the outcome of a centralised and political hegemony, the structure of political authority and within that the interests and in particular the ability politicians have to maintain their power and control. This indicates that there is an institutional or structural fault which creates the conditions for political deception and that this arises from the nature of elite-orientated democracies. This is a formal procedural problem about centralised power, ineffective mechanisms of accountability, lack of due process and democratic control.

Political deceits are intrinsic to the process of wielding power and to the nature of political authority when power and authority are insufficiently checked and controlled. Lies are possible in elite democracies because the absence of control not only provides politicians with incentives to lie to maintain office, but provides easy opportunities for them to lie to cover up private gain or to promote selective interests.

Some forms of political lies are inevitable in elite democracies not just for procedural reasons, but because they are structurally functional to the preservation of elite democracy. They are necessary to prevent dissent and to maintain and promote the economic, social and political interests of private groups. They are a reflection of the power of these groups to achieve their will at the expense of the common good. If this function did not need to be obscured there would be no need for lies.

Given this, perhaps it would be more 'realistic' for political realists to concentrate on changing those aspects of political and economic life that need change in order to reduce the ability and need for secrecy and lies in politics, rather than defend them as necessary or justified.

The struggle for democratic accountability: constraining and exposing official lying and seeking the truth

These conclusions seek to offer findings about practice as well as about our theoretical understanding and analytical explanations of the phenomenon of lying in politics. In this part we ask: if an adequately and accurately informed public is crucial to democratic practice, how can it be more thoroughly realised? Two kinds of answers are explored. First, the measures that should be expected of the state and its institutions and servants to improve the flow of information from governments and make them more accountable. Included here will be assessment of such measures as Freedom of Information legislation, which has existed in the USA and many other democratic countries for some years, but has also only just been put on the agenda in the UK. What are the lessons for future practice of government personnel and for future reform? A second, less commonly discussed, issue explores what citizens and bodies in civil society can do to equip themselves with more complete information, in the teeth of a political climate of secrecy and lies, what Chomsky calls 'intellectual self-defence'. Here again, we will have recourse to the cases, seeking to extract lessons of what modes of public investigation have led to revelations, and what combination of scepticism, muckraking and questioning might have revealed more, earlier. Beyond that we will explore what old and new methods can be used in this era of information technology by citizens and groups who are not content to be left in the dark or to be mystified.

What should be expected of the state?

Our general discussion of contexts and practices in the USA and the UK have shown that these states consistently fall short of providing the openness and accuracy of information, especially about policies and the policy-making process in controversial areas, required to guarantee accountability and participation. The detailed case-studies further substantiate this conclusion as well as charting major instances where governments actively lied. Moreover, one characteristic shared by these cases is that in each of them the deception was eventually uncovered. One must assume that there are other parts of the iceberg which remain below the surface. These findings clearly imply reform of institutions, their practices and cultures. But what changes are needed depends on one's answers to the issues of explanation of why the phenomenon occurs, which we explored in Chapter 3. If lying is seen as inherent in the character of politics or of the modern state or of capitalist democracies in general, that would support either a pessimistic view of making significant changes or point to sweeping social as well as political reform as a prerequisite. For those who located some, if not all, the slippage from democratic norms more at the level of the particular states and their structures, then constitutional and administrative reform might be expected to change the practice significantly.

High on the list of requirements for accountability is freedom of information legislation. The arguments for such FOI Acts are familiar, and will not be rehearsed here. However, the experience of the USA, where an Act has been on the statute books for over 20 years, can be instructive. It certainly acts as an effective device for individuals to get information about what information governments hold about them, and for facilitating investigation of certain broader policy issues – certainly compared with Britain. However, the persistence of official deception implies that this is not a sufficient condition to ensure adequate informing of the public. One shortcoming in practice lies in the fact that FOI's ability to reduce secrecy depends on what information is classified as 'secret' or beyond limits according to the law in the first place. Moreover, it does not ensure the accuracy of such information as is released to the public. Much depends on these and other actual provisions in a FOI: Sweden's allows for much more openness than that in the U.S, for instance (see Robertson, 1982).

The UK Government of John Major did adopt a code of 'open government', but resisted legislation which would entrench any 'right' to information. The conventional argument against it has always been that revelations about the policy-making process would inhibit the freedom of civil servants in proffering advice, which reputedly was a cornerstone of the principle of 'cabinet responsibility'. The new Labour government came to power having maintained a manifesto commitment to FOI since 1974, and immediately promised legislation. But its introduction onto the Parliamentary agenda has been postponed and the soon-to-be-published draft bill does reportedly have an unduly long list of exclusions: as well as security services, the list includes law enforcement functions of the police, immigration and other government departments, privatised utilities, and civil service advice to ministers. Under this last provision, much of what was painfully extracted from the Scott and BSE inquiries would not ordinarily be available. Official proposals also seem to envisage continuation of the measure introduced into the 1989 rewriting of the Official Secrets Act that there will be no 'public interest' defence for whistle-blowers.

Another set of issues have arisen with the developments of Information Technology. At an official level, IT makes possible the electronic distribution of government documents, reports, statistics, and on a larger-scale than by print. However, both the US and the UK Governments, bent on 'privatisation', have introduced or are considering commercial channels for this distribution. More information *may* be available, but at a price, and thus not readily available for the less affluent citizen, or for campaigning groups rather than businesses. This relates to a more fundamental political issue: whether the information superhighway takes a hierarchical form, or the 'flatter', more dispersed model of the Internet, which has, arguably, much more democratic potential (see Kranich, 1995). This issue is made more complex as a more hierarchical structure could facilitate the 'invasion of public space' either to allow more government control ('pornography' is the common justification here) or monopolisation by IT corporate giants. Certainly the protection of public space (by shaping the information highway on the 'model of the library rather than the shopping mall') is one of the reforming measures that is crucial. The task of doing this seems likely to be harder in the USA (Hirschkop, 1996) than in the UK and Europe (Wheeler, 1998), where academic, non-commercial elements of the web are still resisting commercialisation.

Intellectual self-defence

There have been major debates in the literature and in politics around FOI and what other demands/requirements the state should have to fulfill. The consequent issue of what rights and recourse individuals and associations in civil society should have when governments maintain secrecy and are suspected of lying, even in the teeth of laws on openness, is hardly ever raised. Certainly if 'democracy' is defined as depending as much on the attributes of the political system, and of civil society and not just of the state, then this implies not only rights but duties to break through and around government's secrecy, lying and obfuscation. But are there any practical guidelines as to how this 'Lifting the Lid', as Northmore (1996) calls it, might be done? Certainly the case-studies in this volume offer some answers to this broad question through a consideration of their processes of unravelling. With hindsight we know much about what really occurred and about the official deception involved in these cases because all but the war on drugs eventually became the subject of some sort of official inquiry, whose reports, and even evidence sometimes, entered the public record. These documents themselves, and not just the summaries presented in our chapters and other literature, repay study, even if they are now matters of history, for what they reveal about the kind of practices that can be expected of those in authority – their motives, attitudes and techniques of deception. They also suggest another possibility for popular investigation: the study of the routine and mundane in official publications and, now, electronic information. Among examples, the Pergau Dam affair might be cited: it was the routine report of the Public Accounts Committee of the Commons that was the initial source of much of the evidence, which was then picked up on by the press and campaigning groups. Northmore (1996) offers a handy list of UK official handbooks which can be read to reveal information and prompt questions on foreign policy and other matters of state; Negrine (1996) offers a similar insight into the use of official economic data. Chomsky, whose views have been discussed in this volume, repays a reading for his method of argumentation is one based on a wealth of empirical information, often derived from official documents which he uses to find out what governments do not want known, especially the 'real' nature of policy. He also uses the media that he pillories for its subservience to good effect; one of his techniques is to compare systematically different sources, including the foreign reporting of events. A master of both of these techniques was the Washington-based journalist, I. F. Stone, who put out his own weekly paper single-handedly for almost 20 years. In seeking to expose, but in a manner that was sober and accurate enough that readers of all political persuasions would 'take my findings and analyses seriously', but where he could lay 'no claim to "inside stuff" or private sources of the government', he used painstaking searching of what was in the public domain to take 'the flotsam of the week's news and make it sing' (Middleton, 1973: 312).

The role of the media as a source of revelation rather than deception is certainly part of the equation. In several of our cases, press investigations played their part in creating a climate where denial was difficult to maintain, and helped to precipitate inquiries: the Watergate scandal UK comes particularly to mind. But commentators on both sides of the Atlantic have bewailed the decline of 'investigative journalism' (as distinct from the other kind, presumably?).

A crucial source for some of the revelations have been 'whistleblowers' – notably, 'Deep Throat' in Watergate, some drug enforcement officials, Ponting over the sinking of the *Belgrano*, a small number of scientists over BSE. Such people should be regarded as the heroes of civil society, but in UK they are given no legal protection and little, if any, boost by the media or organised opinion in either country. The passing on of any such revelations might be expected to be easier in the IT era.

Interest groups, campaigning organisations and other associations of civil society have played a role as sources and conduits of alternative information and exposés. The Pergau arms-for-aid issue was investigated and government was pursued through the courts by the World Development Movement; anti-Indochina War groups helped expose issues such as the bombing of Laos; environmental groups provide alerts nowadays on environmental health and pollution concerns. Again, their investigations and the dissemination of any findings can be aided by the Internet. But more of this kind of alternative information is required and might be forthcoming as people realise that some sources are available and the public is not entirely condemned to knowing only what those in power want them to know. Such work must be based on a healthy and democratic scepticism about information and its sources. The maxim of Mandy Rice-Davies, a woman caught up in the scandal of the 1950s involving the UK Defence Minister Profumo, is a usefully sceptical watchword for scrutinising the activities of those in power. When challenged by the press with a peer of the realm's denial that he had had an affair with her, she simply said, 'he would say that wouldn't he?'

Bibliography

Allison, G., *Essence of Decision: Explaining the Cuban Missile Crisis*, Boston, Mass: Little, Brown, 1971.

Almond, G. A., 'Public Opinion and National Security Policy', *Public Opinion Quarterly*, 20, 1956.

Aquinas, T., *Summa Theologica*, trans. by the Fathers of the English Dominican Province, London: Burns Oates and Washbourne Ltd, 1922.

Arendt, H., *Crisis of the Republic*, New York: Harcourt Brace Jovanovich, Inc., 1972.

Armstrong, S., M. Byrne and T. Blanton, *Secret Military Assistance to Iran and the Contras: A Chronology of Events and Individuals*, Washington: National Security Archives, 1987.

Augustine, Saint, 'Lying', and 'Against Lying' in *Treatises on Various Subjects*, ed. R. J. Deferrari, *Fathers of the Church*, Vol. 16, Washington, DC: Catholic University of America Press, 1952.

Bailey, M., *Oilgate: The Sanctions Scandal*, Seven Oaks: Coronet, 1979.

Bailey, S. K., 'The Public Interest: Some Operational Dilemmas' in Friedrich (ed.), 1962.

Barker, Anthony, 'The Inquiry's Procedures', *Parliamentary Affairs*, 50(1), 1997(1).

Barker, Anthony, 'Practising to Deceive: Whitehall, Arms Exports and the Scott Inquiry', *Political Quarterly*, 1997(2).

Beard, C., *An Analytic Study of American Foreign Policy*, Chicago: Quadrangle, 1966.

Beck, M., *Secret Contenders: The Myth of Cold War Counterintelligence*, New York: Sheridan Square Publications, 1984.

Bennett Report, *Report of the Committee of Inquiry into Police Interrogation Procedures in Northern Ireland*, Cmnd 7397, 1979.

Bernstein, C. and B. Woodward, *All the President's Men*, New York: Simon and Schuster, 1974.

Bingham, T. and S. Gray, *Report on the Supply of Petroleum and Petroleum Products to Rhodesia*, London: HMSO, 1978.

Birkinshaw, P., 'Freedom of Information', *Parliamentary Affairs*, 50(1), 1997.

Blackstock, N., *COINTELPRO: The FBI's Secret War on Political Freedom*, 2nd edn, New York: Pathfinder Books,1988.

Bok, S., *Lying: Moral Choice in Public and Private Life*, Sussex: Harvester, 1978.

Boyle, R., *Flower of the Dragon: the Breakdown of the U.S. Army in Vietnam*, San Francisco: Ramparts Press, 1972.

Boyle, K., T. Hadden and P. Hillyard, *Ten Years On in Northern Ireland: The Legal Control of Political Violence*, London: Cobden Trust, 1980.

Brown, H., *Thinking about National Security: Defence and Foreign Policy in a Dangerous World*, Boulder, Colorado: Westview Press, 1983.

Bunyan, T., *The History and Practice of Political Police in Britain*, London: Quartet Books, 1977.

Cameron Report, *Disturbances in Northern Ireland: Report of the Commission Appointed by the Governor of Northern Ireland*, Cmnd 532, Belfast: HMSO, 1969.

Camus, A., *Collected Plays*, London: Hamish Hamilton, 1965.

Canham-Clyne, J., 'Business as Usual: Iran-Contra and the National Security State', *World Politics*, 9(4), 1992.

Caro, R., *Means of Ascent*, Vol. 2: The Years of Lyndon Johnson, New York: Knopf, 1990.

Cassinelli, C.W., 'The Public Interest in Political Ethics' in Friedrich (ed.), 1962.

Castells, M., *The Information Age: Economy, Society and Culture, Vol. III: End of the Millennium*, Oxford: Blackwell, 1998.

Chabod, F., *Machiavelli and the Renaissance*, Cambridge, Mass: Harvard University Press, 1958.

Chomsky, N., *Necessary Illusions: Thought Control in Democratic Society*, London: Pluto, 1989.

Churchill, W. and J. Vander Wall, *Agents of Repression. The FBI's Secret War against the Black Panther Party and the American Indian Movement*, Boston: South End Press, 1988.

Cliffe, L., 'The Racial Implications of Britain's Sanctions Cover-up', *SAGE Race Relations Abstract*, 4(3), August 1979.

Cliffe, L. 'The Politics of Lying', *Red Pepper*, May 1996.

Coady, C. A. J., 'Politics and the Problem of Dirty Hands' in P. Singer (ed.) *A Companion to Ethics*, Oxford: Blackwell, 1991.

Cohen, J. and J. Rogers, 'Knowledge, Morality and Hope: The Social Thought of Noam Chomsky', *New Left Review*, 187, 1991.

Committee of Public Accounts, Seventeenth Report, *Pergau Hydro-Electric Project*, House of Commons, 1993–4, 155, London: HMSO, 1994.

Congressional Quarterly, *The Iran-Contra Puzzle*, Washington, DC: 1987.

Consumers in Europe Group, *BSE: Briefing and recommendations from Consumers in Europe Group*, London: Consumers in Europe Group, 1996

Cowley, C., *Guns, Lies and Spies*, London: Hamish Hamilton, 1992.

Croce, B., *Elementi di politica*, Bari: Laterza, 1925.

Curtis, L., *Ireland: The Propaganda War*, London: Pluto, 1984.

Dash, S., *Justice Denied: A Challenge to Lord Widgery's Report on 'Bloody Sunday'*, New York: International League for the Rights of Man, 1972.

Dealler, S. F., 'Bovine Spongiform Encephalopathy (BSE): The Potential Effect of the Epidemic on the Human Population', *British Food Journal*, 95(8), 1993.

Dealler, S. F., *Lethal Legacy* , London: Bloomsbury Publishing, 1996.

Dealler, S. F. and J. T. Kent, 'BSE: an update on the statistical evidence', *British Food Journal*, 97(8), 1995.

Destler, I. M., *Presidents, Bureaucrats and Foreign Policy*, Princeton: Princeton University Press, 1974.

Doig, A., 'Truth-Telling and Power', *Parliamentary Affairs*, 50(1), 1997.

Dorril, S. and R. Ramsay, *Smear! Wilson and the Secret State*, London: Grafton, 1992.

Dorril, S., *The Silent Conspiracy: Inside the Intelligence Services in the 1990s*, London: Mandarin, 1993.

Draper, T., *A Very Thin Line: The Iran-Contra Affairs*, New York: Hill & Wang, 1991.

Elliot, M., *Mad Cows and Englishmen*, London, BBC2, 15 and 22 February, 1 and 8 March 1998.

Epstein E., *Agency of Fear: Opiates and Political Power in America* (revised edition), London: Verso, 1991.

European Parliament, Committee on the Environment, Committee on Agriculture Public Health and Consumer Protection and Rural Development, *BSE – CJD: Our Health at Risk*, Brussels: Official Documents from Europe, 1996.

European Parliament (1997(1)), Temporary Committee of Inquiry, *Report on alleged contraventions or maladministration in the implementation of Community law in relation to BSE, without prejudice to the jurisdiction of the Community and national courts* (Ortega Report), Part A.I., Brussels: European Parliament, DOC EN//RR/319/319544 (A4-0020/97/PART A.I), 1997.

European Parliament (1997(2)), Temporary Committee of Inquiry, *Report on alleged contraventions or maladministration in the implementation of Community law in relation to BSE*, Part A: III. Minority Opinions, Brussels, European Parliament, DOC EN//RR/319/319621 (A4-0020/97/PART A.III), 1997.

European Parliament (1997(3)), *Resolution on the results of the Temporary Committee of Inquiry into BSE*, Brussels: European Parliament, Resolutions B4-0078, 0079, 0080, 0083, and 0096/97, 1997.

Foreign Affairs Committee, Third Report. *Public Expenditure: The Pergau Hydro-Electric Project, Malaysia, The Aid And Trade Provision And Related Matters.* Report, together with the Proceedings of the Committee. Volume I. House of Commons, 1993–4, 271-I, London: HMSO, 1994(1).

Foreign Affairs Committee, Third Report. *Public Expenditure: The Pergau Hydro-Electric Project, Malaysia, The Aid And Trade Provision And Related Matters.* Minutes of Evidence and Appendices. Volume II. House of Commons, 1993–4, 271-II, London: HMSO, 1994(2).

Foreign and Commonwealth Office, *Department Report 1993*, Cmnd 2202, London: HMSO, 1993.

Friedman, L. and W. F. Levantrosser (eds), *Watergate and afterward: The Legacy of Richard Nixon*, Westport: Greenwood Press, 1992.

Friedrich, C. J. (ed.), *NOMOS V: The Public Interest*, New York: Atherton, 1962.

Friedrich, C. J., *The Pathology of Politics*, New York: Harper & Row, 1972.

Galnor, I. (ed.), *Government Secrecy in Democracies*, New York: Harper & Row, 1977.

Gamara, E., 'Fighting Drugs in Bolivia: U.S. and Bolivian perceptions at Odds', in Leons and Sanabria (eds), 1997.

Gavshon, A. and D. Rice, *The Sinking of the Belgrano*, London: Secker & Warburg, 1984.

George, A. L. and E. O. Keohane, 'The Concept of the National Interest' in A. L. George (ed.), *Presidential Decision Making in Foreign Policy: The Effective Use of Information and Advice*, Boulder, Colorado: Westview Press, 1980.

Gerth, H. H. and C. Wright Mills (eds), *From Max Weber: Essays in Sociology*, Oxford: Oxford University Press, 1946.

Gibbs, D. N., 'Secrecy and International Relations', *Journal of Peace Research*, Vol. 32, No. 2, 1995.

Gifford, C., *Deregulation, Disasters and BSE*, European Labour Forum, n.d. (1996).

Gill, P., *Policing Politics: Security, Intelligence and the Liberal Democratic State*, London: Frank Cass, 1994.

Goodin, R., *Manipulatory Politics*, New Haven: Yale University Press, 1980.

Gravel, M., The Pentagon Papers: *The Defense Department's History of US Decision Making in Vietnam*, Boston: Beacon Press, 1971.

Greer, S., 'The Supergrass System' in Jennings (ed.), 1990.

Grieder, W., *Who Will Tell the People? The Betrayal of American Democracy*, New York: Simon & Shuster, 1992.

Grotius, H., *On the Law of War and Peace*, Bk.3, trans. F. W. Kelsey, Indianapolis: Bobbs-Merrill Company, 1925.

Guelke, A., 'Policing in Northern Ireland', in B. Hadfield (ed.), *Northern Ireland: Politics and the Constitution*, Buckingham: Open University Press, 1992.

Halliday, F., *The Making of the Second Cold War*, London: Verso, 1983.

Hampshire, S., 'Morality and Pessimism' in Hampshire (ed.), 1978.

Hampshire, S. (ed.), *Public and Private Morality*, Cambridge: Cambridge University Press, 1978.

Harden, I. and N. Lewis, *The Noble Lie: The British Constitution and the Rule of Law*, London: Hutchinson, 1986.

Hargreaves, C., *Snow Fields: the War on Cocaine in the Andes*, London: Zed Press, 1992.

Her Majesty's Government, *The Report of the Rt. Hon. Sir Richard Scott's Inquiry: Government Press Pack*, London: HMSO, 1996.

Herman, E., 'Gatekeeper versus propaganda model: a critical American perspective' in P. Golding, G. Murdock and P. Schlesinger (eds), *Communicating Politics: Mass Communications and the Political Process*, Leicester: Leicester University Press, 1986.

Herman, E. and N. Chomsky, *Manufacturing Consent: The Political Economy of the Mass Media*, New York: Pantheon, 1988/ London: Vintage Books, 1994.

Hirschkop, K., 'Democracy and the New Technologies', *Monthly Review*, 48(3), July–August 1996.

Hoffman, F., 'The Panama Press Pool Deployment: A Critique', in Matthews (ed.), 1991.

Holt, T. A., and P. J. Phillips, 'Bovine Spongiform Encephalopathy', *British Medical Journal*, 296(6636), 1988.

Hooper, D., *Official Secrets: the Use and Abuse of the Act*, London: Secker and Warburg, 1987.

Huntingdon, S., *Political Order in Changing Societies*, New Haven: Yale University Press, 1968.

Ingham, B., *Kill the Messenger*, London: Fontana, 1991.

Inouye, D. and L. Hamilton, *Report of the Congressional Committees Investigating the Iran–Contra Affair*, Washington: Government Printing Office, 17 November 1987.

Irish Government, *Bloody Sunday and the Report of the Widgery Tribunal: The Irish Government's Assessment of the New Material*, presented to the British Government in June 1997.

Jennings, A. (ed.), *Justice Under Fire: The Abuse of Civil Liberties in Northern Ireland*, London: Pluto, 1990.

Jones, W. T., 'Public Roles, Private Rolés and Different Moral Assessments of Role Performance', *Ethics*, 94, 1984.

Karnow, S., *Vietnam: A History*, Harmondsworth: Penguin Books, 1984.

Karp, W., *Indispensable Enemies: The Politics of Misrule in America*, Baltimore, MD: Penguin Books, 1973.

Kassop, N., 'President Nixon's Dismissal of Special prosecutor Archibald Cox: An Analysis of the Constitutionality and Legality of an Exercise of Presidential Removal Power', in Friedman and Levantrosser (eds), 1992.

Keller, W., *The Liberals and J. Edgar Hoover: the Rise and Fall of a Domestic Intelligence State*, Princeton: Princeton University Press, 1989.

Kerry Report, *Drugs, Law Enforcement and Foreign Policy*, Senate Committee on Foreign Relations, Sub-Committee on Terrorism, Narcotics and International Relations, Washington, US,: Government Printing Office, 1989.

Kincaid, J., 'Secrecy and Democracy: The Unresolved Legacy of the Pentagon Papers', in Friedman and Levantrosser (eds), 1992.

Koen, Ross Y., *The China Lobby in American Politics*, New York: Macmillan, 1960.

Kolko, G., *Vietnam: Anatomy of a War, 1940–1975*, London: Unwin, 1986.

Kolko, G., *Confronting the Third World: United States Foreign Policy, 1945–1980*, New York: Pantheon, 1988.

Kranich, N., 'Staking a Claim in Cyberspace: Ensuring a Public Place on the Info Highway', in G. Ruggiero and S. Sahulka (eds), *The New American Crisis: Radical Analyses of the Problems Facing America Today*, New York: New Press, 1995.

Krasner, S. D., *Defending the National Interest*, Princeton, New Jersey: Princeton University Press, 1978.

Kruger, H., *The Great Heroin Coup: Drugs, Intelligence and International Fascism*, Boston: South End Press, 1980.

Kutler, S.(ed.), *Abuse of Power: The New Nixon Tapes*, New York: Touchstone 1998.

Kwitny, J., *The Crimes of Patriots: A True Tale of Dope, Dirty Money, and the CIA*, New York: W. W. Norton, 1987.

Lacey, R. W., *Mad Cow Disease: The History of BSE in Britain*, Channel Isles: Cypelsa Publications, 1994.

Leigh, D., *The Wilson Plot: The Intelligence Services and the Discrediting of a Prime Minister 1945–1976*, London: Heinemann, 1988.

Leigh, D., *Betrayed. The Real Story of the Matrix Churchill Trial*, London: Bloomsbury, 1993.

Leons, M. and H. Sanabria (eds), *Coca, Cocaine and the Bolivian Reality*, Binghampton: State University of New York, 1997.

Levine, M., *Deep Cover: The Inside Story of How DEA Infighting, Incompetence, and Subterfuge Lost Us the Biggest Battle of the Drug War*, New York: Delacorte Press, 1990.

Levy, D., *The Debate over Vietnam*, Baltimore, MD: Johns Hopkins University Press, 1991.

Littauer, R. and N. Uphoff (eds), *The Air War in Indochina*, Boston: Beacon Press, 1972.

Markovits, A. and M. Silverstein (eds), *The Politics of Scandal: Power and Process in Liberal Democracies*, New York: Holmes & Meier,1988.

Marshall, J., P. Scott and J. Hunter, *The Iran–Contra Connection: Secret Teams and Covert Operations in the Reagan Era*, Montreal: Black Rose Books, 1987.

Matthews, L. (ed.), *Newsmen and National Defense: Is Conflict Inevitable?*, Washington, DC: Brassey's, 1991.

McCann, E., *Bloody Sunday in Derry: What Really Happened*, Dingle, Co. Kerry: Brandon, 1992.

McCoy, A., *The Politics of Heroin: CIA Complicity in the Global Drug Trade*, Boston: Lawrence Hill Books, 1991.

McNamara, R., with B. van de Mark, *In Retrospect: The Tragedy and Lessons of Vietnam*, New York: Times Books, 1995.

Meinecke, F., *Machiavellianism*, trans. Douglas Scott, London: Routledge, 1957.

Michael J., *The Politics of Secrecy: Confidential Government and the Public Right to Know*, Harmondsworth, Penguin, 1982.

Middleton, N. (ed.), *The Best of 'I.F. Stone's Weekly'*: *Pages from a Radical Newspaper*, Harmondsworth: Penguin Books, 1973.

Miller, D., *Don't Mention the War: Northern Ireland, Propaganda and Media*, London: Pluto, 1994.

Miller, D., *Export or Die: Britain's Defence Trade with Iran and Iraq*, London: Cassell, 1996.

Milne, S., *The Enemy Within: MI5, Maxwell and the Scargill Affair*, London: Verso, 1994.

Monopolies and Mergers Commission, *Supply of Animal Waste in Great Britain*, London: HMSO, Cmnd 9470, 1985.

Monopolies and Mergers Commission, *Prosper de Mulder and Croda International: A Report on the Proposed Takeover*, London: HMSO, Cmnd 1611, 1991.

Monopolies and Mergers Commission, *Supply of Animal Waste in Great Britain*, London: HMSO, Cmnd 2340, 1993.

Morgan, K. L., 'Bovine Spongiform Encephalopathy: time to take scrapie seriously', *Veterinary Record*, 122(8), April 1988.

Morgenthau, H. J., *Politics among Nations: The Struggle for Peace and Power*, 4th edition, New York: Knopf, 1967.

Mullan, D. (ed.), *Eyewitness: Bloody Sunday*, Dublin: Wolfhound Press, 1997.

Murray, R., *The SAS in Ireland*, Dublin: Mercier Press, 1990.

Nagel, T., 'Ruthlessness in Public Life' in Hampshire (ed.), 1978.

Narang, H. K., *Creutzfeld-Jakob Disease, Bovine Spongiform Encephalopathy, Scrapie: From Sheep to Cow to Man*, Newcastle: H. H. Publishing, 1997.

Narang, H. K., *Death on the Menu: CJD Victims – Diagnosis and Cure: Families devastated by 'Mad Cow' Disease Reveal their Tragic Stories*, Newcastle: H. H. Publishing, 1997.

Narang, H. K., *BSE Inquiry Submission*, Statement No. 113, Harash Narang, 1998.

National Audit Office, *Pergau Hydro-Electric Project*, House of Commons 1992–3, 908, London: HMSO, 1993.

National Audit Office, *Appropriation Accounts 1993–4*, volume 2: Class II – Foreign and Commonwealth Office, House of Commons 1994–5, 100-II, London: HMSO, 1995.

Negrine, R., *The Communication of Politics*, London: Sage, 1996.

Negrine, R.,'The Communication of Political Information and the Creation of an Informed Citizenry', Chapter 1 of Negrine, 1996.

Negrine, R., 'The Inquiry's Media Coverage', *Parliamentary Affairs*, 50(1), 1997.

Nincic, M., *Democracy and Foreign Policy: The Fallacy of Political Realism*, New York: Columbia University Press, 1992.

Nolan, Lord, *Standards in Public Life*, First Report of the Committee on Standards in Public Life, vol. 1: Report. Cmnd. 2850-I, 1994–5, London: HMSO, 1995.

Northmore, D., *Lifting the Lid: A Guide to Investigative Research*, London: Cassell, 1996.

Norton-Taylor, R., *Truth is a Difficult Concept: Inside the Scott Inquiry.* London: Guardian Books, 1995.

Norton-Taylor, R., M. Lloyd and S. Cook, *Knee Deep in Dishonour: the Scott Report and its Aftermath*, London: Gollancz, 1996.

Office International des Epizooites, Regional Commission for Europe, Recommendation No.2. *Scrapie and other spongiform encephalopathies with special reference to bovine spongiform encephalopathy (BSE).* Adopted 5 October 1990. London: Official Documents from Europe, 1992.

O'Neill, O., 'Messy Morality and the Art of the Possible', *Proceedings of the Aristotelaian Society*, Supplementary Volume LXIV, 1990.

Padover, S. K. (ed.), *The Complete Madison*, New York: Harper, 1953.

Perry, M., 'The Measurement of British Unemployment: The Political and Social Controversies; Chapter 4 of *The Measurement of Unemployment in Europe with Special Reference to Britain, France and Poland*, Ph.D. thesis, University of Manchester, 1993, pp. 181–229.

Phythian, M. and W. Little, 'Parliament and Arms Sales: Lessons of the Matrix Churchill Affair', *Parliamentary Affairs*, 46, 1993.

Ponting, C., *The Right to Know: the Inside Story of the 'Belgrano' Affair*, London: Sphere Books, 1985.

Prados, J., *Presidents' Secret Wars: CIA and Pentagon Covert Operations since World War 2*, New York: Morrow, 1986.

Prouty, L., *The Secret Team: The CIA and its Allies in Control of the World*, New York: Ballantine Books, 1973.

Pyper, R., *The British Civil Service*, London: Prentice-Hall, 1995.

R. v Ponting, *Criminal Law Review*, 318, 1985.

Renard, R., *The Burmese Connection: Illegal Drugs and the Making of the Golden Triangle*, Boulder: L. Rienner, 1996.

Report of the European Commission on Human Rights, 1976: Ireland v. U.K of Great Britain and Northern Ireland, Application No. 5310/71.

Rhodes, R., 'A Terrifying New Plague', *Newsweek*, 24 March 1997.

Robertson, K. G., *Public Secrets: A Study on the Development of Government Secrecy*, London: Macmillan, 1982.

Rogers, A., *Secrecy and Power in the British State: A History of the Official Secrets Act*, London: Pluto, 1997.

Ross, S., *Washington Babylon: Sex, Scandal and Corruption in American Politics from 1702 to the Present*, London: Alison & Busby, 1989.

Rourke, F., *Secrecy and Publicity*, Baltimore: Johns Hopkins Press, 1966.

Rusbridger, J., *The Intelligence Game: Illusions and Delusions of International Espionage*, London: I. B. Tauris, 1991.

Scarman Report, *Violence and Civil Disturbances in Northern Ireland in 1969: Report of the Tribunal of Inquiry*, Cmnd 566, Belfast: HMSO, 1972.

Schlesinger, P., 'From Production to Propaganda', *Media, Culture and Society*, Vol. 11, 1989.

Schubert, G., 'Is There a Public Interest Theory?' in Friedrich (ed.), 1962.

Scott, P. D., 'Foreword' in Kruger, 1980.

Scott, P. D. and J. Marshall, *Cocaine Politics: Drugs, Armies and the CIA in Central America*, Berkeley: University of California Press, 1991.

Scott, R., *Report of the Inquiry into the Export of Defence Equipment and Dual-use Goods to Iraq and Related Prosecutions with the Proceedings of the Committee.* House of Commons, Session 1995–6, HC 115, London: HMSO, 1996.

Select Committee on Members' Interests (1990), *Parliamentary Lobbying Minutes of Evidence and Appendices.* House of Commons, Session 1989–90, 283, House of Commons, Session 1987–8, 518 and Session 1988–9, 44, London: HMSO, 1990.

Senate Committee on Foreign Relations, *The Gulf of Tonkin: 1964 Incidents*, Washington: U.S. Government Printing Office, 1968.

Shaoul, J., *BSE: For Services Rendered? The Drive for Profits in the Meat Industry*, Manchester: Department of Accounting and Finance, University of Manchester, 1996.

Sheehan, N., *The Pentagon Papers – as published by the New York Times*, New York: Bantam Books, 1971.

Shils, E., *The Torment of Secrecy*, London: Heinemann, 1956.

Silverstein, M.,'Watergate and the American Political System', in Markovits and Silverstein, 1988.

Sorauf, F. J., 'The Public Interest Reconsidered' *Journal of Politics*, XIX, 1957.

Sorauf, F. J., 'The Conceptual Muddle' in Friedrich (ed.), 1962.

Southwood, R., *Report of the working party on bovine spongiform encephalopathy*, London: HMSO, 1989.

Stalker, J., *Stalker*, London: Harrap, 1988.

Starr K., *Referral to the U.S. House of Representatives*, pursuant to Title 28, U.S. Code 595 (c), (Clinton: the Starr Report), submitted by The Office of the Independent Counsel, 9 September, 1998.

Stockwell, J., *In Search of Enemies*, New York: W. W. Norton, 1978.

Strasbourg Notebook (1997(1)), *BSE – Commission President responds – BSE Enquiry Report*, Brussels: 18 February 1997.

Strasbourg Notebook (1997(2)) *BSE – UK Condemned – Commission Warned*, Brussels: 19 February 1997.

Tant, A.P., 'The Politics of Official Statistics', *Government & Opposition*, 30.2, 1995.

Thompson, B., 'Under the Scott-Light: British Government Seen Through the Scott Report', *Parliamentary Affairs* 50(1), 1997.

Thoumi, F., *Political Economy and Illegal Drugs in Columbia*, Boulder: L. Rienner, 1995.

Thurlow, R., *The Secret State: British Intelligence in the Twentieth Century*, Oxford: Blackwell, 1994.

Toro, M., *Mexico's 'War' on Drugs: Cause and Consequences*, Boulder: L. Rienner, 1995.

Tower, J., *President's Special Review Board* (The Tower Commission), 26 February, (Washington: U.S. Government Printing Office, 1987.

Trade and Industry Committee, *Second Report. Exports To Iraq: Project Babylon And Long Range Guns. Report together with the proceedings of the Committee*. House of Commons, Session 1991–2, HC 86, London: HMSO, 1992.

Treverton, G., *Covert Action: The Limits of Intervention in the Post-war World*, New York: Basic Books, 1987.

Trotsky, L., *Their Morals and Ours*, New York: Pathfinder Press, 1973.

Tyrrell, D. A. J., *Consultative committee on research into spongiform encephalopathies*, London: HMSO, 1990.

U.S. Senate, *Alleged Assassination Plots Involving Foreign Leaders*, An Interim Report of the Select Committee to Study Governmental Operations with Respect to Intelligence Activities, Report 94-465, Washington: U.S. Government Printing Office, 1975.

United Nations Drug Control Programme, *World Drug Report*, Oxford: Oxford University Press, 1997.

Urban, M., *Big Boys Rules: The Secret Struggle against the IRA*, London: Faber, 1992.

Walsh, *Final Report of the Independent Counsel for Iran-Contra Matters* (The Walsh Report), (U.S. Court of Appeal for the District of Columbia Circuit, Division for the Purpose of Appointing Independent Counsel, Division No. 86–6), 1994.

Walsh, D., *The Bloody Sunday Tribunal of Inquiry: a Resounding Defeat for Truth, Justice and the Rule of Law*, University of Limerick, 1997.

Walsh L., *Firewall: The Iran-Contra Conspiracy & Cover-up*, New York: W. W. Norton, 1997.

Walzer, M. 'Political Action and the Problem of Dirty Hands' *Philosophy and Public Affairs,*Vol. 2, No. 2, 1973.

Washington Office on Latin America (WOLA), *Clear and Present Dangers: The U.S. Military and the War on Drugs in the Andes*, Washington: October 1991.

Wells, G. A. H. et al., 'A Novel Progressive Spongiform Encephalopathy in Cattle', *Veterinary Record* 121(18), October 1987.

Wheeler, M., 'Democracy and the Information Super-Highway', *Democratisation*, Vol. 5. No. 2, 1998.

Widgery Report, *Report of the Tribunal Appointed to the Inquiry into the Events on Sunday, 30 January 1972 which Led to the Loss of Life in Connection with the Procession in Londonderry on that day*, HC 220, London: HMSO, 1972.

Williams, B., 'Politics and Morality' in Hampshire (ed.), 1978.

Wise, D., *The Politics of Lying: Government Deception, Secrecy and Power*, New York: Vintage Books, 1973.

World Development Movement, *The Pergau Dam Scandal*, London: World Development Movement, 1995(1).

World Development Movement, *Gunrunners Gold: How the Public's Money Finances Arms Sales*, London: World Development Movement, 1995(2).

Woodward, B., *Veil: the Secret Wars of the CIA 1981–1987*, New York: Simon & Schuster, 1987.

Wright, G., *The Destruction of a Nation: United States' Policy towards Angola since 1945* London: Pluto Press, 1997.

Wright, P., *Spycatcher: The Candid Autobiography of a Senior Intelligence Officer*, New York: Dell, 1987.

Wroe, A., *Lives, Lies and the Iran–Contra Affair*, London: I. B. Tauris, 1991.

Index